PYTHON PLAYGROUND

PYTHON PLAYGROUND

Geeky Projects for the Curious Programmer

by Mahesh Venkitachalam

**no starch
press**

San Francisco

Printed in USA

First printing

19 18 17 16 15   1 2 3 4 5 6 7 8 9

ISBN-10: 1-59327-604-4
ISBN-13: 978-1-59327-604-1

Text stock is SFI Certified

Publisher: William Pollock
Production Editor: Serena Yang
Cover Illustration: Josh Ellingson
Interior Design: Octopod Studios
Developmental Editor: William Pollock
Technical Reviewers: Nicholas Kramer and Raviprakash Jayaraman
Copyeditor: Kim Wimpsett
Compositor: Kathleen Miller
Proofreader: Paula L. Fleming

Figure 8-4 was created by Fred Hsu (March 2005) and has been reproduced under the Creative Commons Attribution-Share Alike 3.0 Unported license.

For information on distribution, translations, or bulk sales, please contact No Starch Press, Inc. directly:

No Starch Press, Inc.
245 8th Street, San Francisco, CA 94103
phone: 415.863.9900; info@nostarch.com
www.nostarch.com

Library of Congress Cataloging-in-Publication Data

Venkitachalam, Mahesh.
  Python playground : geeky projects for the curious programmer / by Mahesh Venkitachalam.
      pages cm
  Includes index.
  ISBN 978-1-59327-604-1 -- ISBN 1-59327-604-4
 1. Python (Computer program language) 2. Electronic apparatus and appliances--Automatic control.
3. Arduino (Programmable controller)--Programming. 4. Raspberry Pi (Computer)--Programming. I.
Title.
  QA76.73.P98.V46 2015
  005.13'3--dc23
                              2014046103

For my parents,
A.V. Venkitachalam and N. Saraswathy,
for giving me the greatest gift of all—
an education

&

For Hema
$$H = M^2A$$

BRIEF CONTENTS

CONTENTS IN DETAIL

5
BOIDS: SIMULATING A FLOCK   71

PART III: FUN WITH IMAGES   87

6
ASCII ART   89

7
PHOTOMOSAICS   101

PART V: HARDWARE HACKING   233

12
INTRODUCTION TO THE ARDUINO   235

13
LASER AUDIO DISPLAY

14
A RASPBERRY PI–BASED WEATHER MONITOR

ACKNOWLEDGMENTS

Writing a book is like running a marathon. Or so I've been told. But what I do know is that writing this book tested the limits of my endurance, and I couldn't have done it without my personal cheerleading squad of close friends and family.

First of all, I'd like to thank my wife Hema for her constant love, encouragement, and patience throughout the two years it took to complete this work. I thank my friend Raviprakash Jayaraman for being a co-conspirator in all my dubious projects, for being a technical reviewer for this book, and for interesting lunches, movies, and trips to the S.P. Road Zoo. I thank my friend Seby Kallarakkal for pushing me to pursue this book and for all the interesting discussions we had together. I am grateful to my pal Dr. Santosh Hemachandra for helpful discussions on fast Fourier transforms. I'd like to thank Karthikeyan Chellappa for helping me test out the installation of Python modules and for our running sessions around Kaikondrahalli Lake. I would also like to thank Matthew Denham (with whom I conversed on reddit) for his help on the mathematics of Spirographs.

I'd like to thank Tyler Ortman and Bill Pollock of No Starch Press, for accepting my book proposal, and Serena Yang, for her professional work in editing the book. I'd like to thank Nicholas Kramer for his technical review of the book.

I thank my parents A.V. Venkitachalam and N. Saraswathy for providing me with an education far beyond their financial means. Finally, I thank all my teachers who inspired me. I hope to remain a student all my life.

INTRODUCTION

 Welcome to *Python Playground*! Within these pages, you'll find 14 exciting projects designed to encourage you to explore the world of programming with Python. The projects cover a wide range of topics, such as drawing Spirograph-like patterns, creating ASCII art, 3D rendering, and projecting laser patterns in sync with music. In addition to being fun in and of themselves, these projects are designed to be jumping-off points for you to explore your own ideas by expanding on each of the projects.

Who Is This Book For?

Python Playground is written for anyone curious about how to use programming to understand and explore ideas. The projects in this book assume that you know basic Python syntax and basic programming concepts and that you're familiar with high-school level mathematics. I've done my best to explain in detail the math you need for all projects.

This book is not intended to be your first book on Python. I won't walk you through the basics. I will, however, show you how to use Python to solve a variety of real-world problems in a series of nontrivial projects. As you work through the projects, you'll explore the nuances of the Python programming language and learn how to work with some popular Python libraries. But perhaps even more importantly, you'll learn how to break down a problem into parts, develop an algorithm to solve that problem, and then implement a solution from the ground up using Python. It can be difficult to solve real-world problems because they are often open-ended and require expertise in various domains. But Python offers the tools to facilitate problem-solving. Overcoming difficulties and finding solutions to real problems is the most important part of your journey on the way to becoming an expert programmer.

What's in This Book?

Let's take a quick tour through the chapters in this book.

Part I: Warming Up

Chapter 1 will show you how to parse iTunes playlist files and gather useful information from them, such as track lengths and common tracks. In **Chapter 2**, we use parametric equations and Turtle graphics to draw curves like the ones generated by a Spirograph.

Part II: Simulating Life

This part is about using mathematical models to simulate phenomena. In **Chapter 3**, you'll learn how to implement the Conway's Game of Life algorithm to generate dynamic patterns that create other patterns as a sort of simulation of artificial life. **Chapter 4** will show you how to create realistic plucked string sounds using the Karplus-Strong algorithm. Then, in **Chapter 5**, you'll learn how to implement the Boids algorithm to simulate the flocking behavior of birds.

Part III: Fun with Images

This part will introduce you to reading and manipulating 2D images with Python. **Chapter 6** shows you how to create ASCII art from an image. In **Chapter 7**, you'll make a photomosaic, and in **Chapter 8**, you'll learn how to generate autostereograms, which create the illusion of a 3D image.

Part IV: Enter 3D

The projects in this part use the OpenGL 3D graphics library. **Chapter 9** introduces the basics of using OpenGL to create simple 3D graphics. In **Chapter 10**, you'll create a particle simulation—a fountain of fireworks that uses math and OpenGL shaders for computation and rendering. Then in

Chapter 11, you'll use OpenGL shaders to implement a volume ray casting algorithm to render volumetric data—a technique commonly used for medical imaging such as MRI and CT scans.

Part V: Hardware Hacking

In the final part, you'll use Python to explore the Arduino microcontroller and the Raspberry Pi. In **Chapter 12**, you'll use the Arduino to read and plot sensor data from a simple circuit. In **Chapter 13**, you'll combine Python with an Arduino to control two rotating mirrors and a laser to produce a laser show that responds to sound. In **Chapter 14**, you'll use the Raspberry Pi to build a web-based weather monitoring system.

Why Python?

Python is an ideal language for exploring programming. As a multiparadigm language, it provides you with a lot of flexibility in how you structure your programs. You can use Python as a *scripting* language to simply execute code, as a *procedural* language to organize your program into a collection of functions which call each other, or as an *object-oriented* language that uses classes, inheritance, and modules to build up a hierarchy. This flexibility allows you to choose the programming style most suited to a particular project.

When you develop using a more traditional language like C or C++, you have to compile and link your code before you can run it. With Python, you can run it directly after editing. (Under the hood, Python compiles your code into an intermediate bytecode that is then run by the Python interpreter, but these processes are transparent to you, the user.) In practice, the process of modifying and running your code over and over is much less cumbersome with Python.

Furthermore, the Python interpreter is a very handy tool for checking code syntax, getting help with modules, doing quick computations, and even testing code under development. For example, when I write Python code, I keep three windows open: a text editor, a shell, and a Python interpreter. As I develop code in the editor, I import my functions or classes into the interpreter and test them as I go.

Python has a very small set of simple and powerful data structures. If you already understand strings, lists, tuples, dictionaries, list comprehensions, and basic control structures such as for and while loops, you're off to a great start. Python's succinct and expressive syntax makes it easy to do complex operations with just a few lines of code. And once you're familiar with Python's built-in and third-party modules, you'll have an arsenal of tools to tackle real problems like the ones covered on this book. There are standard ways to call C/C++ code from Python and vice versa, and because you can find libraries to do almost anything in Python, it's easy to combine Python with other language modules in bigger projects. This is why Python is considered a great *glue* language—it makes it easy to combine diverse software components. The hardware projects at the end of this book demonstrate how Python can work side by side with Arduino code and JavaScript. Real software projects often use a mix of software technologies, and Python fits very well into such layered architectures.

The following example demonstrates the ease of working with Python. While developing code for the Raspberry Pi weather monitor in Chapter 14, I wrote this string looking at the oscilloscope output from the temperature/humidity sensor:

```
0011011100000000000110100000000001010001
```

Since I don't speak binary (especially at 7 AM on a Sunday morning), I fired up the Python interpreter and entered:

```
>>> str = '0011011100000000000110100000000001010001'
>>> len(str)
40
>>> [int(str[i:i+8], 2) for i in range(0, 40, 8)]
[55, 0, 26, 0, 81]
```

This code splits up the 40-bit string into five 8-bit integers, which I can actually interpret. The data above is decoded as a 55.0 percent humidity reading at a temperature of 26.0 degrees centigrade, and the checksum is 55 + 26 = 81.

This example demonstrates the practical use of the Python interpreter as a very power calculator. You don't need to write a complete program to do quick computations; just open up the interpreter and get going. This is just one of the many reasons why I love Python, and why I think you will too.

Python Versions

This book was built with Python 3.3.3, but all code is compatible with Python 2.7.x and 3.x.

The Code in This Book

I've done my best throughout this book to walk you through the code for each project in detail, piece by piece. You can either enter the code yourself or download the complete source code (using the Download Zip option) for all programs in the book at *https://github.com/electronut/pp/*.

You'll find several exciting projects in the following pages. I hope you have as much fun playing with them as I had creating them. And don't forget to explore further with the exercises presented at the end of each project. I wish you many happy hours of programming with *Python Playground*!

PART I

WARMING UP

"In the beginner's mind there are many possibilities;
in the expert's mind there are few."
—Shunryu Suzuki

1

PARSING ITUNES PLAYLISTS

Our Python expedition begins with a simple project that finds duplicate music tracks in iTunes playlist files and plots various statistics such as track lengths and ratings. You'll start by taking a look at the iTunes playlist format and then learn how to extract information from these files using Python. To plot this data, you'll use the `matplotlib` library.

In this project, you will learn the about the following topics:

- XML and property list (p-list) files
- Python lists and dictionaries
- Using Python set objects
- Using `numpy` arrays
- Histograms and scatter plots

- Making simple plots with the `matplotlib` library
- Creating and saving data files

Anatomy of the iTunes Playlist File

The information in an iTunes library can be exported into playlist files. (Choose **File ▸ Library ▸ Export Playlist** in iTunes.) The playlist files are written in Extensible Markup Language (XML), a text-based language designed to represent text-based information hierarchically. It consists of a tree-like collection of user-defined tags in the form `<myTag>`, each of which can have attribute and child tags with additional information.

When you open a playlist file in a text editor, you'll see something like this abbreviated version:

```
    <?xml version="1.0" encoding="UTF-8"?>
❶  <!DOCTYPE plist PUBLIC "-//Apple Computer//DTD PLIST 1.0//EN" "http://www
    .apple.com/DTDs/PropertyList-1.0.dtd">
❷  <plist version="1.0">
❸  <dict>
❹  <key>Major Version</key><integer>1</integer>
        <key>Minor Version</key><integer>1</integer>
        --snip--
❺      <key>Tracks</key>
        <dict>
            <key>2438</key>
            <dict>
            <key>Track ID</key><integer>2438</integer>
            <key>Name</key><string>Yesterday</string>
            <key>Artist</key><string>The Beatles</string>
            <key>Composer</key><string>Lennon [John], McCartney [Paul]</string>
            <key>Album</key><string>Help!</string>
            </dict>
            --snip--
        </dict>
❻      <key>Playlists</key>
        <array>
            <dict>
                <key>Name</key><string>Now</string>
                <key>Playlist ID</key><integer>21348</integer>
                --snip--
                <array>
                    <dict>
                        <key>Track ID</key><integer>6382</integer>
                    </dict>
                    --snip--
                </array>
            </dict>
        </array>
    </dict>
    </plist>
```

The <dict> and <key> tags relate to the way a property list (p-list) file represents objects as *dictionaries*, which are data structures that link a key with a value to make it easy to find a corresponding value. P-list files use dictionaries of dictionaries, where values associated with a key in one dictionary are often themselves yet another dictionary (or even a list of dictionaries).

The <xml> tag identifies the file as XML. Following this opening tag, a *document type declaration (DTD)* defines the structure of the XML document ❶. As you can see, Apple defines this structure at a uniform resource locator (URL) visible in the tag.

At ❷, the file declares the top-level <plist> tag whose only child element is the dictionary <dict> ❸. This dictionary contains various keys including, at ❹, Major Version, Minor Version, and so on, but you're interested in the Tracks key at ❺. Notice that the value corresponding to this key is also a dictionary, which maps an integer track ID to another dictionary containing elements such as Name, Artist, and so on. Each track in a music collection has a unique track ID key.

The playlist order is defined at ❻ by Playlists, a child of the top-level dictionary.

Requirements

In this project, we'll use the built-in module plistlib to read the playlist files. We'll also use the matplotlib library for plotting and numpy arrays to store data.

The Code

The goals in this project are to find duplicates in your music collection, identify tracks shared between playlists, plot the distribution of track durations, and graph the relationship between song ratings and length.

As your music collection grows, you'll invariably end up with duplicate songs. To identify duplicates, search the names in the dictionary associated with the Tracks key (discussed earlier) for duplicates and use track length as an additional criterion to detect duplicates, since a track with the same name but a different length is likely unique.

To find tracks shared between two or more playlists, you'll export the collections as playlist files, gather the track names for each playlist, and compare them as sets to discover common tracks by finding the intersection between sets.

While gathering data from your music collection, you'll create a couple of plots with the powerful matplotlib (*http://matplotlib.org/*) plotting package developed by the late John Hunter. You'll draw a histogram to show the distribution of track durations and a scatter plot to compare song ratings with song length.

To see the full project code, skip ahead to "The Complete Code" on page 11.

Finding Duplicates

You'll start by finding duplicate tracks with the findDuplicates() method, as shown here:

```
      def findDuplicates(fileName):
          print('Finding duplicate tracks in %s...' % fileName)
          # read in a playlist
❶        plist = plistlib.readPlist(fileName)
          # get the tracks from the Tracks dictionary
❷        tracks = plist['Tracks']
          # create a track name dictionary
❸        trackNames = {}
          # iterate through the tracks
❹        for trackId, track in tracks.items():
              try:
❺                name = track['Name']
                 duration = track['Total Time']
                 # look for existing entries
❻                if name in trackNames:
                     # if a name and duration match, increment the count
                     # round the track length to the nearest second
❼                    if duration//1000 == trackNames[name][0]//1000:
                         count = trackNames[name][1]
❽                        trackNames[name] = (duration, count+1)
                 else:
                     # add dictionary entry as tuple (duration, count)
❾                    trackNames[name] = (duration, 1)
              except:
                  # ignore
                  pass
```

At ❶, the readPlist() method takes a p-list file as input and returns the top-level dictionary. You access the Tracks dictionary at ❷, and at ❸, you create an empty dictionary to keep track of duplicates. At ❹, you begin iterating through the Tracks dictionary using the items() method, which is commonly used in Python to retrieve both the key and the value of a dictionary as you iterate through it.

At ❺, you retrieve the name and duration of each track in the dictionary. You check to see whether the current track name already exists in the dictionary being built by using the in keyword ❻. If so, the program checks whether the track lengths of the existing and newly found tracks are identical ❼ by dividing the track length of each by 1,000 with the // operator to convert milliseconds to seconds and then rounding to the nearest second. (Of course, this means that two tracks that differ in length only by milliseconds are considered to be the same length.) If you determine that the two track lengths are equal, you get the value associated with name, which is the tuple (duration, count), and increment count at ❽. If this is the first time the program has come across the track name, it creates a new entry for it, with a count of 1 ❾.

You enclose the body of the code's main for loop in a try block because some music tracks may not have the track name defined. In that case, you skip the track and include only pass (which does nothing) in the except section.

Extracting Duplicates

To extract duplicates, you use this code:

```
      # store duplicates as (name, count) tuples
❶     dups = []
      for k, v in trackNames.items():
❷         if v[1] > 1:
              dups.append((v[1], k))
      # save duplicates to a file
❸     if len(dups) > 0:
          print("Found %d duplicates. Track names saved to dup.txt" % len(dups))
      else:
          print("No duplicate tracks found!")
❹     f = open("dups.txt", "w")
      for val in dups:
❺         f.write("[%d] %s\n" % (val[0], val[1]))
      f.close()
```

At ❶, you create an empty list to hold the duplicates. Next, you iterate through the trackNames dictionary, and if count (accessed with v[1] because it's the second element in the tuple) is greater than 1, you append a tuple with (name, count) to the list. At ❸, the program prints information about what it has found and then saves that information to a file using the open() method ❹. At ❺, you iterate through the dups list, writing out the duplicate entries.

Finding Tracks Common Across Multiple Playlists

Now let's look at how you find music tracks that are common across multiple playlists:

```
def findCommonTracks(fileNames):
    # a list of sets of track names
❶   trackNameSets = []
    for fileName in fileNames:
        # create a new set
❷       trackNames = set()
        # read in playlist
❸       plist = plistlib.readPlist(fileName)
        # get the tracks
        tracks = plist['Tracks']
        # iterate through the tracks
        for trackId, track in tracks.items():
            try:
                # add the track name to a set
❹               trackNames.add(track['Name'])
```

```
        except:
            # ignore
            pass
        # add to list
❺      trackNameSets.append(trackNames)
    # get the set of common tracks
❻    commonTracks = set.intersection(*trackNameSets)
    # write to file
    if len(commonTracks) > 0:
❼        f = open("common.txt", "w")
        for val in commonTracks:
            s = "%s\n" % val
❽            f.write(s.encode("UTF-8"))
        f.close()
        print("%d common tracks found. "
            "Track names written to common.txt." % len(commonTracks))
    else:
        print("No common tracks!")
```

First, you pass a list of playlist filenames to findCommonTracks(), which creates an empty list ❶ to store a set of objects created from each playlist. The program then iterates through each file in the list. For each file, you create a Python set object called trackNames ❷; then as in findDuplicates(), you use plistlib to read in the file ❸ and get the Tracks dictionary. Next, you iterate through each track in this dictionary and add the trackNames object ❹. Once the program has finished with all tracks in a file, it adds this set to trackNameSets ❺.

At ❻, you use the set.intersection() method to get the set of tracks that are common among the sets. (You use the Python * operator to unpack the argument lists.) If the program finds any tracks that are common among sets, it writes the track names to a file. At ❼, you open the file, and the two lines that follow do the actual writing. Use encode() to format the output and to ensure that any Unicode characters are handled correctly ❽.

Collecting Statistics

Next, use the plotStats() method to collect statistics for the track names:

```
def plotStats(fileName):
    # read in a playlist
❶    plist = plistlib.readPlist(fileName)
    # get the tracks from the playlist
    tracks = plist['Tracks']
    # create lists of song ratings and track durations
❷    ratings = []
    durations = []
    # iterate through the tracks
    for trackId, track in tracks.items():
        try:
❸            ratings.append(track['Album Rating'])
            durations.append(track['Total Time'])
```

```
    except:
        # ignore
        pass

    # ensure that valid data was collected
❹  if ratings == [] or durations == []:
        print("No valid Album Rating/Total Time data in %s." % fileName)
        return
```

The goal here is to gather ratings and track durations and then do some plotting. At ❶ and in the lines that follow, you read the playlist file and get access to the Tracks dictionary. Next, you create two empty lists to store ratings and durations ❷. (Ratings in iTunes playlists are stored as integers in the range [0, 100]). Iterating through the tracks, you get and append the ratings and durations to the appropriate lists at ❸. Finally, the sanity check at ❹ makes sure you collected valid data from the playlist file.

Plotting Your Data

You're now ready to plot some data.

```
    # scatter plot
❶  x = np.array(durations, np.int32)
    # convert to minutes
❷  x = x/60000.0
❸  y = np.array(ratings, np.int32)
❹  pyplot.subplot(2, 1, 1)
❺  pyplot.plot(x, y, 'o')
❻  pyplot.axis([0, 1.05*np.max(x), -1, 110])
❼  pyplot.xlabel('Track duration')
❽  pyplot.ylabel('Track rating')

    # plot histogram
    pyplot.subplot(2, 1, 2)
❾  pyplot.hist(x, bins=20)
    pyplot.xlabel('Track duration')
    pyplot.ylabel('Count')

    # show plot
❿  pyplot.show()
```

At ❶, you put the data for the track durations into a 32-bit integer array using numpy.array() (imported as np in the code); then at ❷, you use numpy to apply an operation to every element in the array. In this case, you're converting the duration in milliseconds to seconds by dividing each value by 60 × 1000. You store the track ratings in another numpy array, y, at ❸.

Use matplotlib to draw two plots in the same figure. At ❹, the arguments to subplot()—namely, (2, 1, 1)—tell matplotlib that the figure should have two rows (2) and one column (1) and that the next plot should go in the first row (1). You create the plot at ❺ by calling plot(), and the o tells matplotlib to use circles to represent the data.

At ❻, you set slightly inflated ranges for both the x-axis and y-axis to produce some padding between the plot and the axes. At ❼ and ❽, you set the text for the x-axis and y-axis labels.

Now you plot the duration histogram in the second row of the same figure using the matplotlib method hist() ❾. The bins argument sets the number of data partitions, each of which is used for adding counts in that range. Finally, you call show() ❿, and matplotlib displays your beautiful graph in a new window.

Command Line Options

Now let's look at the main() method of the program to see how it handles command line arguments:

```
def main():
    # create parser
    descStr = """
    This program analyzes playlist files (.xml) exported from iTunes.
    """
❶  parser = argparse.ArgumentParser(description=descStr)
    # add a mutually exclusive group of arguments
❷  group = parser.add_mutually_exclusive_group()

    # add expected arguments
❸  group.add_argument('--common', nargs='*', dest='plFiles', required=False)
❹  group.add_argument('--stats', dest='plFile', required=False)
❺  group.add_argument('--dup', dest='plFileD', required=False)

    # parse args
❻  args = parser.parse_args()

    if args.plFiles:
        # find common tracks
        findCommonTracks(args.plFiles)
    elif args.plFile:
        # plot stats
        plotStats(args.plFile)
    elif args.plFileD:
        # find duplicate tracks
        findDuplicates(args.plFileD)
    else:
❼      print("These are not the tracks you are looking for.")
```

Most projects in this book have command line arguments. Rather than trying to parse them by hand and creating a mess, delegate this mundane task to Python's argparse module. At ❶, you create an ArgumentParser object for this purpose. The program can be used to do three different things such as find common tracks among playlists, plot statistics, or find duplicate tracks in a playlist. However, it can do only one of them at a time, and you don't want it to crash if the user decides to specify two or more of these options at the same time. The argparse module provides a solution to this challenge in the form of mutually exclusive argument groups. At ❷, you use the parser.add_mutually_exclusive_group() method to create such a group.

At ❸, ❹, and ❺, you specify the command line options mentioned earlier and enter the variable names (args.plFiles, args.plFile, and args.plFileD) the parsed values should be stored in. The actual parsing is done at ❻. Once the arguments are parsed, you pass them to the appropriate functions, findCommonTracks(), plotStats(), and findDuplicates(), as discussed earlier in this chapter.

To see whether an argument was parsed, test the appropriate variable name in args. For example, if the user did not use the --common option (which finds common tracks among playlists), args.plFiles should be set to None after parsing.

You handle the case in which the user didn't enter any arguments at ❼.

The Complete Code

Here is the complete program. You can also find the code and some test data for this project at *https://github.com/electronut/pp/tree/master/playlist/*.

```python
import re, argparse
import sys
from matplotlib import pyplot
import plistlib
import numpy as np

def findCommonTracks(fileNames):
    """
    Find common tracks in given playlist files,
    and save them to common.txt.
    """
    # a list of sets of track names
    trackNameSets = []
    for fileName in fileNames:
        # create a new set
        trackNames = set()
        # read in playlist
        plist = plistlib.readPlist(fileName)
        # get the tracks
        tracks = plist['Tracks']
        # iterate through the tracks
        for trackId, track in tracks.items():
            try:
                # add the track name to a set
                trackNames.add(track['Name'])
            except:
                # ignore
                pass
        # add to list
        trackNameSets.append(trackNames)
```

```python
        # get the set of common tracks
        commonTracks = set.intersection(*trackNameSets)
        # write to file
        if len(commonTracks) > 0:
            f = open("common.txt", 'w')
            for val in commonTracks:
                s = "%s\n" % val
                f.write(s.encode("UTF-8"))
            f.close()
            print("%d common tracks found. "
                  "Track names written to common.txt." % len(commonTracks))
        else:
            print("No common tracks!")

def plotStats(fileName):
    """
    Plot some statistics by reading track information from playlist.
    """
    # read in a playlist
    plist = plistlib.readPlist(fileName)
    # get the tracks from the playlist
    tracks = plist['Tracks']
    # create lists of song ratings and track durations
    ratings = []
    durations = []
    # iterate through the tracks
    for trackId, track in tracks.items():
        try:
            ratings.append(track['Album Rating'])
            durations.append(track['Total Time'])
        except:
            # ignore
            pass

    # ensure that valid data was collected
    if ratings == [] or durations == []:
        print("No valid Album Rating/Total Time data in %s." % fileName)
        return

    # scatter plot
    x = np.array(durations, np.int32)
    # convert to minutes
    x = x/60000.0
    y = np.array(ratings, np.int32)
    pyplot.subplot(2, 1, 1)
    pyplot.plot(x, y, 'o')
    pyplot.axis([0, 1.05*np.max(x), -1, 110])
    pyplot.xlabel('Track duration')
    pyplot.ylabel('Track rating')

    # plot histogram
    pyplot.subplot(2, 1, 2)
    pyplot.hist(x, bins=20)
    pyplot.xlabel('Track duration')
    pyplot.ylabel('Count')
```

```python
        # show plot
        pyplot.show()


def findDuplicates(fileName):
    """
    Find duplicate tracks in given playlist.
    """
    print('Finding duplicate tracks in %s...' % fileName)
    # read in playlist
    plist = plistlib.readPlist(fileName)
    # get the tracks from the Tracks dictionary
    tracks = plist['Tracks']
    # create a track name dictionary
    trackNames = {}
    # iterate through tracks
    for trackId, track in tracks.items():
        try:
            name = track['Name']
            duration = track['Total Time']
            # look for existing entries
            if name in trackNames:
                # if a name and duration match, increment the count
                # round the track length to the nearest second
                if duration//1000 == trackNames[name][0]//1000:
                    count = trackNames[name][1]
                    trackNames[name] = (duration, count+1)
            else:
                # add dictionary entry as tuple (duration, count)
                trackNames[name] = (duration, 1)
        except:
            # ignore
            pass
    # store duplicates as (name, count) tuples
    dups = []
    for k, v in trackNames.items():
        if v[1] > 1:
            dups.append((v[1], k))
    # save duplicates to a file
    if len(dups) > 0:
        print("Found %d duplicates. Track names saved to dup.txt" % len(dups))
    else:
        print("No duplicate tracks found!")
    f = open("dups.txt", 'w')
    for val in dups:
        f.write("[%d] %s\n" % (val[0], val[1]))
    f.close()

# gather our code in a main() function
def main():
    # create parser
    descStr = """
This program analyzes playlist files (.xml) exported from iTunes.
    """

    parser = argparse.ArgumentParser(description=descStr)
```

```
    # add a mutually exclusive group of arguments
    group = parser.add_mutually_exclusive_group()

    # add expected arguments
    group.add_argument('--common', nargs='*', dest='plFiles', required=False)
    group.add_argument('--stats', dest='plFile', required=False)
    group.add_argument('--dup', dest='plFileD', required=False)

    # parse args
    args = parser.parse_args()

    if args.plFiles:
        # find common tracks
        findCommonTracks(args.plFiles)
    elif args.plFile:
        # plot stats
        plotStats(args.plFile)
    elif args.plFileD:
        # find duplicate tracks
        findDuplicates(args.plFileD)
    else:
        print("These are not the tracks you are looking for.")

# main method
if __name__ == '__main__':
    main()
```

Running the Program

Here is a sample run of the program:

```
$ python playlist.py --common test-data/maya.xml test-data/rating.xml
```

Here is the output:

```
5 common tracks found. Track names written to common.txt.
$ cat common.txt
God Shuffled His Feet
Rubric
Floe
Stairway To Heaven
Pi's Lullaby
moksha:playlist mahesh$
```

Now let's plot some statistics for the tracks.

```
$ python playlist.py --stats test-data/rating.xml
```

Figure 1-1 shows the output from this sample run.

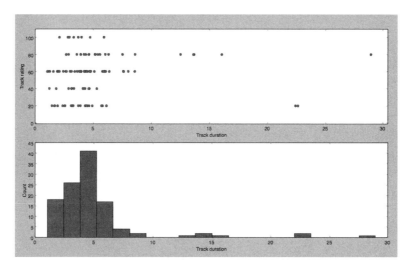

Figure 1-1: Sample run of playlist.py

Summary

In this project, we developed a program that analyzes iTunes playlists and, in the process, learned some useful Python constructs. In upcoming projects, you'll build on some of the basics covered here to explore a wide range of interesting topics and delve deeper into Python.

Experiments!

Here are a few ways you could build on this program:

1. When finding duplicate tracks, you considered track duration as an additional criterion to determine whether two tracks were identical. But when finding common tracks, you used only track names to make comparisons. Incorporate track duration as an additional check in `findCommonTracks()`.

2. In the `plotStats()` method, you used the matplotlib `hist()` method to compute and display the histogram. Write code to compute the histogram manually and display it without using the `hist()` method. To display a plot as a bar chart, read up on bar charts in the `matplotlib` documentation.

3. Several mathematical formulas exist for calculating a correlation coefficient, which measures the strength of a relationship between two variables. Read up on correlation and calculate a correlation value for a rating/duration scatter plot using your own music data. Consider other scatter plots you can make with data gleaned from your playlists.

2

SPIROGRAPHS

You can use a Spirograph toy (shown in Figure 2-1) to draw mathematical curves. The toy consists of two different sized rings with plastic teeth, one large and one small. The small one has several holes. You put a pen or pencil through one of the holes and then rotate the smaller wheel inside the larger one (which has gears on its inside), keeping the pen in contact with the outer wheel, to draw an endless number of complex and wonderfully symmetric patterns.

In this project, you'll use Python to create an animation of Spirograph-like drawing curves. Our *spiro.py* program will use Python and parametric equations to describe the motion of the program's Spirograph's rings and draw the curves (which I call *spiros*). You'll save the completed drawings as PNG image files and use command line options to specify parameters or to generate random spiros.

Figure 2-1: A Spirograph toy

In this project, you'll learn how to draw spiros on your computer. You'll also learn how to do the following:

- Create graphics with the turtle module.
- Use parametric equations.
- Use mathematical equations to generate curves.
- Draw a curve using lines.
- Use a timer to animate graphics.
- Save graphics to image files.

A word of caution about this project: I've chosen to use the turtle module for this project mainly for illustrative purposes and because it's fun, but turtle is slow and not ideal for creating graphics when performance is critical. (What do you expect from turtles?) If you want to draw something fast, there are better ways to do so, and you'll explore some of these options in upcoming projects.

Parametric Equations

In this section, you will look at a simple example of using *parametric equations* to draw a circle. Parametric equations express the coordinates of the points of a curve as functions of a variable, called a *parameter*. They make it easy to draw curves because you can just plug parameters into equations to produce a curve.

NOTE   *If you'd rather not get into this math right now, you can skip ahead to the next section, which talks about the equations specific to the Spirograph project.*

Let's begin by considering that the equation used to describe a circle with radius r, centered at the origin of a two-dimensional plane, is. A circle consists of all the points at the x- and y-coordinates that satisfy this equation.

Now, consider the following equations:

$$x = r\cos(\theta)$$
$$y = r\sin(\theta)$$

These equations are a *parametric* representation of a circle, where the angle θ is the parameter. Any value of (x, y) in these equations will satisfy the equation for a circle described earlier, $x^2 + y^2 = r^2$. If you vary θ from 0 to 2π, you can use these equations to compute a corresponding x-and-y coordinate along the circle. Figure 2-2 shows this scheme.

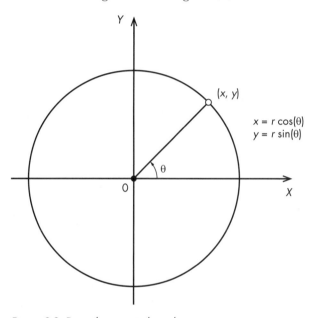

Figure 2-2: Describing a circle with a parametric equation

Remember, these two equations apply to a circle centered at the origin of the coordinate system. You can put a circle at any point in the xy plane by translating the center of the circle to the point (a, b). So the more general parametric equations then become $x = a + r\cos(\theta)$ and $y = b + r\cos(\theta)$. Now let's look at the equations that describe your spiros.

Spirograph Equations

Figure 2-3 shows a mathematical model of Spirograph-like motion. The model has no gears because they're used in the toy only to prevent slippage, and here you don't have to worry about anything slipping.

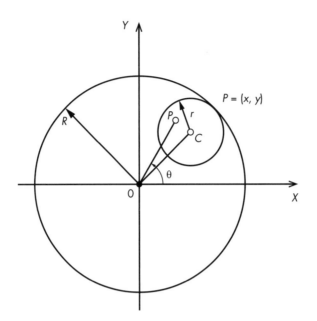

Figure 2-3: Spirograph mathematical model

In Figure 2-3, C is the center of the smaller circle, and P is the pen's tip. The radius of the bigger circle is R, and that of the smaller circle is r. You express the ratio of the radii as follows:

$$k = \frac{r}{R}$$

You express the ratio of segment PC to the smaller circle's radius r as the variable l ($l = PC / r$), which determines how far the pen tip is from the center of the small circle. You then combine these variables to represent the motion of P to produce these parametric equations:

$$x = R\left((1-k)\cos(\theta) + lk\cos\left(\frac{1-k}{k}\theta \right) \right)$$

$$y = R\left((1-k)\sin(\theta) + lk\sin\left(\frac{1-k}{k}\theta \right) \right)$$

NOTE   *These curves are called hypotrochoids and epitrochoids. Although the equations may look a bit scary, the derivation is pretty straightforward. See the Wikipedia page if you'd like to explore the math.*[1]

---

1. *http://en.wikipedia.org/wiki/Spirograph/*

Figure 2-4 shows how you use these equations to produce a curve that varies based on the parameters used. By varying the parameters R, r, and l, you can produce an endless variety of fascinating curves.

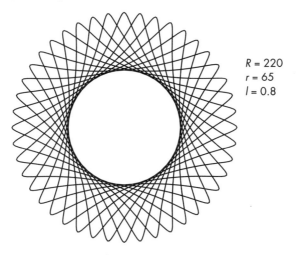

R = 220
r = 65
l = 0.8

Figure 2-4: A sample curve

You draw the curve as a series of lines between points. If the points are close enough, the drawing looks like a smooth curve.

If you've played with a real Spirograph, you know that depending on the parameters used, Spirographs can require many revolutions to complete. To determine when to stop drawing, you use the *periodicity* of the Spirograph (how long before the Spirograph starts repeating itself) by looking at the ratio of the radii of the inner and outer circles:

$$\frac{r}{R}$$

You reduce this fraction by dividing the numerator and denominator by the *greatest common divisor (GCD)*, and the numerator tells you how many periods the curve needs to complete itself. For example, in Figure 2-4, the GCD of (r, R) is 5.

$$\frac{r}{R} = \frac{65}{220}$$

Here is the reduced form of this fraction:

$$\frac{(65 / 5)}{(220 / 5)} = \frac{13}{44}$$

This tells you that in 13 revolutions, the curve will start repeating itself. The number 44 tells you the number of times the smaller circle revolves about its center, which gives you a hint to the shape of the curve. If you count them in Figure 2-4, you'll see that the number of petals or lobes in the drawing is exactly 44!

Once you express the radii ratio in the reduced form r/R, the range for the parameter θ to draw the spiro is $[0, 2\pi r]$. This tells you when to stop drawing a particular spiro. Without know the ending range of the angle, you would be looping around, repeating the curve unnecessarily.

Turtle Graphics

You'll use Python's turtle module to create your drawings; it's a simple drawing program modeled after the idea of a turtle dragging its tail through the sand, creating patterns. The turtle module includes methods you can use to set the position and color of the pen (the turtle's tail) and many other useful functions for drawing. As you will see, all you need is a handful of graphics functions to create cool-looking spiros.

For example, this program uses turtle to draw a circle. Enter the following code, save it as *drawcircle.py*, and run it in Python:

```
    import math
❶   import turtle

    # draw the circle using turtle
    def drawCircleTurtle(x, y, r):
        # move to the start of circle
❷       turtle.up()
❸       turtle.setpos(x + r, y)
❹       turtle.down()

        # draw the circle
❺       for i in range(0, 365, 5):
❻           a = math.radians(i)
❼           turtle.setpos(x + r*math.cos(a), y + r*math.sin(a))

❽   drawCircleTurtle(100, 100, 50)
❾   turtle.mainloop()
```

You start by importing the turtle module at ❶. Next, you define the drawCircleTurtle() method, which calls up() at ❷. This tells Python to move the pen up; in other words, take the pen off the virtual paper so that it won't draw as you move the turtle. You want to position the turtle before you start drawing.

At ❸, you set the turtle's position to the first point on the horizontal axis: $(x + r, y)$, where (x, y) is the center of the circle. Now you're ready to draw, so you call down() at ❹. At ❺, you start a loop using range(0, 365, 5), which increments the variable i in steps of 5 from 0 to 360. The i variable is the angle parameter you'll pass into the parametric circle equation, but first you convert it from degrees to radians at ❻. (Most computer programs require radians for angle-based calculations.)

At ❼, you compute the circle's coordinates using the parametric equations discussed previously, and set the turtle position accordingly, which draws a line from the last turtle position to the newly calculated one. (Technically, you're producing an *N*-sided polygon, but because you're using small angles, *N* will be very large, and the polygon will look like a circle.)

At ❽, you call `drawCircleTurtle()` to draw the circle, and at ❾, you call `mainloop()`, which keeps the tkinter window open so that you can admire your circle. (tkinter is the default GUI library used by Python.)

Now you're ready to draw some spiros!

Requirements

You'll use the following to create your spiros:

- The turtle module for drawing
- Pillow, a fork of the *Python Imaging Library (PIL)*, to save the spiro images

The Code

First, define a class Spiro to draw the curves. You'll use this class to draw a single curve in one go (using the draw() method) and to animate a set of random spiros using a timer and the update() method. To draw and animate the Spiro objects, you'll use a class called SpiroAnimator.

To see the full project code, skip ahead to "The Complete Code" on page 31.

The Spiro Constructor

Here is the Spiro constructor:

```
# a class that draws a Spirograph
class Spiro:
    # constructor
    def __init__(self, xc, yc, col, R, r, l):

        # create the turtle object
❶       self.t = turtle.Turtle()
        # set the cursor shape
❷       self.t.shape('turtle')
        # set the step in degrees
❸       self.step = 5
        # set the drawing complete flag
❹       self.drawingComplete = False

        # set the parameters
❺       self.setparams(xc, yc, col, R, r, l)

        # initialize the drawing
❻       self.restart()
```

The Spiro constructor creates a new turtle object at ❶, which will help you draw multiple spiros simultaneously. At ❷, you set the shape of the turtle cursor to a turtle. (You'll find other choices in the turtle documentation at *https://docs.python.org/3.3/library/turtle.html*.) You set the angle increment for the parametric drawing to 5 degrees at ❸, and at ❹, you set a flag that you'll use during the animation, which produces a bunch of spiros.

At ❺ and ❻, you call setup functions, as discussed next.

The Setup Functions

Let's now take a look at the setparams() method, which helps initialize a Spiro object, as shown here:

```
    # set the parameters
    def setparams(self, xc, yc, col, R, r, l):
        # the Spirograph parameters
❶      self.xc = xc
        self.yc = yc
❷      self.R = int(R)
        self.r = int(r)
        self.l = l
        self.col = col
        # reduce r/R to its smallest form by dividing with the GCD
❸      gcdVal = gcd(self.r, self.R)
❹      self.nRot = self.r//gcdVal
        # get ratio of radii
        self.k = r/float(R)
        # set the color
        self.t.color(*col)
        # store the current angle
❺      self.a = 0
```

At ❶, you store the coordinates of the center of the curve. Then you convert the radius of each circle (R and r) to an integer and store the values at ❷. At ❸, you use the gcd() method from the built-in Python module fractions to compute the GCD of the radii. You'll use this information to determine the periodicity of the curve, which you save as self.nRot at ❹. Finally, at ❺, you store the current angle, a, which you'll use to create the animation.

The restart() Method

Next, the restart() method resets the drawing parameters for the Spiro object and gets it ready for a redraw:

```
    # restart the drawing
    def restart(self):
        # set the flag
❶      self.drawingComplete = False
        # show the turtle
❷      self.t.showturtle()
```

```
                    # go to the first point
❸                   self.t.up()
❹                   R, k, l = self.R, self.k, self.l
                    a = 0.0
❺                   x = R*((1-k)*math.cos(a) + l*k*math.cos((1-k)*a/k))
                    y = R*((1-k)*math.sin(a) - l*k*math.sin((1-k)*a/k))
❻                   self.t.setpos(self.xc + x, self.yc + y)
❼                   self.t.down()
```

Here you use a Boolean flag drawingComplete to determine whether the drawing has been completed, and you initialize the flag at ❶. This flag is useful while multiple Spiro objects are being drawn because it allows you to keep track of whether a particular spiro is complete. At ❷, you show the turtle cursor, in case it was hidden. You lift up the pen at ❸ so you can move to the first position at ❻ without drawing a line. At ❹, you're just using some local variables to keep the code compact. Then, at ❺, you compute the x- and y-coordinates with the angle a set to 0 to get the curve's starting point. Finally, at ❼, you've finished, and you set the pen down. The setpos() call will draw the actual line.

The draw() Method

The draw() method draws the curve in one continuous line.

```
                # draw the whole thing
                def draw(self):
                    # draw the rest of the points
                    R, k, l = self.R, self.k, self.l
❶                   for i in range(0, 360*self.nRot + 1, self.step):
❷                       a = math.radians(i)
                        x = R*((1-k)*math.cos(a) + l*k*math.cos((1-k)*a/k))
                        y = R*((1-k)*math.sin(a) - l*k*math.sin((1-k)*a/k))
                        self.t.setpos(self.xc + x, self.yc + y)
                    # drawing is now done so hide the turtle cursor
❸                   self.t.hideturtle()
```

At ❶, you iterate through the complete range of the parameter i, which is expressed in degrees as 360 times nRot. Compute the x- and y-coordinates for each value of the i parameter at ❷, and at ❸, hide the cursor because you've finished drawing.

Creating the Animation

The update() method shows the drawing method you use to draw the curve segment by segment to create an animation.

```
                # update by one step
                def update(self):
                    # skip the rest of the steps if done
❶                   if self.drawingComplete:
                        return
```

```
                    # increment the angle
❷                   self.a += self.step
                    # draw a step
                    R, k, l = self.R, self.k, self.l
                    # set the angle
❸                   a = math.radians(self.a)
                    x = self.R*((1-k)*math.cos(a) + l*k*math.cos((1-k)*a/k))
                    y = self.R*((1-k)*math.sin(a) - l*k*math.sin((1-k)*a/k))
                    self.t.setpos(self.xc + x, self.yc + y)
                    # if drawing is complete, set the flag
❹                   if self.a >= 360*self.nRot:
                        self.drawingComplete = True
                        # drawing is now done so hide the turtle cursor
                        self.t.hideturtle()
```

At ❶, the update() method checks to see whether the drawingComplete flag is set; if not, it continues through the rest of the code. At ❷, update() increments the current angle. Beginning at ❸, it calculates the (x, y) position corresponding to the current angle and moves the turtle there, drawing the line segment in the process.

When I discussed the Spirograph equations, I talked about the periodicity of the curve. A Spirograph starts repeating itself after a certain angle. At ❹, you see whether the angle has reached the full range computed for this particular curve. If so, you set the drawingComplete flag because the drawing is complete. Finally, you hide the turtle cursor so you can see your beautiful creation.

The SpiroAnimator Class

The SpiroAnimator class will let you draw random spiros simultaneously. This class uses a timer to draw the curves one segment at a time; this technique updates the graphics periodically and lets the program process events such as button presses, mouse clicks, and so on. But this timer technique requires some restructuring in the drawing code.

```
# a class for animating Spirographs
class SpiroAnimator:
    # constructor
    def __init__(self, N):
        # set the timer value in milliseconds
❶       self.deltaT = 10
        # get the window dimensions
❷       self.width = turtle.window_width()
        self.height = turtle.window_height()
        # create the Spiro objects
❸       self.spiros = []
        for i in range(N):
            # generate random parameters
❹           rparams = self.genRandomParams()
            # set the spiro parameters
❺           spiro = Spiro(*rparams)
            self.spiros.append(spiro)
```

```
       # call timer
❻      turtle.ontimer(self.update, self.deltaT)
```

At ❶, the SpiroAnimator constructor sets deltaT to 10, which is the time interval in milliseconds you'll use for the timer. At ❷, you store the dimensions of the turtle window. Then you create an empty array at ❸, which you'll populate with Spiro objects. These encapsulate the Spirograph drawing and then loop *N* times (N is passed into SpiroAnimator in the constructor), create a new Spiro object at ❺, and add it to the list of Spiro objects. The rparams here is a tuple that you need to pass into the Spiro constructor. However, the constructor expects a list of arguments, so you use the Python * operator to convert a tuple to a list of arguments.

Finally, at ❻, you set the turtle.ontimer() method to call update() every deltaT milliseconds.

Notice at ❹ that you call a helper method called genRandomParams(). You'll look at that next.

The genRandomParams() Method

You'll use the genRandomParams() method to generate random parameters to send to each Spiro object as it's created in order to create a wide variety of curves.

```
       # generate random parameters
       def genRandomParams(self):
           width, height = self.width, self.height
❶          R = random.randint(50, min(width, height)//2)
❷          r = random.randint(10, 9*R//10)
❸          l = random.uniform(0.1, 0.9)
❹          xc = random.randint(-width//2, width//2)
❺          yc = random.randint(-height//2, height//2)
❻          col = (random.random(),
                  random.random(),
                  random.random())
❼          return (xc, yc, col, R, r, l)
```

To generate random numbers, you use two methods from the random Python module: randint(), which returns random integers in the specified range, and uniform(), which does the same for floating-point numbers. At ❶, you set R to a random integer between 50 and the value of half the smallest dimension of your window, and at ❷, you set r to between 10 and 90 percent of R.

Then at ❸, you set *l* to a random fraction between 0.1 and 0.9. At ❹ and ❺, you select a random point on the screen to place the center of the spiro by selecting random x- and y-coordinates from within the screen boundaries. Assign a random color to the curve at ❻ by setting random values to the red, green, and blue color components. Finally, at ❼, all of your calculated parameters are returned as a tuple.

Restarting the Program

We'll use another restart() method to restart the program.

```
# restart spiro drawing
    def restart(self):
        for spiro in self.spiros:
            # clear
            spiro.clear()
            # generate random parameters
            rparams = self.genRandomParams()
            # set the spiro parameters
            spiro.setparams(*rparams)
            # restart drawing
            spiro.restart()
```

This loops through all the Spiro objects, clears the previous drawing for each, assigns new spiro parameters, and then restarts the program.

The update() Method

The following code shows the update() method in SpiroAnimator, which is called by the timer to update all the Spiro objects used in the animation:

```
    def update(self):
        # update all spiros
❶      nComplete = 0
        for spiro in self.spiros:
            # update
❷          spiro.update()
            # count completed spiros
❸          if spiro.drawingComplete:
                nComplete += 1
        # restart if all spiros are complete
❹      if nComplete == len(self.spiros):
            self.restart()
        # call the timer
❺      turtle.ontimer(self.update, self.deltaT)
```

The update() method uses a counter nComplete to track the number of Spiro objects being drawn. After you initialize at ❶, it loops through the list of Spiro objects, updates them at ❷, and increments the counter at ❸ if a Spiro is completed.

Outside the loop at ❹, you check the counter to determine whether all the objects have finished drawing. If so, you restart the animation with fresh spiros by calling the restart() method. At the end of a restart() at ❺, you call the timer method, which calls update() again after deltaT milliseconds.

Showing or Hiding the Cursor

Finally, you use the following method to toggle the turtle cursor on and off. This can be used to make the drawing go faster.

```
# toggle turtle cursor on and off
def toggleTurtles(self):
    for spiro in self.spiros:
        if spiro.t.isvisible():
            spiro.t.hideturtle()
        else:
            spiro.t.showturtle()
```

Saving the Curves

Use the saveDrawing() method to save the drawings as PNG image files.

```
    # save drawings as PNG files
    def saveDrawing():
        # hide the turtle cursor
❶      turtle.hideturtle()
        # generate unique filenames
❷      dateStr = (datetime.now()).strftime("%d%b%Y-%H%M%S")
        fileName = 'spiro-' + dateStr
        print('saving drawing to %s.eps/png' % fileName)
        # get the tkinter canvas
❸      canvas = turtle.getcanvas()
        # save the drawing as a postscipt image
❹      canvas.postscript(file = fileName + '.eps')
        # use the Pillow module to convert the postscript image file to PNG
❺      img = Image.open(fileName + '.eps')
❻      img.save(fileName + '.png', 'png')
        # show the turtle cursor
❼      turtle.showturtle()
```

At ❶, you hide the turtle cursor so that you won't see it in the final drawing. Then, at ❷, you use datetime() to generate unique names for the image files by using the current time and date (in the *day-month-year-hour-minute-second* format). You append this string to *spiro-* to generate the filename.

The turtle program uses user interface (UI) windows created by tkinter, and you use the canvas object of tkinter to save the window in the Embedded PostScript (EPS) file format at ❸ and ❹. Because EPS is vector based, you can use it to print your images at high resolution, but PNG is more versatile, so you use Pillow to open the EPS file at ❺ and save it as a PNG file at ❻. Finally, at ❼, you unhide the turtle cursor.

Parsing Command Line Arguments and Initialization

Like in Chapter 1, you use argparse in the main() method to parse command line options sent to the program.

```
❶    parser = argparse.ArgumentParser(description=descStr)

     # add expected arguments
❷    parser.add_argument('--sparams', nargs=3, dest='sparams', required=False,
                         help="The three arguments in sparams: R, r, l.")

     # parse args
❸    args = parser.parse_args()
```

At ❶, you create the argument parser object, and at ❷, you add the --sparams optional argument to the parser. You make the call that does the actual parsing at ❸.

Next, the code sets up some turtle parameters.

```
❶    # set the width of the drawing window to 80 percent of the screen width
     turtle.setup(width=0.8)

❷    # set the cursor shape to turtle
     turtle.shape('turtle')

❸    # set the title to Spirographs!
     turtle.title("Spirographs!")
     # add the key handler to save our drawings
❹    turtle.onkey(saveDrawing, "s")
     # start listening
❺    turtle.listen()

❻    # hide the main turtle cursor
     turtle.hideturtle()
```

At ❶, you use setup() to set the width of the drawing window to 80 percent of the screen width. (You could also give setup() specific height and origin parameters.) You set the cursor shape to turtle at ❷, and you set the title of the program window to *Spirographs!* at ❸. At ❹, you use onkey() with saveDrawing to save the drawing when you press S. Then, at ❺, you call listen() to make the window listen for user events. Finally, at ❻, you hide the turtle cursor.

Once the command line arguments are parsed, the rest of the code proceeds as follows:

```
❶    # check for any arguments sent to --sparams and draw the Spirograph
     if args.sparams:
❷        params = [float(x) for x in args.sparams]
         # draw the Spirograph with the given parameters
         col = (0.0, 0.0, 0.0)
❸        spiro = Spiro(0, 0, col, *params)
❹        spiro.draw()
```

```
        else:
            # create the animator object
❺          spiroAnim = SpiroAnimator(4)
            # add a key handler to toggle the turtle cursor
❻          turtle.onkey(spiroAnim.toggleTurtles, "t")
            # add a key handler to restart the animation
❼          turtle.onkey(spiroAnim.restart, "space")

        # start the turtle main loop
❽      turtle.mainloop()
```

At ❶, you first check whether any arguments were given to --sparams; if so, you extract them from the string and use a *list comprehension* to convert them into floats at ❷. (A list comprehension is a Python construct that lets you create a list in a compact and powerful way. For example, a = [2*x for x in range(1, 5)] creates a list of the first four even numbers.)

At ❸, you use any extracted parameters to construct the Spiro object (with the help of the Python * operator, which converts the list into arguments). Then, at ❹, you call draw(), which draws the spiro.

Now, if no arguments were specified on the command line, you enter random mode. At ❺, you create a SpiroAnimator object, passing it the argument 4, which tells it to create four drawings. At ❻, use onkey to capture any presses of the T key so that you can use it to toggle the turtle cursors (toggleTurtles), and at ❼, handle presses of the spacebar (space) so that you can use it to restart the animation at any point. Finally, at ❽, you call mainloop() to tell the tkinter window to stay open, listening for events.

The Complete Code

Here is the complete Spirograph program. You can also download the code for this project from *https://github.com/electronut/pp/blob/master/spirograph/spiro.py*.

```
import sys, random, argparse
import numpy as np
import math
import turtle
import random
from PIL import Image
from datetime import datetime
from fractions import gcd

# a class that draws a Spirograph
class Spiro:
    # constructor
    def __init__(self, xc, yc, col, R, r, l):

        # create the turtle object
        self.t = turtle.Turtle()
        # set the cursor shape
        self.t.shape('turtle')
```

```
        # set the step in degrees
        self.step = 5
        # set the drawing complete flag
        self.drawingComplete = False

        # set the parameters
        self.setparams(xc, yc, col, R, r, l)

        # initialize the drawing
        self.restart()

    # set the parameters
    def setparams(self, xc, yc, col, R, r, l):
        # the Spirograph parameters
        self.xc = xc
        self.yc = yc
        self.R = int(R)
        self.r = int(r)
        self.l = l
        self.col = col
        # reduce r/R to its smallest form by dividing with the GCD
        gcdVal = gcd(self.r, self.R)
        self.nRot = self.r//gcdVal
        # get ratio of radii
        self.k = r/float(R)
        # set the color
        self.t.color(*col)
        # store the current angle
        self.a = 0

    # restart the drawing
    def restart(self):
        # set the flag
        self.drawingComplete = False
        # show the turtle
        self.t.showturtle()
        # go to the first point
        self.t.up()
        R, k, l = self.R, self.k, self.l
        a = 0.0
        x = R*((1-k)*math.cos(a) + l*k*math.cos((1-k)*a/k))
        y = R*((1-k)*math.sin(a) - l*k*math.sin((1-k)*a/k))
        self.t.setpos(self.xc + x, self.yc + y)
        self.t.down()

    # draw the whole thing
    def draw(self):
        # draw the rest of the points
        R, k, l = self.R, self.k, self.l
        for i in range(0, 360*self.nRot + 1, self.step):
            a = math.radians(i)
            x = R*((1-k)*math.cos(a) + l*k*math.cos((1-k)*a/k))
            y = R*((1-k)*math.sin(a) - l*k*math.sin((1-k)*a/k))
            self.t.setpos(self.xc + x, self.yc + y)
```

```python
        # drawing is now done so hide the turtle cursor
        self.t.hideturtle()

    # update by one step
    def update(self):
        # skip the rest of the steps if done
        if self.drawingComplete:
            return
        # increment the angle
        self.a += self.step
        # draw a step
        R, k, l = self.R, self.k, self.l
        # set the angle
        a = math.radians(self.a)
        x = self.R*((1-k)*math.cos(a) + l*k*math.cos((1-k)*a/k))
        y = self.R*((1-k)*math.sin(a) - l*k*math.sin((1-k)*a/k))
        self.t.setpos(self.xc + x, self.yc + y)
        # if drawing is complete, set the flag
        if self.a >= 360*self.nRot:
            self.drawingComplete = True
            # drawing is now done so hide the turtle cursor
            self.t.hideturtle()

    # clear everything
    def clear(self):
        self.t.clear()

# a class for animating Spirographs
class SpiroAnimator:
    # constructor
    def __init__(self, N):
        # set the timer value in milliseconds
        self.deltaT = 10
        # get the window dimensions
        self.width = turtle.window_width()
        self.height = turtle.window_height()
        # create the Spiro objects
        self.spiros = []
        for i in range(N):
            # generate random parameters
            rparams = self.genRandomParams()
            # set the spiro parameters
            spiro = Spiro(*rparams)
            self.spiros.append(spiro)
        # call timer
        turtle.ontimer(self.update, self.deltaT)

    # restart spiro drawing
    def restart(self):
        for spiro in self.spiros:
            # clear
            spiro.clear()
            # generate random parameters
            rparams = self.genRandomParams()
```

```
            # set the spiro parameters
            spiro.setparams(*rparams)
            # restart drawing
            spiro.restart()

        # generate random parameters
        def genRandomParams(self):
            width, height = self.width, self.height
            R = random.randint(50, min(width, height)//2)
            r = random.randint(10, 9*R//10)
            l = random.uniform(0.1, 0.9)
            xc = random.randint(-width//2, width//2)
            yc = random.randint(-height//2, height//2)
            col = (random.random(),
                    random.random(),
                    random.random())
            return (xc, yc, col, R, r, l)

        def update(self):
            # update all spiros
            nComplete = 0
            for spiro in self.spiros:
                # update
                spiro.update()
                # count completed spiros
                if spiro.drawingComplete:
                    nComplete += 1
            # restart if all spiros are complete
            if nComplete == len(self.spiros):
                self.restart()
            # call the timer
            turtle.ontimer(self.update, self.deltaT)

        # toggle turtle cursor on and off
        def toggleTurtles(self):
            for spiro in self.spiros:
                if spiro.t.isvisible():
                    spiro.t.hideturtle()
                else:
                    spiro.t.showturtle()

# save drawings as PNG files
def saveDrawing():
    # hide the turtle cursor
    turtle.hideturtle()
    # generate unique filenames
    dateStr = (datetime.now()).strftime("%d%b%Y-%H%M%S")
    fileName = 'spiro-' + dateStr
    print('saving drawing to %s.eps/png' % fileName)
    # get the tkinter canvas
    canvas = turtle.getcanvas()
    # save the drawing as a postscipt image
    canvas.postscript(file = fileName + '.eps')
    # use the Pillow module to convert the poscript image file to PNG
    img = Image.open(fileName + '.eps')
```

```python
        img.save(fileName + '.png', 'png')
        # show the turtle cursor
        turtle.showturtle()

# main() function
def main():
    # use sys.argv if needed
    print('generating spirograph...')
    # create parser
    descStr = """This program draws Spirographs using the Turtle module.
When run with no arguments, this program draws random Spirographs.

Terminology:

R: radius of outer circle
r: radius of inner circle
l: ratio of hole distance to r
"""
    parser = argparse.ArgumentParser(description=descStr)

    # add expected arguments
    parser.add_argument('--sparams', nargs=3, dest='sparams', required=False,
                        help="The three arguments in sparams: R, r, l.")

    # parse args
    args = parser.parse_args()

    # set the width of the drawing window to 80 percent of the screen width
    turtle.setup(width=0.8)

    # set the cursor shape to turtle
    turtle.shape('turtle')

    # set the title to Spirographs!
    turtle.title("Spirographs!")
    # add the key handler to save our drawings
    turtle.onkey(saveDrawing, "s")
    # start listening
    turtle.listen()

    # hide the main turtle cursor
    turtle.hideturtle()

    # check for any arguments sent to --sparams and draw the Spirograph
    if args.sparams:
        params = [float(x) for x in args.sparams]
        # draw the Spirograph with the given parameters
        col = (0.0, 0.0, 0.0)
        spiro = Spiro(0, 0, col, *params)
        spiro.draw()
    else:
        # create the animator object
        spiroAnim = SpiroAnimator(4)
        # add a key handler to toggle the turtle cursor
        turtle.onkey(spiroAnim.toggleTurtles, "t")
```

```
        # add a key handler to restart the animation
        turtle.onkey(spiroAnim.restart, "space")

    # start the turtle main loop
    turtle.mainloop()

# call main
if __name__ == '__main__':
    main()
```

Running the Spirograph Animation

Now it's time to run your program.

```
$ python spiro.py
```

By default, the *spiro.py* program draws random spiros, as shown in
Figure 2-5. Pressing S saves the drawing.

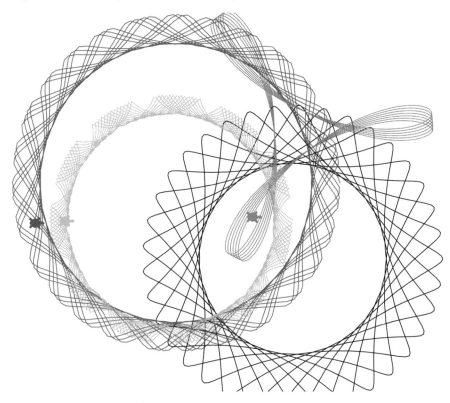

Figure 2-5: A sample run of spiro.py

Now run the program again, this time passing in parameters on the command line to draw a particular spiro.

```
$ python spiro.py --sparams 300 100 0.9
```

Figure 2-6 shows the output. As you can see, this code draws a single spiro with the parameters specified by the user, in contrast to Figure 2-5, which displays an animation of several random spiros.

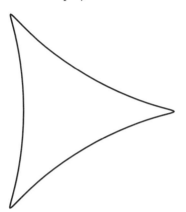

Figure 2-6: A sample run of spiro.py *with specific parameters*

Summary

In this project, you learned how to create Spirograph-like curves. You also learned how to adjust the input parameters to generate a variety of different curves and to animate them on screen. I hope you enjoy creating these spiros. (You'll find a surprise in Chapter 13, where you'll learn how to project spiros onto a wall!)

Experiments!

Here are some ways to experiment further with spiros.

1. Now that you know how to draw circles, write a program to draw random *spirals*. Find the equation for a *logarithmic spiral* in parametric form and then use it to draw the spirals.

2. You might have noticed that the turtle cursor is always oriented to the right as the curves are drawn, but that's not how turtles move! Orient the turtle so that, as the curve is being drawn, it faces in the direction of drawing. (Hint: calculate the direction vector between successive points for every step and reorient the turtle using the turtle.setheading() method.)

3. Try drawing a Koch snowflake, a fractal curve constructed using recursion (a function that calls itself), with the turtle. You can structure your recursive function call like this:

```
# recursive Koch snowflake
def kochSF(x1, y1, x2, y2, t):
    # compute intermediate points p2, p3
    if segment_length > 10:
        # recursively generate child segments
        # flake #1
        kochSF(x1, y1, p1[0], p1[1], t)
        # flake #2
        kochSF(p1[0], p1[1], p2[0], p2[1], t)
        # flake #3
        kochSF(p2[0], p2[1], p3[0], p3[1], t)
        # flake #4
        kochSF(p3[0], p3[1], x2, y2, t)
    else:
        # draw
        # ...
```

If you get really stuck, you can find my solution at *http://electronut.in/koch-snowflake-and-the-thue-morse-sequence/*.

PART II

SIMULATING LIFE

"First, let's assume the cow is a sphere . . ."
—Anonymous physics joke

3

CONWAY'S GAME OF LIFE

 You can use a computer to study a system
by creating a mathematical model for that
system, writing a program to represent the
model, and then letting the model evolve over
time. There are many kinds of computer simulations,
but I'll focus on a famous one called Conway's Game
of Life, the work of the British mathematician John Conway. The Game of
Life is an example of a *cellular automaton*, a collection of colored cells on a
grid that evolve through a number of time steps according to a set of rules
defining the states of neighboring cells.

In this project, you'll create an $N{\times}N$ grid of cells and simulate the evo-
lution of the system over time by applying the rules of Conway's Game of
Life. You'll display the state of the game at each time step and provide ways
to save the output to a file. You'll set the initial condition of the system to
either a random distribution or a predesigned pattern.

This simulation consists of the following components:

- A property defined in one- or two-dimensional space
- A mathematical rule to change this property for each step in the simulation
- A way to display or capture the state of the system as it evolves

The cells in Conway's Game of Life can be either ON or OFF. The game starts with an initial condition, in which each cell is assigned one state and mathematical rules determine how its state will change over time. The amazing thing about Conway's Game of Life is that with just four simple rules the system evolves to produce patterns that behave in incredibly complex ways, almost as if they were alive. Patterns include "gliders" that slide across the grid, "blinkers" that flash on and off, and even replicating patterns.

Of course, the philosophical implications of this game are also significant, because they suggest that complex structures can evolve from simple rules without following any sort of preset pattern.

Here are some of the main concepts covered in this project:

- Using `matplotlib` `imshow` to represent a 2D grid of data
- Using `matplotlib` for animation
- Using the `numpy` array
- Using the `%` operator for boundary conditions
- Setting up a random distribution of values

How It Works

Because the Game of Life is built on a grid of nine squares, every cell has eight neighboring cells, as shown in Figure 3-1. A given cell (i, j) in the simulation is accessed on a grid $[i][j]$, where i and j are the row and column indices, respectively. The value of a given cell at a given instant of time depends on the state of its neighbors at the previous time step.

Conway's Game of Life has four rules.

1. If a cell is ON and has fewer than two neighbors that are ON, it turns OFF.
2. If a cell is ON and has either two or three neighbors that are ON, it remains ON.
3. If a cell is ON and has more than three neighbors that are ON, it turns OFF.
4. If a cell is OFF and has exactly three neighbors that are ON, it turns ON.

These rules are meant to mirror some basic ways that a group of organisms might fare over time: underpopulation and overpopulation kill cells by turning a cell OFF when it has fewer than two neighbors or more than three, and cells stay ON and reproduce by turning another cell from OFF to ON when the population is balanced. But what about cells at the edge of the grid? Which cells are their neighbors? To answer this question, you need to think about *boundary conditions*, the rules that govern what happens to cells at the edges or boundaries of the grid. I'll

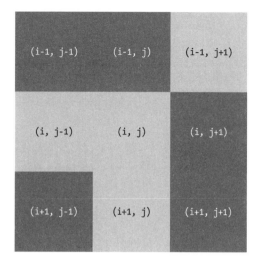

Figure 3-1: Eight neighboring cells

address this question by using *toroidal boundary conditions*, meaning that the square grid wraps around so that its shape is a torus. As shown in Figure 3-2, the grid is first warped so that its horizontal edges (A and B) join to form a cylinder, and then the cylinder's vertical edges (C and D) are joined to form a torus. Once the torus has been formed, all cells have neighbors because the whole space has no edge.

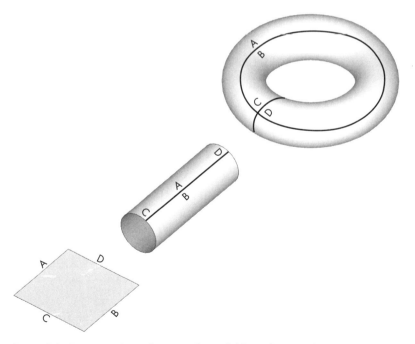

Figure 3-2: Conceptual visualization of toroidal boundary conditions

NOTE *This is similar to how boundaries work in Pac-Man. If you go off the top of the screen, you appear on the bottom. If you go off the left side of the screen, you appear on the right side. This kind of boundary condition is common in 2D simulations.*

Here's a description of the algorithm you'll use to apply the four rules and run the simulation:

1. Initialize the cells in the grid.
2. At each time step in the simulation, for each cell (i, j) in the grid, do the following:
   a. Update the value of cell (i, j) based on its neighbors, taking into account the boundary conditions.
   b. Update the display of grid values.

Requirements

You'll use numpy arrays and the matplotlib library to display the simulation output, and you'll use the matplotlib animation module to update the simulation. (See Chapter 1 for a review of matplotlib.)

The Code

You'll develop the code for the simulation bit by bit inside the Python interpreter by examining the pieces needed for different parts. To see the full project code, skip ahead to "The Complete Code" on page 49.

First, import the modules you'll be using for this project:

```
>>> import numpy as np
>>> import matplotlib.pyplot as plt
>>> import matplotlib.animation as animation
```

Now let's create the grid.

Representing the Grid

To represent whether a cell is alive (ON) or dead (OFF) on the grid, you'll use the values 255 and 0 for ON and OFF, respectively. You'll display the current state of the grid using the imshow() method in matplotlib, which represents a matrix of numbers as an image. Enter the following:

```
❶ >>> x = np.array([[0, 0, 255], [255, 255, 0], [0, 255, 0]])
❷ >>> plt.imshow(x, interpolation='nearest')
   plt.show()
```

At ❶, you define a 2D numpy array of shape (3, 3), where each element of the array is an integer value. You then use the plt.show() method to display this matrix of values as an image, and you pass in the interpolation option as 'nearest' at ❷ to get sharp edges for the cells (or they'd be fuzzy).

Figure 3-3 shows the output of this code.

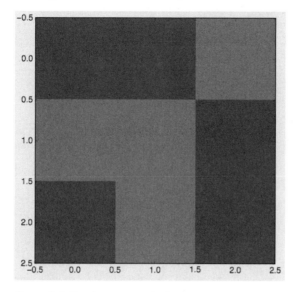

Figure 3-3: Displaying a grid of values

Notice that the value of 0 (OFF) is shown in dark gray and 255 (ON) is shown in light gray, which is the default colormap used in imshow().

Initial Conditions

To begin the simulation, set an initial state for each cell in the 2D grid. You can use a random distribution of ON and OFF cells and see what kind of patterns emerge, or you can add some specific patterns and see how they evolve. You'll look at both approaches.

To use a random initial state, use the choice() method from the random module in numpy. Enter the following:

```
np.random.choice([0, 255], 4*4, p=[0.1, 0.9]).reshape(4, 4)
```

Here is the output:

```
array([[255, 255, 255, 255],
       [255, 255, 255, 255],
       [255, 255, 255, 255],
       [255, 255, 255, 0]])
```

np.random.choice chooses a value from the given list [0, 255], with the probability of the appearance of each value given in the parameter p=[0.1, 0.9]. Here, you ask for 0 to appear with a probability of 0.1 (or 10 percent) and for 255 to appear with a probability of 90 percent. (The two values in p must add up to 1.) Because this choice() method creates a one-dimensional array of 16 values, you use .reshape to make it a two-dimensional array.

To set up the initial condition to match a particular pattern instead of just filling in a random set of values, initialize the two-dimensional grid to zeros and then use a method to add a pattern at a particular row and column in the grid, as shown here:

```
def addGlider(i, j, grid):
    """adds a glider with top left cell at (i, j)"""
❶   glider = np.array([[0, 0, 255],
                       [255, 0, 255],
                       [0, 255, 255]])
❷   grid[i:i+3, j:j+3] = glider
❸ grid = np.zeros(N*N).reshape(N, N)
❹ addGlider(1, 1, grid)
```

At ❶, you define the glider pattern (an observed pattern that moves steadily across the grid) using a numpy array of shape (3, 3). At ❷, you can see how you use the numpy slice operation to copy this pattern array into the simulation's two-dimensional grid, with its top-left corner placed at the coordinates you specify as i and j. You create an $N{\times}N$ array of zeros at ❸, and at ❹, you call the addGlider() method to initialize the grid with the glider pattern.

Boundary Conditions

Now we can think about how to implement the toroidal boundary conditions. First, let's see what happens at the right edge of a grid of size $N{\times}N$. The cell at the end of row i is accessed as grid[i][N-1]. Its neighbor to the right is grid[i][N], but according to the toroidal boundary conditions, the value accessed as grid[i][N] should be replaced by grid[i][0]. Here's one way to do that:

```
if j == N-1:
    right = grid[i][0]
else:
    right = grid[i][j+1]
```

Of course, you'd need to apply similar boundary conditions to the left, top, and bottom sides of the grid, but doing so would require adding a lot more code because each of the four edges of the grid would need to be tested. A much more compact way to accomplish this is with Python's modulus (%) operator, as shown here:

```
>>> N = 16
>>> i1 = 14
>>> i2 = 15
>>> (i1+1)%N
15
>>> (i2+1)%N
0
```

As you can see, the % operator gives the remainder for the integer division by N. You can use this operator to make the values wrap around at the edge by rewriting the grid access code like this:

```
right = grid[i][(j+1)%N]
```

Now when a cell is on the edge of the grid (in other words, when j = N-1), asking for the cell to the right with this method will give you (j+1)%N, which sets j back to 0, making the right side of the grid wrap to the left side. When you do the same for the bottom of the grid, it wraps around to the top.

Implementing the Rules

The rules of the Game of Life are based on the number of neighboring cells that are ON or OFF. To simplify the application of these rules, you can calculate the total number of neighboring cells in the ON state. Because the ON states have a value of 255, you can just sum the values of all the neighbors and divide by 255 to get the number of ON cells. Here is the relevant code:

```
                    # apply Conway's rules
                    if grid[i, j] == ON:
❶                       if (total < 2) or (total > 3):
                            newGrid[i, j] = OFF
                    else:
                        if total == 3:
❷                           newGrid[i, j] = ON
```

At ❶, any cell that is ON is turned OFF if it has fewer than two neighbors that are ON or if it has more than three neighbors that are ON. The code at ❷ applies only to OFF cells: a cell is turned ON if exactly three neighbors are ON.

Now it's time to write the complete code for the simulation.

Sending Command Line Arguments to the Program

The following code sends command line arguments to your program:

```
# main() function
def main():
    # command line argumentss are in sys.argv[1], sys.argv[2], ...
    # sys.argv[0] is the script name and can be ignored
    # parse arguments
❶   parser = argparse.ArgumentParser(description="Runs Conway's Game of Life
        simulation.")
    # add arguments
❷   parser.add_argument('--grid-size', dest='N', required=False)
❸   parser.add_argument('--mov-file', dest='movfile', required=False)
❹   parser.add_argument('--interval', dest='interval', required=False)
❺   parser.add_argument('--glider', action='store_true', required=False)
    args = parser.parse_args()
```

The main() function begins by defining command line parameters for the program. You use the argparse class at ❶ to add command line options to the code, and then you add various options to it in the following lines. At ❷, you specify the simulation grid size *N*, and at ❸, you specify the filename for the saved *.mov* file. At ❹, you set the animation update interval in milliseconds, and at ❺, you start the simulation with a glider pattern.

Initializing the Simulation

Continuing through the code, you come to the following section, which initializes the simulation:

```
# set grid size
N = 100
if args.N and int(args.N) > 8:
    N = int(args.N)

# set animation update interval
updateInterval = 50
if args.interval:
    updateInterval = int(args.interval)

# declare grid
grid = np.array([])
# check if "glider" demo flag is specified
if args.glider:
    grid = np.zeros(N*N).reshape(N, N)
    addGlider(1, 1, grid)
else:
    # populate grid with random on/off - more off than on
    grid = randomGrid(N)
```

The ❶ marks the line `grid = np.array([])`.

Still within the main() function, this portion of the code applies any parameters called at the command line, once the command line options have been parsed. For example, the lines that follow ❶ set up the initial conditions, either a random pattern by default or a glider pattern.

Finally, you set up the animation.

```
# set up the animation
fig, ax = plt.subplots()
img = ax.imshow(grid, interpolation='nearest')
ani = animation.FuncAnimation(fig, update, fargs=(img, grid, N, ),
                              frames=10,
                              interval=updateInterval,
                              save_count=50)

# number of frames?
# set the output file
if args.movfile:
    ani.save(args.movfile, fps=30, extra_args=['-vcodec', 'libx264'])

plt.show()
```

The ❶ marks the line `fig, ax = plt.subplots()` and ❷ marks the line `ani = animation.FuncAnimation(...)`.

At ❶, you configure the `matplotlib` plot and animation parameters. At ❷, `animation.FuncAnimation()` calls the function `update()`, defined earlier in the program, which updates the grid according to the rules of Conway's Game of Life using toroidal boundary conditions.

The Complete Code

Here is the complete program for your Game of Life simulation. You can also download the code for this project from *https://github.com/electronut/pp/ blob/master/conway/conway.py*.

```
import sys, argparse
import numpy as np
import matplotlib.pyplot as plt
import matplotlib.animation as animation

ON = 255
OFF = 0
vals = [ON, OFF]

def randomGrid(N):
    """returns a grid of NxN random values"""
    return np.random.choice(vals, N*N, p=[0.2, 0.8]).reshape(N, N)

def addGlider(i, j, grid):
    """adds a glider with top-left cell at (i, j)"""
    glider = np.array([[0,    0, 255],
                       [255,  0, 255],
                       [0,  255, 255]])
    grid[i:i+3, j:j+3] = glider

def update(frameNum, img, grid, N):
    # copy grid since we require 8 neighbors for calculation
    # and we go line by line
    newGrid = grid.copy()
    for i in range(N):
        for j in range(N):
            # compute 8-neghbor sum using toroidal boundary conditions
            # x and y wrap around so that the simulation
            # takes place on a toroidal surface
            total = int((grid[i, (j-1)%N] + grid[i, (j+1)%N] +
                        grid[(i-1)%N, j] + grid[(i+1)%N, j] +
                        grid[(i-1)%N, (j-1)%N] + grid[(i-1)%N, (j+1)%N] +
                        grid[(i+1)%N, (j-1)%N] + grid[(i+1)%N, (j+1)%N])/255)
            # apply Conway's rules
            if grid[i, j] == ON:
                if (total < 2) or (total > 3):
                    newGrid[i, j] = OFF
            else:
                if total == 3:
                    newGrid[i, j] = ON
```

```python
        # update data
        img.set_data(newGrid)
        grid[:] = newGrid[:]
        return img,

# main() function
def main():
    # command line arguments are in sys.argv[1], sys.argv[2], ...
    # sys.argv[0] is the script name and can be ignored
    # parse arguments
    parser = argparse.ArgumentParser(description="Runs Conway's Game of Life
        simulation.")
  # add arguments
    parser.add_argument('--grid-size', dest='N', required=False)
    parser.add_argument('--mov-file', dest='movfile', required=False)
    parser.add_argument('--interval', dest='interval', required=False)
    parser.add_argument('--glider', action='store_true', required=False)
    parser.add_argument('--gosper', action='store_true', required=False)
    args = parser.parse_args()

    # set grid size
    N = 100
    if args.N and int(args.N) > 8:
        N = int(args.N)

    # set animation update interval
    updateInterval = 50
    if args.interval:
        updateInterval = int(args.interval)

    # declare grid
    grid = np.array([])
    # check if "glider" demo flag is specified
    if args.glider:
        grid = np.zeros(N*N).reshape(N, N)
        addGlider(1, 1, grid)
    else:
        # populate grid with random on/off - more off than on
        grid = randomGrid(N)

    # set up the animation
    fig, ax = plt.subplots()
    img = ax.imshow(grid, interpolation='nearest')
    ani = animation.FuncAnimation(fig, update, fargs=(img, grid, N, ),
                                  frames=10,
                                  interval=updateInterval,
                                  save_count=50)

    # number of frames?
    # set the output file
    if args.movfile:
        ani.save(args.movfile, fps=30, extra_args=['-vcodec', 'libx264'])

    plt.show()
```

```
# call main
if __name__ == '__main__':
    main()
```

Running the Game of Life Simulation

Now run the code:

```
$ python3 conway.py
```

This uses the default parameters for the simulation: a grid of 100×100 cells and an update interval of 50 milliseconds. As you watch the simulation, you'll see how it progresses to create and sustain various patterns over time, as in Figure 3-4.

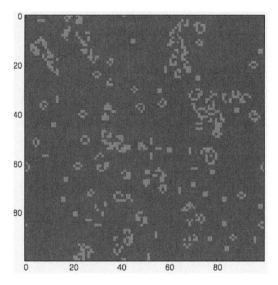

Figure 3-4: Game of Life in progress

Figure 3-5 shows some of the patterns to look for in the simulation. Besides the glider, look for a three-cell blinker and static patterns such as a block or loaf shape.

Now change things up a bit by running the simulation with these parameters:

```
$ python conway.py --grid-size 32 --interval 500 --glider
```

This creates a simulation grid of 32×32, updates the animation every 500 milliseconds, and uses the initial glider pattern shown in the bottom right of Figure 3-5.

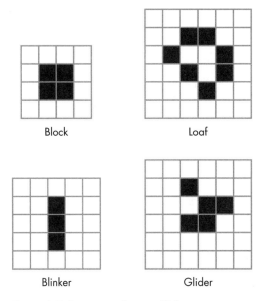

Block   Loaf

Blinker   Glider

Figure 3-5: Patterns in Game of Life

Summary

In this project, you explored Conway's Game of Life. You learned how to set up a basic computer simulation based on some rules and how to use `matplotlib` to visualize the state of the system as it evolves.

My implementation of Conway's Game of Life emphasizes simplicity over performance. You can speed up the computations in Game of Life in many different ways, and a tremendous amount of research has been done on how to do this. You'll find a lot of this research with a quick Internet search.

Experiments!

Here are some ways to experiment further with Conway's Game of Life.

1. Write an `addGosperGun()` method to add the pattern shown in Figure 3-6 to the grid. This pattern is called the *Gosper Glider Gun*. Run the simulation and observe what the gun does.

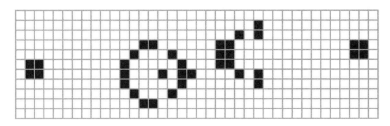

Figure 3-6: Gosper Glider Gun

2. Write a readPattern() method that reads in an initial pattern from a text file and uses it to set the initial conditions for the simulation. Here is a suggested format for this file:

8
0 0 0 255 ...

The first line of the file defines N, and the rest of the file is just $N \times N$ integers (0 or 255) separated by whitespace. You can use Python methods such as open and file.read to do this. This exploration will help you study how any given pattern evolves with the rules of the Game of Life. Add a --pattern-file command line option to use this file while running the program.

4

GENERATING MUSICAL OVERTONES WITH THE KARPLUS-STRONG ALGORITHM

One of the main characteristics of any musical sound is its pitch, or *frequency*. This is the number of vibrations per second in hertz (Hz). For example, the third string from the top of an acoustic guitar produces an D note with a frequency of 146.83 Hz. This is a sound you can approximate by creating a sine wave with a frequency of 146.83 Hz on a computer, as shown in Figure 4-1.

Unfortunately, if you play this sine wave on your computer, it won't sound anything like a guitar or a piano. What makes a computer sound so different from a musical instrument when playing the same note?

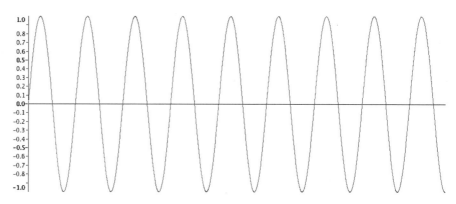

Figure 4-1: Sine wave at 146.83 Hz

When you pluck a string on the guitar, the instrument produces a mix of frequencies with varying intensity, as shown in the *spectral plot* in Figure 4-2. The sound is most intense when the note is first struck, and the intensity dies off over time. The dominant frequency you hear when you pluck the D string on the guitar, called the *fundamental frequency*, is 146.83 Hz, but you also hear certain multiples of that frequency called *overtones*. The sound of any instrument is comprised of this fundamental frequency and overtones, and it's the combination of these that makes a guitar sound like a guitar.

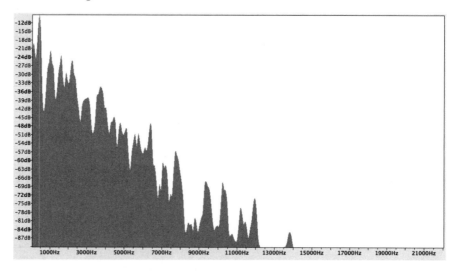

Figure 4-2: Spectral plot of note D4 played on guitar

As you can see, to simulate the sound of a plucked string instrument on the computer, you need to be able to generate both the fundamental frequency and the overtones. The trick is to use the Karplus-Strong algorithm.

In this project, you'll generate five guitar-like notes of a musical scale (a series of related notes) using the Karplus-Strong algorithm. You'll visualize the algorithm used to generate these notes and save the sounds as WAV files. You'll also create a way to play them at random and learn how to do the following:

- Implement a ring buffer using the Python deque class.
- Use numpy arrays and ufuncs.
- Play WAV files using pygame.
- Plot a graph using matplotlib.
- Play the pentatonic musical scale.

In addition to implementing the Karplus-Strong algorithm in Python, you'll also explore the WAV file format and see how to generate notes within a pentatonic musical scale.

How It Works

The Karplus-Strong algorithm can simulate the sound of a plucked string by using a *ring buffer* of displacement values to simulate a string tied down at both ends, similar to a guitar string.

A ring buffer (also known as a *circular buffer*) is a fixed-length buffer (just an array of values) that wraps around itself. In other words, when you reach the end of the buffer, the next element you access will be the first element in the buffer. (See "Implementing the Ring Buffer with deque" on page 61 for more about ring buffers.)

The length (N) of the ring buffer is related to the fundamental frequency of vibration according to the equation $N = S/f$, where S is the sampling rate and f is the frequency.

At the start of the simulation, the buffer is filled with random values in the range [−0.5, 0.5], which you might think of as representing the random displacement of a plucked string as it vibrates.

In addition to the ring buffer, you use a *samples buffer* to store the intensity of the sound at any particular time. The length of this buffer and the sampling rate determine the length of the sound clip.

The Simulation

The simulation proceeds until the sample buffer is filled in a kind of feedback scheme, as shown in Figure 4-3. For each step of the simulation, you do the following:

1. Store the first value from the ring buffer in the samples buffer.
2. Calculate the average of the first two elements in the ring buffer.
3. Multiply this average value by an attenuation factor (in this case, 0.995).
4. Append this value to the end of the ring buffer.
5. Remove the first element of the ring buffer.

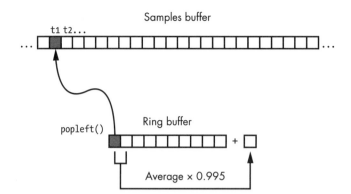

Figure 4-3: Ring buffer and the Karplus-Strong algorithm

To simulate a plucked string, fill a ring buffer with numbers that represent the energy of the wave. The sample buffer, which represents the final sound data, is created by iterating through the values in the ring buffer. Use an averaging scheme (explained in a moment) to update values in the ring buffer.

This feedback scheme is designed to simulate the energy traveling through a vibrating string. According to physics, for a vibrating string, the fundamental frequency is inversely proportional to its length. Since we are interested in generating sounds of a certain frequency, we choose a ring buffer length that is inversely proportional to that frequency. The averaging that happens in step 1 of the simulation acts as a *low-pass filter* that cuts off higher frequencies and allows lower frequencies through, thereby eliminating higher *harmonics* (that is, larger multiples of the fundamental frequency) because you're mainly interested in the fundamental frequency. Finally, you use the attenuation factor to simulate the loss of energy as the wave travels back and forth along the string.

The samples buffer that you use in step 1 of the simulation represents the amplitude of the generated sound over time. To calculate the amplitude at any given time, you update the ring buffer by calculating the average of its first two elements and multiplying the result by an attenuation factor. This calculated value is then appended to the end of the ring buffer, and the first element is removed.

Now let's look at a simple example of the algorithm in action. The following table represents a ring buffer at two consecutive time steps. Each value in the ring buffer represents the amplitude of the sound. The buffer has five elements, and they are initially filled with some numbers.

Time step 1	0.1	−0.2	0.3	0.6	−0.5
Time step 2	−0.2	0.3	0.6	−0.5	−0.199

As you go from time step 1 to step 2, apply the Karplus-Strong algorithm as follows. The first value in the first row, 0.1, is removed, and all subsequent values from time step 1 are added in the same order to the second row, which represents time step 2. The last value in time step 2 is the attenuated average of the first and last values of time step 1, which is calculated as $0.995 \times ((0.1 + -0.5) \div 2) = -0.199$.

Creating WAV Files

The *Waveform Audio File Format (WAV)* is used to store audio data. This format is convenient for small audio projects because it is simple and doesn't require you to deal with complicated compression techniques.

In its simplest form, WAV files consist of a series of bits representing the amplitude of the recorded sound at a given point in time, called the *resolution*. You'll use 16-bit resolution in this project. WAV files also have a set *sampling rate*, which is the number of times the audio is *sampled*, or read, every second. In this project, you use a sampling rate of 44,100 Hz, the rate used in audio CDs. Let's generate a five-second audio clip of a 220 Hz sine wave using Python. First, you represent a sine wave using this formula:

$$A = \sin(2\pi f t)$$

Here, A is the amplitude of the wave, f is the frequency, and t is the current time index. Now you rewrite this equation as follows:

$$A = \sin(2\pi f i/R)$$

In this equation, i is the index of the sample, and R is the sampling rate. Using these two equations, you can create a WAV file for a 200 Hz sine wave as follows:

```
import numpy as np
import wave, math

sRate = 44100
nSamples = sRate * 5
❶ x = np.arange(nSamples)/float(sRate)
❷ vals = np.sin(2.0*math.pi*220.0*x)
❸ data = np.array(vals*32767, 'int16').tostring()
file = wave.open('sine220.wav', 'wb')
❹ file.setparams((1, 2, sRate, nSamples, 'NONE', 'uncompressed'))
file.writeframes(data)
file.close()
```

At ❶ and ❷, you create a numpy array (see Chapter 1) of amplitude values, according to the second sine wave equation. The numpy array is a fast and convenient way to apply functions to arrays such as the sin() function.

At ❸, the computed sine wave values in the range [–1, 1] are scaled to 16-bit values and converted to a string so they can be written to a file. At ❹, you set the parameters for the WAV file; in this case, it's a single-channel (mono), two-byte (16-bit), uncompressed format. Figure 4-4 shows the generated *sine220.wav* file in Audacity, a free audio editor. As expected, you see a sine wave of frequency 220 Hz, and when you play the file, you hear a 220 Hz tone for five seconds.

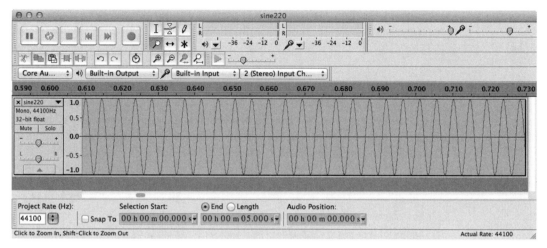

Figure 4-4: A sine wave at 220 Hz

The Minor Pentatonic Scale

A *musical scale* is a series of notes in increasing or decreasing pitch or frequency. A *musical interval* is the difference between two pitches. Usually, all notes in a piece of music are chosen from a particular scale. A *semitone* is a basic building block of a scale and is the smallest musical interval in Western music. A *tone* is twice the length of a semitone. The *major scale,* one of the most common musical scales, is defined by the interval pattern *tone-tone-semitone-tone-tone-tone-semitone.*

We will briefly go into the pentatonic scale here, since we want to generate musical notes in that scale. This section will tell you how we came up with the frequency numbers used by our program to generate these notes using the Karplus-Strong algorithm. The *pentatonic scale* is a five-note musical scale. For example, the famous American song "Oh! Susanna" is based on a pentatonic scale. A variant of this scale is the minor pentatonic scale.

This scale is given by the note sequence *(tone+semitone)-tone-tone-(tone+semitone)-tone.* Thus, the C minor pentatonic scale consists of the notes C, E-flat, F, G, and B-flat. Table 4-1 lists the frequencies of the five notes of a minor pentatonic scale that you will generate using the Karplus-Strong algorithm. (Here, C4 designates C in the fourth octave of a piano, or *middle C,* by convention.)

Table 4-1: Notes in a Minor Pentatonic Scale

Note	Frequency (Hz)
C4	261.6
E-flat	311.1
F	349.2
G	392.0
B-flat	466.2

Requirements

In this project, you'll use the Python wave module to create audio files in WAV format. You'll use numpy arrays for the Karplus-Strong algorithm and the deque class from Python collections to implement the ring buffer. You'll also play back the WAV files with the pygame module.

The Code

Now let's develop the various pieces of code required to implement the Karplus-Strong algorithm and then put them together for the complete program. To see the full project code, skip ahead to "The Complete Code" on page 65.

Implementing the Ring Buffer with deque

Recall from earlier that the Karplus-Strong algorithm uses a ring buffer to generate a musical note. You'll implement the ring buffer using Python's deque container (pronounced "deck")—part of Python's collections module—which provides specialized container data types in an array. You can insert and remove elements from the beginning (head) or end (tail) of a deque (see Figure 4-5). This insertion and removal process is a 0(1), or a "constant time" operation, which means it takes the same amount of time regardless of how big the deque container gets.

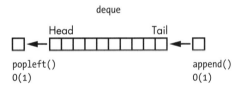

Figure 4-5: Ring buffer using deque

The following code shows how you would use deque in Python:

```
>>> from collections import deque
❶ >>> d = deque(range(10))
>>> print(d)
deque([0, 1, 2, 3, 4, 5, 6, 7, 8, 9])
❷ >>> d.append(-1)
>>> print(d)
deque([0, 1, 2, 3, 4, 5, 6, 7, 8, 9, -1])
❸ >>> d.popleft()
0
>>> print d
deque([1, 2, 3, 4, 5, 6, 7, 8, 9, -1])
```

At ❶, you create the deque container by passing in a list created by the range() method. At ❷, you append an element to the end of the deque container, and at ❸, you pop (remove) the first element from the head of the deque. Both these operations happen quickly.

Implementing the Karplus-Strong Algorithm

You also use a deque container to implement the Karplus-Strong algorithm for the ring buffer, as shown here:

```
# generate note of given frequency
def generateNote(freq):
    nSamples = 44100
    sampleRate = 44100
    N = int(sampleRate/freq)
    # initialize ring buffer
❶    buf = deque([random.random() - 0.5 for i in range(N)])
    # initialize samples buffer
❷    samples = np.array([0]*nSamples, 'float32')
    for i in range(nSamples):
❸        samples[i] = buf[0]
❹        avg = 0.996*0.5*(buf[0] + buf[1])
        buf.append(avg)
        buf.popleft()

    # convert samples to 16-bit values and then to a string
    # the maximum value is 32767 for 16-bit
❺    samples = np.array(samples*32767, 'int16')
❻    return samples.tostring()
```

At ❶, you initialize deque with random numbers in the range [−0.5, 0.5]. At ❷, you set up a float array to store the sound samples. The length of this array matches the sampling rate, which means the sound clip will be generated for one second.

The first element in deque is copied to the samples buffer at ❸. At ❹, and in the lines that follow, you can see the low-pass filter and attenuation in action. At ❺, the samples array is converted into a 16-bit format by multiplying each value by 32,767 (a 16-bit signed integer can take only values from −32,768 to 32,767), and at ❻, it is converted to a string representation for the wave module, which you'll use to save this data to a file.

Writing a WAV File

Once you have the audio data, you can write it to a WAV file using the Python wave module.

```
def writeWAVE(fname, data):
    # open file
❶    file = wave.open(fname, 'wb')
    # WAV file parameters
    nChannels = 1
    sampleWidth = 2
    frameRate = 44100
    nFrames = 44100
    # set parameters
❷    file.setparams((nChannels, sampleWidth, frameRate, nFrames,
                    'NONE', 'noncompressed'))
```

```
❸     file.writeframes(data)
      file.close()
```

At ❶, you create a WAV file, and at ❷, you set its parameters using a single-channel, 16-bit, uncompressed format. Finally, at ❸, you write the data to the file.

Playing WAV Files with pygame

Now you'll use the Python pygame module to play the WAV files generated by the algorithm. pygame is a popular Python module used to write games. It's built on top of the Simple DirectMedia Layer (SDL) library, a high-performance, low-level library that gives you access to sound, graphics, and input devices on a computer.

For convenience, you encapsulate the code in a NotePlayer class, as shown here:

```
      # play a WAV file
      class NotePlayer:
          # constructor
          def __init__(self):
❶             pygame.mixer.pre_init(44100, -16, 1, 2048)
              pygame.init()
              # dictionary of notes
❷             self.notes = {}
          # add a note
          def add(self, fileName):
❸             self.notes[fileName] = pygame.mixer.Sound(fileName)
          # play a note
          def play(self, fileName):
              try:
❹                 self.notes[fileName].play()
              except:
                  print(fileName + ' not found!')
          def playRandom(self):
              """play a random note"""
❺             index = random.randint(0, len(self.notes)-1)
❻             note = list(self.notes.values())[index]
              note.play()
```

At ❶ , you preinitialize the pygame mixer class with a sampling rate of 44,100, 16-bit signed values, a single channel, and a buffer size of 2,048. At ❷, you create a dictionary of notes, which stores the pygame sound objects against the filenames. Next, in NotePlayer's add() method ❸, you create the sound object and store it in the notes dictionary.

Notice in play() how the dictionary is used at ❹ to select and play the sound object associated with a filename. The playRandom() method picks a random note from the five notes you've generated and plays it. Finally, at ❺, randint() selects a random integer from the range [0, 4] and at ❻ picks a note to play from the dictionary.

The main() Method

Now let's look at the main() method, which creates the notes and handles various command line options to play the notes.

```
    parser = argparse.ArgumentParser(description="Generating sounds with
        Karplus String Algorithm")
    # add arguments
❶   parser.add_argument('--display', action='store_true', required=False)
    parser.add_argument('--play', action='store_true', required=False)
    parser.add_argument('--piano', action='store_true', required=False)
    args = parser.parse_args()

    # show plot if flag set
    if args.display:
        gShowPlot = True
        plt.ion()

    # create note player
    nplayer = NotePlayer()

    print('creating notes...')
    for name, freq in list(pmNotes.items()):
        fileName = name + '.wav'
❷       if not os.path.exists(fileName) or args.display:
            data = generateNote(freq)
            print('creating ' + fileName + '...')
            writeWAVE(fileName, data)
        else:
            print('fileName already created. skipping...')

        # add note to player
❸       nplayer.add(name + '.wav')

        # play note if display flag set
        if args.display:
❹           nplayer.play(name + '.wav')
            time.sleep(0.5)

    # play a random tune
    if args.play:
        while True:
            try:
❺               nplayer.playRandom()
                # rest - 1 to 8 beats
❻               rest = np.random.choice([1, 2, 4, 8], 1,
                                        p=[0.15, 0.7, 0.1, 0.05])
                time.sleep(0.25*rest[0])
            except KeyboardInterrupt:
                exit()
```

First, you set up some command line options for the program using argparse, as discussed in earlier projects. At ❶, if the --display command line option was used, you set up a matplotlib plot to show how the waveform evolves during the Karplus-Strong algorithm. The ion() call enables interactive mode for matplotlib. You then create an instance of the NotePlayer class, generating the notes in a pentatonic scale using the generateNote() method. The frequencies for the five notes are defined in the global dictionary pmNotes.

At ❷, you use the os.path.exists() method to see whether the WAV file has been created. If so, you skip the computation. (This is a handy optimization if you're running this program several times.)

Once the note is computed and the WAV file created, you add the note to the NotePlayer dictionary at ❸ and then play it at ❹ if the display command line option is used.

At ❺, if the –play option is used, the playRandom() method in NotePlayer plays a note at random from the five notes. For a note sequence to sound even remotely musical, you need to add rests between the notes played, so you use the random.choice() method from numpy at ❻ to choose a random rest interval. This method also lets you choose the probability of the rest interval, which you set so that a two-beat rest is the most probable and an eight-beat rest the least probable. Try changing these values to create your own style of random music!

The Complete Code

Now let's put the program together. The complete code is shown here and can also be downloaded from *https://github.com/electronut/pp/blob/master/karplus/ks.py.*

```
import sys, os
import time, random
import wave, argparse, pygame
import numpy as np
from collections import deque
from matplotlib import pyplot as plt

# show plot of algorithm in action?
gShowPlot = False

# notes of a Pentatonic Minor scale
# piano C4-E(b)-F-G-B(b)-C5
pmNotes = {'C4': 262, 'Eb': 311, 'F': 349, 'G':391, 'Bb':466}

# write out WAV file
def writeWAVE(fname, data):
    # open file
    file = wave.open(fname, 'wb')
    # WAV file parameters
    nChannels = 1
    sampleWidth = 2
    frameRate = 44100
    nFrames = 44100
```

```python
    # set parameters
    file.setparams((nChannels, sampleWidth, frameRate, nFrames,
                    'NONE', 'noncompressed'))
    file.writeframes(data)
    file.close()

# generate note of given frequency
def generateNote(freq):
    nSamples = 44100
    sampleRate = 44100
    N = int(sampleRate/freq)
    # initialize ring buffer
    buf = deque([random.random() - 0.5 for i in range(N)])
    # plot of flag set
    if gShowPlot:
        axline, = plt.plot(buf)
    # initialize samples buffer
    samples = np.array([0]*nSamples, 'float32')
    for i in range(nSamples):
        samples[i] = buf[0]
        avg = 0.995*0.5*(buf[0] + buf[1])
        buf.append(avg)
        buf.popleft()
        # plot of flag set
        if gShowPlot:
            if i % 1000 == 0:
                axline.set_ydata(buf)
                plt.draw()

    # convert samples to 16-bit values and then to a string
    # the maximum value is 32767 for 16-bit
    samples = np.array(samples*32767, 'int16')
    return samples.tostring()

# play a WAV file
class NotePlayer:
    # constructor
    def __init__(self):
        pygame.mixer.pre_init(44100, -16, 1, 2048)
        pygame.init()
        # dictionary of notes
        self.notes = {}
    # add a note
    def add(self, fileName):
        self.notes[fileName] = pygame.mixer.Sound(fileName)
    # play a note
    def play(self, fileName):
        try:
            self.notes[fileName].play()
        except:
            print(fileName + ' not found!')
    def playRandom(self):
        """play a random note"""
        index = random.randint(0, len(self.notes)-1)
```

```python
        note = list(self.notes.values())[index]
        note.play()

# main() function
def main():
    # declare global var
    global gShowPlot

    parser = argparse.ArgumentParser(description="Generating sounds with
        Karplus String Algorithm")
    # add arguments
    parser.add_argument('--display', action='store_true', required=False)
    parser.add_argument('--play', action='store_true', required=False)
    parser.add_argument('--piano', action='store_true', required=False)
    args = parser.parse_args()

    # show plot if flag set
    if args.display:
        gShowPlot = True
        plt.ion()

    # create note player
    nplayer = NotePlayer()

    print('creating notes...')
    for name, freq in list(pmNotes.items()):
        fileName = name + '.wav'
        if not os.path.exists(fileName) or args.display:
            data = generateNote(freq)
            print('creating ' + fileName + '...')
            writeWAVE(fileName, data)
        else:
            print('fileName already created. skipping...')

        # add note to player
        nplayer.add(name + '.wav')

        # play note if display flag set
        if args.display:
            nplayer.play(name + '.wav')
            time.sleep(0.5)

    # play a random tune
    if args.play:
        while True:
            try:
                nplayer.playRandom()
                # rest - 1 to 8 beats
                rest = np.random.choice([1, 2, 4, 8], 1,
                                        p=[0.15, 0.7, 0.1, 0.05])
                time.sleep(0.25*rest[0])
            except KeyboardInterrupt:
                exit()
```

```
# random piano mode
if args.piano:
    while True:
        for event in pygame.event.get():
            if (event.type == pygame.KEYUP):
                print("key pressed")
                nplayer.playRandom()
                time.sleep(0.5)

# call main
if __name__ == '__main__':
    main()
```

Running the Plucked String Simulation

To run the code for this project, enter this in a command shell:

```
$ python3 ks.py -display
```

As you can see in Figure 4-6, the matplotlib plot shows how the Karplus-Strong algorithm converts the initial random displacements to create waves of the desired frequency.

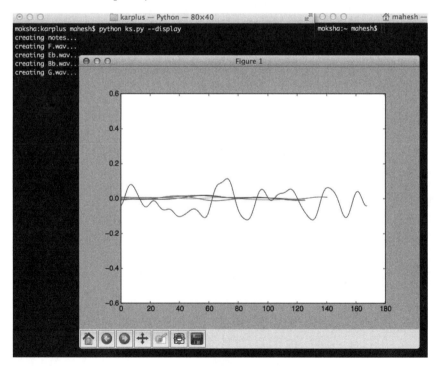

Figure 4-6: Sample run of Karplus-Strong algorithm

Now try playing a random note using this program.

```
$ python ks.py -play
```

This should play a random note sequence using the generated WAV files of the pentatonic musical scale.

Summary

In this project, you used the Karplus-Strong algorithm to simulate the sound of plucked strings and played notes from generated WAV files.

Experiments!

Here are some ideas for experiments:

1. Use the techniques you learned in this chapter to create a method that replicates the sound of two strings of different frequencies vibrating together. Remember, the Karplus-Strong algorithm produces sound amplitudes that can be added together (before scaling to 16-bit values for WAV file creation). Now add a time delay between the first and second string plucks.

2. Write a method to read music from a text file and generate musical notes. Then play the music using these notes. You can use a format where the note names are followed by integer rest time intervals, like this: C4 1 F4 2 G4 1 . . . .

3. Add a --piano command line option to the project. When the project is run with this option, the user should be able to press the A, S, D, F, and G keys on a keyboard to play the five musical notes. (Hint: use pygame.event.get and pygame.event.type.)

5

BOIDS: SIMULATING A FLOCK

Look closely at a flock of birds or a school of fish, and you'll notice that although the groups are composed of individual creatures, the group as a whole seems to have a life of its own. The birds in a flock align with each other as they move and flow over and around obstacles. They break formation when disturbed or startled but then regroup, as if controlled by some larger force.

In 1986, Craig Reynolds created a realistic-looking simulation of the flocking behavior of birds called the *Boids* model. One remarkable thing about the Boids model (named after the stereotypical New Yorker's pronunciation of the word *birds*) is that only three simple rules govern the interaction between individuals in the flock, yet the model produces behavior similar to that of a real flock. The Boids model is widely studied and has even been used to animate computer-generated swarms like the marching penguins in the movie *Batman Returns* (1992).

In this project, you'll use Reynolds's three rules to create a Boids simulation of the flocking behavior of *N* birds and plot their positions and directions of movement over time. You'll also provide a method to add a bird to the flock as well as a scatter effect that you can use to study the effect of a local disturbance on the flock. Boids is called an N-*body simulation* because it models a dynamic system of *N* particles that exert forces on each other.

How It Works

The three core rules of the Boids simulation are as follows:

Separation   Keep a minimum distance between the boids.

Alignment   Point each boid in the average direction of movement of its local flockmates.

Cohesion   Move each boid toward the center of mass of its local flockmates.

Boids simulations can add other rules, too, such as ones to avoid obstacles or scatter the flock when it's disturbed, as you'll learn in the following sections. This version of Boids implements these core rules for every step in the simulation:

- For all boids in the flock, do the following:
    - Apply the three core rules.
    - Apply any additional rules.
    - Apply all boundary conditions.
- Update the positions and velocities of the boids.
- Plot the new positions and velocities.

As you will see, these simple rules create a flock with evolving, complex behavior.

Requirements

These are the Python tools you'll be using in this simulation:

- numpy arrays to store the positions and velocities of the boids
- The matplotlib library to animate the boids
- argparse to process command line options
- The scipy.spatial.distance module, which has some really neat methods for calculating distances between points

NOTE   *I chose to use* matplotlib *for boids as a matter of simplicity and convenience. To draw a huge number of boids as fast as possible, you might use something like the OpenGL library. You'll explore graphics in more detail in Part 3 of this book.*

The Code

First, you'll compute the position and velocities of the boids. Next, you'll set up the boundary conditions for the simulation, look at how the boids are drawn, and implement the Boids simulation rules discussed earlier. Finally, you'll add some interesting events to the simulation by adding boids and scattering the flock. To see the full project code, skip ahead to "The Complete Code" on page 82.

Computing the Position and Velocities of the Boids

The Boids simulation needs to compute the position and velocities of the boids at each step by pulling information from numpy arrays. At the beginning of the simulation, you place all boids in approximately the center of the screen, with their velocities set in random directions.

```
❶ import math
❷ import numpy as np

❸ width, height = 640, 480

❹ pos = [width/2.0, height/2.0] + 10*np.random.rand(2*N).reshape(N, 2)
❺ angles = 2*math.pi*np.random.rand(N)
❻ vel = np.array(list(zip(np.sin(angles), np.cos(angles))))
```

You begin by importing the math module used in the calculations that follow at ❶. At ❷, you import the numpy library as np (to save some typing). Then you set the width and height of the simulation window on the screen ❸. At ❹, you create a numpy array pos by adding a random displacement of 10 units to the center of the window. The code np.random.rand(2*N) creates a one-dimensional array of 2N random numbers in the range [0, 1]. The reshape() call then converts this into a two-dimensional array of shape (N, 2), which you'll use to store the boids' positions. Notice, too, the numpy broadcasting rules in action here: the 1×2 array is added to each element in the N×2 array.

Next, you create an array of random unit velocity vectors (these are vectors of magnitude 1.0, pointing in random directions) using the following method: given an angle t, the pair of numbers $(\cos(t), \sin(t))$ lie on a circle of radius 1.0, centered at the origin $(0, 0)$. If you draw a line from the origin to a point on this circle, it becomes a unit vector that depends on the angle A. So if you choose A at random, you end up with a random velocity vector. Figure 5-1 illustrates this scheme.

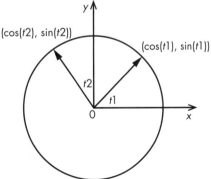

Figure 5-1: Generating random unit velocity vectors

At ❺, you generate an array of *N* random angles in the range [0, 2pi], and at ❻, you create an array using the random vector method discussed earlier and group the coordinates using the built-in zip() method. Here is a simple example of zip(). This joins two lists into a list of tuples.

```
>>> zip([0, 1, 2], [3, 4, 5])
[(0, 3), (1, 4), (2, 5)]
```

Here you've generated two arrays, one with random positions clustered within a 10-pixel radius around the center of the screen and the other with unit velocities pointing in random directions. This means that at the start of the simulation, the boids will all hover around the center of the screen, pointed in random directions.

Setting Boundary Conditions

Birds fly in the boundless sky, but the boids must play in limited space. To create that space, you'll create boundary conditions as you did with the toroidal boundary condition in the Conway simulation in Chapter 3. In this case, you'll apply a *tiled boundary condition* (actually the continuous space version of the boundary condition you used in Chapter 3).

Think of the Boids simulation as taking place in a tiled space: when a boid moves out of a tile, it moves in from the opposite direction to an identical tile. The main difference between the toroidal and tiled boundary conditions is that this Boids simulation won't take place on a discrete grid; instead, the birds move over a continuous region. Figure 5-2 shows what those tiled boundary conditions look like. Look at the tile in the middle. The birds flying out to the right are entering the tile on the right, but the boundary conditions ensure that they actually come right back into the center tile through the tile at the left. You can see the same thing happening at the top and bottom tiles.

Here is how you implement the tiled boundary conditions for the Boids simulation:

```
    def applyBC(self):
        """apply boundary conditions"""
        deltaR = 2.0
        for coord in self.pos:
❶          if coord[0] > width + deltaR:
                coord[0] = - deltaR
            if coord[0] < - deltaR:
                coord[0] = width + deltaR
            if coord[1] > height + deltaR:
                coord[1] = - deltaR
            if coord[1] < - deltaR:
                coord[1] = height + deltaR
```

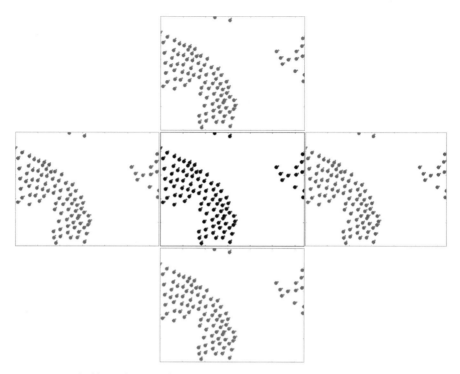

Figure 5-2: Tiled boundary conditions

At ❶, if the x-coordinate is greater than the width of the tile, you set it back to the left edge of the tile. The deltaR in this line provides a slight buffer, which allows the boid to move slightly outside the tile before it starts coming back in from the opposite direction, thus producing a better visual effect. You perform a similar check at the left, top, and bottom edges of the tile.

Drawing a Boid

To build the animation, you need to know the boid's position and velocity, and have a way to indicate both position and direction of motion at each time step.

Plotting the Boid's Body and Head

To animate the boids, you use matplotlib and a little trick to plot both position and velocity. Draw each boid as two circles, as shown in Figure 5-3. The larger circle represents the body, and the smaller one represents the head. Point P marks the center of the body, and H is the center of the head. You calculate the position of H according to the formula $H = P + k \times V$, where V is the velocity of the boid and k is a constant. At any given time, the boid's head is aligned in the direction of motion. This tells the boid's direction of movement, which is better than just drawing the body alone.

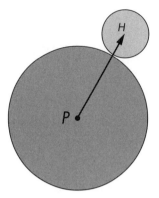

Figure 5-3: Representing a boid

In the following snippet, you draw the boid's body and head as circular markers using `matplotlib`.

```
    fig = plt.figure()
    ax = plt.axes(xlim=(0, width), ylim=(0, height))

❶   pts, = ax.plot([], [], markersize=10, c='k', marker='o', ls='None')
❷   beak, = ax.plot([], [], markersize=4, c='r', marker='o', ls='None')
❸   anim = animation.FuncAnimation(fig, tick, fargs=(pts, beak, boids),
                                   interval=50)
```

You set the size and shape of the markers for the boid's body (`pts`) and head (`beak`) at ❶ and ❷, respectively. You also add mouse button events to the animation window at ❸. Now that you know how to draw the body and beak, let's see how to update their positions.

Updating the Boid's Position

Once the animation starts, you need to update both the boid's position and the location of the head, which tells you the direction in which the boid is moving. You do so with this code:

```
❶ vec = self.pos + 10*self.vel/self.maxVel
❷ beak.set_data(vec.reshape(2*self.N)[::2], vec.reshape(2*self.N)[1::2])
```

At ❶, you calculate the position of the head by applying a displacement of 10 units in the direction of the velocity (`vel`). This displacement determines the distance between the beak and the body. At ❷, you update (reshape) the `matplotlib` axis (`set_data`) with the new values of the head position. The `[::2]` picks out the even-numbered elements (x-axis values) from the velocity list, and the `[1::2]` picks out the odd-numbered elements (y-axis values).

Applying the Rules of the Boids

Now you'll implement the three rules of boids in Python. Let's do this the "numpy way," avoiding loops and using highly optimized numpy methods.

```
import numpy as np
from scipy.spatial.distance import squareform, pdist, cdist

    def test2(pos, radius):
        # get distance matrix
❶       distMatrix = squareform(pdist(pos))
        # apply threshold
❷       D = distMatrix < radius
        # compute velocity
❸       vel = pos*D.sum(axis=1).reshape(N, 1) - D.dot(pos)
        return vel
```

You use the squareform() and pdist() methods at ❶ (defined in the scipy library) to calculate the pairwise distances between an array of points. (You do this by picking any two points from the array and computing the distance and then doing that for all such possible pairs.) For example, in this code, you have three points, which means three possible pairs of points:

```
>>> import numpy as np
>>> from scipy.spatial.distance import squareform, pdist
>>> x = np.array([[0.0, 0.0], [1.0, 1.0], [2.0, 2.0]])
>>> squareform(pdist(x))
array([[ 0. , 1.41421356, 2.82842712],
[ 1.41421356, 0. , 1.41421356],
[ 2.82842712, 1.41421356, 0. ]])
```

The squareform() method gives you a 3×3 matrix, where an entry M_{ij} gives the distance between points P_i and P_j. Next, at ❷, you filter this matrix based on distance. Using the same three-point example, you have the following:

```
>>> squareform(pdist(x)) < 1.4
array([[ True, False, False],
[False, True, False],
[False, False, True]], dtype=bool)
```

The < comparison sets the matrix entry for all distance pairs with a distance less than the given threshold, in this case, 1.4. This compact method of expressing what you want is closer to how you actually think about it.

The method at ❸ is a bit more complicated. The D.sum() method sums the True values in the matrix in a column-wise fashion. The reshape is required because the result of the sum is a one-dimensional array of N values (shape $(N,)$), and you want it to be of shape $(N, 1)$ so it's compatible for multiplication with the position array. D.dot() is just the dot product (multiplication) of the matrix and the position vector.

test2 is much smaller than test1, but its real advantage is speed. Let's use the Python timeit module to compare the performance of the previous two approaches. The following code, written inside the Python interpreter, assumes you have the code for the functions test1 and test2 typed in a file named *test.py* in the same directory:

```
>>> from timeit import timeit
>>> timeit('test1(pos, 100)', 'from test import test1, N, pos, width, height',
number=100)
7.880876064300537
>>> timeit('test2(pos, 100)', 'from test import test2, N, pos, width, height',
number=100)
0.036969900131225586
```

On my computer, the numpy code without loops runs about 200 times faster than the code that uses explicit loops! But why? Aren't they both doing more or less the same thing?

The reason is that as an interpreted language, Python is inherently slower than compiled languages like C. The numpy library brings the convenience of Python and performance nearly equal to that of C by providing highly optimized methods that operate on arrays of data. (You'll find that numpy works best when you reorganize your algorithm as steps that operate on entire arrays at once, without looping through individual elements to perform computations.)

Here is the method that applies the three rules for boids using the numpy techniques discussed earlier:

```
    def applyRules(self):
        # apply rule #1: Separation
        D = distMatrix < 25.0
❶      vel = self.pos*D.sum(axis=1).reshape(self.N, 1) - D.dot(self.pos)
❷      self.limit(vel, self.maxRuleVel)

        # distance threshold for alignment (different from separation)
        D = distMatrix < 50.0

        # apply rule #2: Alignment
❸      vel2 = D.dot(self.vel)
        self.limit(vel2, self.maxRuleVel)
        vel += vel2;

        # apply rule #3: Cohesion
❹      vel3 = D.dot(self.pos) - self.pos
        self.limit(vel3, self.maxRuleVel)
        vel += vel3

        return vel
```

When you apply the separation rule at ❶, each boid is "pushed away" from neighboring boids within a certain distance, as discussed at the beginning of this section. At ❷, the calculated velocity is clamped or restricted to a certain maximum value. (Without this check, the values would increase with each time step, and the simulation would go haywire.)

When you apply the alignment rule at ❸, the velocities of all neighboring boids within a radius of 50 units are added up and restricted to a maximum. This is done so that the computed final velocity doesn't increase indefinitely. As a result, any given boid is influenced by and aligns itself with the average velocity of the boids within the specified radius. (The use of the compact numpy syntax for doing this computation makes things simple and fast.)

Finally, when you apply the cohesion rule at ❹, you add a velocity vector for each boid that points to the *centroid* or geometric center of the neighboring boids within a certain radius. You use the Boolean distance matrix and numpy methods to arrive at a compact syntax.

Adding a Boid

The core rules in the Boids simulation will cause the boids to exhibit flocking behavior. But let's make things more interesting by adding a boid to the flock in the middle of a simulation to see how it behaves.

The following code creates a mouse event that will allow you to add a boid by clicking the left mouse button. A boid will appear at the cursor location with a random velocity assigned to it.

```
# add a "button press" event handler
cid = fig.canvas.mpl_connect('button_press_event', buttonPress)
```
❶

At ❶, you use the mpl_connect() method to add a button press event to the matplotlib canvas. The buttonPress() method will be called every time the mouse button is pressed in the simulation window.

Now, to handle the mouse event and actually create your boid, add this code:

```
def buttonPress(self, event):
    """event handler for matplotlib button presses"""
    # left-click to add a boid
    if event.button is 1:
        self.pos = np.concatenate((self.pos,
                                   np.array([[event.xdata, event.ydata]])),
                                  axis=0)
        # generate a random velocity
        angles = 2*math.pi*np.random.rand(1)
        v = np.array(list(zip(np.sin(angles), np.cos(angles))))
        self.vel = np.concatenate((self.vel, v), axis=0)
        self.N += 1
```
❶
❷

❸

At ❶, you ensure that the mouse event is a left-click. At ❷, you append the mouse location given by (event.xdata, event.ydata) to your boid's position array. At ❸, and the lines that follow, you add a random velocity vector to the boid's velocity array and increment the count of boids by 1.

Scattering the Boids

The three simulation rules keep the boids in a flock as they move around. But what happens when the flock is disturbed? To simulate this situation, you can introduce a "scatter" effect: when you right-click in the user interface (UI) window, the flock will scatter. You can think of this as how the flock might respond to the sudden appearance of a predator or a loud noise that spooks the birds. Here's one way to implement this, as a continuation of the buttonPress() method:

```
       # right-click to scatter boids
❶      elif event.button is 3:
           # add scattering velocity
❷          self.vel += 0.1*(self.pos - np.array([[event.xdata, event.ydata]]))
```

At ❶, you check whether the mouse button press is a right-click event. At ❷, you change the velocity for every boid by adding a component in the direction opposite the point where the disturbance arose (that is, where the mouse was clicked). Initially, the boids will fly away from that point, but as you will see, the three rules prevail, and the boids will coalesce again as a flock.

Command Line Arguments

Here's how command line arguments are handled for the boids program:

```
❶  parser = argparse.ArgumentParser(description="Implementing Craig
                                    Reynolds's Boids...")
   # add arguments
   parser.add_argument('--num-boids', dest='N', required=False)
   args = parser.parse_args()

   # set the initial number of boids
   N = 100
   if args.N:
       N = int(args.N)

   # create boids
   boids = Boids(N)
```

The main() method starts by setting up a command line option at ❶, using the familiar argparse module.

The Boids Class

Next, let's look at the Boids class, which represents the simulation.

```
class Boids:
    """class that represents Boids simulation"""
    def __init__(self, N):
        """initialize the Boid simulation"""
        # initial position and velocities
❶       self.pos = [width/2.0, height/2.0] + 10*np.random.rand(2*N).reshape(N, 2)
        # normalized random velocities
        angles = 2*math.pi*np.random.rand(N)
        self.vel = np.array(list(zip(np.sin(angles), np.cos(angles))))
        self.N = N
        # minimum distance of approach
        self.minDist = 25.0
        # maximum magnitude of velocities calculated by "rules"
        self.maxRuleVel = 0.03
        # maximum magnitude of the final velocity
        self.maxVel = 2.0
```

The Boids class handles the initialization, updates the animation, and applies the rules. The position and velocity arrays are initialized at ❶ and in the lines that follow.

boids.tick() is called at each time step to update the animation, as shown here:

```
def tick(frameNum, pts, beak, boids):
    #print frameNum
    """update function for animation"""
    boids.tick(frameNum, pts, beak)
    return pts, beak
```

You also need a way to limit the value of some vectors. Otherwise, the velocities will keep increasing indefinitely with every time step, and the simulation will come apart.

```
    def limitVec(self, vec, maxVal):
        """limit the magnitude of the 2D vector"""
        mag = norm(vec)
        if mag > maxVal:
            vec[0], vec[1] = vec[0]*maxVal/mag, vec[1]*maxVal/mag

❶   def limit(self, X, maxVal):
        """limit the magnitude of 2D vectors in array X to maxValue"""
        for vec in X:
            self.limitVec(vec, maxVal)
```

You define a limit() method at ❶ that clamps the values in an array to a value calculated by the simulation rules.

The Complete Code

Here is the complete program for your Boids simulation. You can also download the code for this project from *https://github.com/electronut/pp/blob/master/boids/boids.py*.

```python
import sys, argparse
import math
import numpy as np
import matplotlib.pyplot as plt
import matplotlib.animation as animation
from scipy.spatial.distance import squareform, pdist, cdist
from numpy.linalg import norm

width, height = 640, 480

class Boids:
    """class that represents Boids simulation"""
    def __init__(self, N):
        """initialize the Boid simulation"""
        # initial position and velocities
        self.pos = [width/2.0, height/2.0] + 10*np.random.rand(2*N).reshape(N, 2)
        # normalized random velocities
        angles = 2*math.pi*np.random.rand(N)
        self.vel = np.array(list(zip(np.sin(angles), np.cos(angles))))
        self.N = N
        # minimum distance of approach
        self.minDist = 25.0
        # maximum magnitude of velocities calculated by "rules"
        self.maxRuleVel = 0.03
        # maximum maginitude of the final velocity
        self.maxVel = 2.0

    def tick(self, frameNum, pts, beak):
        """Update the simulation by one time step."""
        # get pairwise distances
        self.distMatrix = squareform(pdist(self.pos))
        # apply rules:
        self.vel += self.applyRules()
        self.limit(self.vel, self.maxVel)
        self.pos += self.vel
        self.applyBC()
        # update data
        pts.set_data(self.pos.reshape(2*self.N)[::2],
                     self.pos.reshape(2*self.N)[1::2])
        vec = self.pos + 10*self.vel/self.maxVel
        beak.set_data(vec.reshape(2*self.N)[::2],
                      vec.reshape(2*self.N)[1::2])

    def limitVec(self, vec, maxVal):
        """limit the magnitide of the 2D vector"""
        mag = norm(vec)
```

```
        if mag > maxVal:
            vec[0], vec[1] = vec[0]*maxVal/mag, vec[1]*maxVal/mag

def limit(self, X, maxVal):
    """limit the magnitide of 2D vectors in array X to maxValue"""
    for vec in X:
        self.limitVec(vec, maxVal)

def applyBC(self):
    """apply boundary conditions"""
    deltaR = 2.0
    for coord in self.pos:
        if coord[0] > width + deltaR:
            coord[0] = - deltaR
        if coord[0] < - deltaR:
            coord[0] = width + deltaR
        if coord[1] > height + deltaR:
            coord[1] = - deltaR
        if coord[1] < - deltaR:
            coord[1] = height + deltaR

def applyRules(self):
    # apply rule #1: Separation
    D = self.distMatrix < 25.0
    vel = self.pos*D.sum(axis=1).reshape(self.N, 1) - D.dot(self.pos)
    self.limit(vel, self.maxRuleVel)

    # distance threshold for alignment (different from separation)
    D = self.distMatrix < 50.0

    # apply rule #2: Alignment
    vel2 = D.dot(self.vel)
    self.limit(vel2, self.maxRuleVel)
    vel += vel2;

    # apply rule #3: Cohesion
    vel3 = D.dot(self.pos) - self.pos
    self.limit(vel3, self.maxRuleVel)
    vel += vel3

    return vel

def buttonPress(self, event):
    """event handler for matplotlib button presses"""
    # left-click to add a boid
    if event.button is 1:
        self.pos = np.concatenate((self.pos,
                                   np.array([[event.xdata, event.ydata]])),
                                  axis=0)
        # generate a random velocity
        angles = 2*math.pi*np.random.rand(1)
        v = np.array(list(zip(np.sin(angles), np.cos(angles))))
        self.vel = np.concatenate((self.vel, v), axis=0)
        self.N += 1
```

```
                # right-click to scatter boids
                elif event.button is 3:
                    # add scattering velocity
                    self.vel += 0.1*(self.pos - np.array([[event.xdata, event.ydata]]))

    def tick(frameNum, pts, beak, boids):
        #print frameNum
        """update function for animation"""
        boids.tick(frameNum, pts, beak)
        return pts, beak

# main() function
def main():
    # use sys.argv if needed
    print('starting boids...')

    parser = argparse.ArgumentParser(description="Implementing Craig
                                Reynold's Boids...")
    # add arguments
    parser.add_argument('--num-boids', dest='N', required=False)
    args = parser.parse_args()

    # set the initial number of boids
    N = 100
    if args.N:
        N = int(args.N)

    # create boids
    boids = Boids(N)

    # set up plot
    fig = plt.figure()
    ax = plt.axes(xlim=(0, width), ylim=(0, height))

    pts, = ax.plot([], [], markersize=10, c='k', marker='o', ls='None')
    beak, = ax.plot([], [], markersize=4, c='r', marker='o', ls='None')
    anim = animation.FuncAnimation(fig, tick, fargs=(pts, beak, boids),
                                interval=50)

    # add a "button press" event handler
    cid = fig.canvas.mpl_connect('button_press_event', boids.buttonPress)

    plt.show()

# call main
if __name__ == '__main__':
    main()
```

Running the Boids Simulation

Let's see what happens when you run the simulation. Enter the following:

```
$ python3 boids.py
```

The Boids simulation should start, and all boids should cluster around the center of the window. Let the simulation run for a while, and the boids should start to flock as they form a pattern similar to the one shown in Figure 5-4.

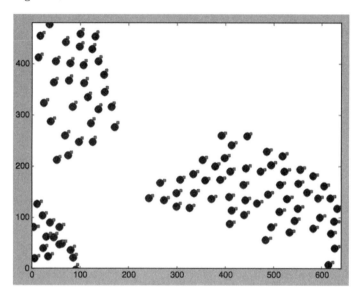

Figure 5-4: Sample run of boids

Click the simulation window. A new boid should appear at that location, and its velocity should change as it encounters the flock. Now right-click. The flock should scatter initially but then recoalesce.

Summary

In this project, you simulated the flocking of birds (or boids) using the three rules proposed by Craig Reynolds. You looked at how to use numpy arrays and how to use explicit loops and numpy methods on entire arrays to improve the speed of computations. You used the scipy.spatial module to perform fast and convenient distance calculations, and you implemented a matplotlib trick that uses two markers to represent both the position and the direction of points. Finally, you added UI interaction in the form of a button press to matplotlib plots.

Experiments!

Here are some ways you might further explore flocking behavior:

1. Implement obstacle avoidance for your flock of boids by writing a new method called avoidObstacle() and applying it right after you apply the three rules, as follows:

```
self.vel += self.applyRules()
self.vel += self.avoidObstacle()
```

The avoidObstacle() method should use a predefined tuple (x, y, R) to add a velocity component to a boid, pushing it away from the obstacle location (x, y), but only when the boid is within radius R of the obstacle. Think of this as the distance at which a boid sees the obstacle and steers away from it. You can specify the (x, y, R) tuple using a command line option.

2. What happens when the boids fly though a strong gust of wind? Simulate this by adding a global velocity component to all the boids at random time steps in the simulation. The boids should temporarily be affected by the wind but return to the flock once the wind stops.

PART III

FUN WITH IMAGES

"You can observe a lot by watching."
—Yogi Berra

6

ASCII ART

In the 1990s, when email ruled and graphics capabilities were limited, it was common to include a signature in your email that contained a graphic made of text, commonly called *ASCII art*. (ASCII is simply a character-encoding scheme.) Figure 6-1 shows a couple of examples. Although the Internet has made sharing images immeasurably easier, the humble text graphic isn't quite dead yet.

ASCII art has its origins in typewriter art created in the late 1800s. In the 1960s, when computers had minimal graphics-processing hardware, ASCII was used to represent images. These days, ASCII art continues as a form of expression on the Internet, and you can find a variety of creative examples online.

```
         \\|//
         (o o)
____oOOo__(_)__oOOo_____

+                                       +
-------------------------------------------+
+-------------------J. RAVIPRAKASH         +
-------------------------------------------+
+Postdoctoral Researcher     | e-mail-->rxj10@psu.edu  +
+Materials Research Laboratory| Tel   -->(814) 865-9931 +
+Pennsylvania State University| fax   -->(814) 863-6734 +
+-------------------------------------------+
+    web page --> http://www.personal.psu.edu/~rxj10    +
-------------------------------------------+
         ||  ||
         oOOo Oooo
```

Figure 6-1: Examples of ASCII art

In this project, you'll use Python to create a program that generates ASCII art from graphical images. The program will let you specify the width of the output (the number of columns of text) and set a vertical scale factor. It also supports two mappings of grayscale values to ASCII characters: a sparse 10-level mapping and a more finely calibrated 70-level mapping.

To generate your ASCII art from an image, you'll learn how to do the following:

- Convert images to grayscale using Pillow, a fork of the Python Imaging Library (PIL)
- Compute the average brightness of a grayscale image using numpy
- Use a string as a quick lookup table for grayscale values

How It Works

This project takes advantage of the fact that from a distance, we perceive grayscale images as the average value of their brightness. For example, in Figure 6-2, you can see a grayscale image of a building and, next to it, an image filled with the average brightness value of the building image. If you look at the images from across the room, they will look similar.

The ASCII art is generated by splitting an image into tiles and replacing the average RGB value of a tile with an ASCII character. From a distance, since our eyes have limited resolution, we sort of see the "average" values in ASCII art while losing the details that would otherwise make the art look less real.

Figure 6-2: Average value of a grayscale image

This program will take a given image and first convert it to 8-bit grayscale so that each pixel has a grayscale value in the range [0, 255] (the range of an 8-bit integer). Think of this 8-bit value as *brightness*, with 0 being black and 255 being white and the values in between being shades of gray.

Next, it will split the image into a grid of $M \times N$ tiles (where M is the number of rows and N the number of columns in the ASCII image). The program will then calculate the average brightness value for each tile in the grid and match it with an appropriate ASCII character by predefining a *ramp* (an increasing set of values) of ASCII characters to represent grayscale values in the range [0, 255]. It will use these values as a lookup table for the brightness values.

The finished ASCII art is just a bunch of lines of text. To display the text, you'll use a constant-width (also called *monospace*) font such as Courier because unless each text character has the same width, the characters in the image won't line up properly along a grid and you'll end up with unevenly spaced and scrambled output.

The *aspect ratio* (the ratio of width to height) of the font used also affects the final image. If the aspect ratio of the space taken up by a character is different from the aspect ratio of the image tile the character is replacing, the final ASCII image will appear distorted. In effect, you're trying to replace an image tile with an ASCII character, so their shapes need to match. For example, if you were to split your image into square tiles and then replace each of the tiles with a font that is stretched in height, the final output would appear stretched vertically.

To address this issue, you'll scale the rows in your grid to match the Courier aspect ratio. (You can send the program command line arguments to modify the scaling to match other fonts.)

In sum, here are the steps the program takes to generate the ASCII image:

1. Convert the input image to grayscale.
2. Split the image into $M \times N$ tiles.
3. Correct M (the number of rows) to match the image and font aspect ratio.

4. Compute the average brightness for each image tile and then look up a suitable ASCII character for each.

5. Assemble rows of ASCII character strings and print them to a file to form the final image.

Requirements

In this project, you'll use Pillow, the friendly fork of the Python Imaging Library, to read in the images, access their underlying data, and create and modify them. You'll also use the numpy library to compute averages.

The Code

You'll begin by defining the grayscale levels used to generate the ASCII art. Then you'll look at how the image is split into tiles and how average brightness is computed for those tiles. Next, you'll work on replacing the tiles with ASCII characters to generate the final output. Finally, you'll set up command line parsing for the program to allow a user to specify the output size, output filename, and so on.

For the full project code, skip to "The Complete Code" on page 95.

Defining the Grayscale Levels and Grid

As the first step in creating your program, define the two grayscale levels used to convert brightness values to ASCII characters as global values.

```
   # 70 levels of gray
❶ gscale1 = "$@B%8&WM#*oahkbdpqwmZO0QLCJUYXzcvunxrjft/\|()1{}[]?-_+~<>i!lI;:,\"^
   `'. "
   # 10 levels of gray
❷ gscale2 = "@%#*+=-:. "
```

The value gscale1 at ❶ is the 70-level grayscale ramp, and gscale2 at ❷ is the simpler 10-level grayscale ramp. Both of these values are stored as strings, with a range of characters that progress from darkest to lightest. (To learn more about how characters are represented as grayscale values, see Paul Bourke's "Character Representation of Grey Scale Images" at *http://paulbourke.net/dataformats/asciiart/*.)

Now that you have your grayscale ramps, you can set up the image. The following code opens the image and splits it into a grid:

```
   # open the image and convert to grayscale
❶ image = Image.open(fileName).convert("L")
   # store the image dimensions
❷ W, H = image.size[0], image.size[1]
   # compute the tile width
❸ w = W/cols
```

```
      # compute the tile height based on the aspect ratio and scale of the font
❹     h = w/scale
      # compute the number of rows to use in the final grid
❺     rows = int(H/h)
```

At ❶, `Image.open()` opens the input image file and `Image.convert()` converts the image to grayscale. The `"L"` stands for *luminance*, a measure of the brightness of an image.

At ❷, you store the width and height of the input image. At ❸, you compute the width of a tile for the number of columns (`cols`) specified by the user. (The program uses a default of 80 columns if the user doesn't set another value in the command line.) For the division at ❸, use floating-point, not integer division, in order to avoid truncation errors while calculating the dimensions of the tiles.

Once you know the width of a tile, you compute its height at ❹ using the vertical scale factor passed in as `scale`. At ❺, use this grid height to compute the number of rows.

The scale factor sizes each tile to match the aspect ratio of the font you are using to display the text so that the final image won't be distorted. The value for `scale` can be passed in as an argument, or it's set to a default of 0.43, which works well for displaying the result in Courier.

Computing the Average Brightness

Next, you compute the average brightness for a tile in the grayscale image. The function `getAverageL()` does the job.

```
❶ def getAverageL(image):
      # get the image as a numpy array
❷     im = np.array(image)
      # get the dimensions
❸     w,h = im.shape
      # get the average
❹     return np.average(im.reshape(w*h))
```

At ❶, the image tile is passed in as a PIL `Image` object. Convert `image` into a numpy array at ❷, at which point `im` becomes a two-dimensional array of brightness for each pixel. At ❸, you store the dimensions (width and height) of the image. At ❹, `numpy.average()` computes the average of the brightness values in the image by using `numpy.reshape()` to first convert the two-dimensional array of the dimensions width and height (`w,h`) into a flat one-dimensional array whose length is a product of the width times the height (`w*h`). The `numpy.average()` call then sums these array values and computes the average.

Generating the ASCII Content from the Image

The main part of the program generates the ASCII content from the image.

```
      # an ASCII image is a list of character strings
❶     aimg = []
```

```
      # generate the list of tile dimensions
      for j in range(rows):
❷        y1 = int(j*h)
         y2 = int((j+1)*h)
         # correct the last tile
         if j == rows-1:
             y2 = H
         # append an empty string
❸        aimg.append("")
         for i in range(cols):
             # crop the image to fit the tile
❹            x1 = int(i*w)
             x2 = int((i+1)*w)
             # correct the last tile
❺            if i == cols-1:
                 x2 = W
             # crop the image to extract the tile into another Image object
❻            img = image.crop((x1, y1, x2, y2))
             # get the average luminance
❼            avg = int(getAverageL(img))
             # look up the ASCII character for grayscale value (avg)
             if moreLevels:
❽                gsval = gscale1[int((avg*69)/255)]
             else:
❾                gsval = gscale2[int((avg*9)/255)]
             # append the ASCII character to the string
❿            aimg[j] += gsval
```

In this section of the program, the ASCII image is first stored as a list
of strings, which is initialized at ❶. Next, you iterate through the calculated
number of row image tiles, and at ❷ and the following line, you calculate
the starting and ending y-coordinates of each image tile. Although these
are floating-point calculations, truncate them to integers before passing
them to an image-cropping method.

Next, because dividing the image into tiles creates edge tiles of the same
size only when the image width is an integer multiple of the number of columns, correct for the y-coordinate of the tiles in the last row by setting the
y-coordinate to the image's actual height. By doing so, you ensure that the
top edge of the image isn't truncated.

At ❸, you add an empty string into the ASCII as a compact way to represent the current image row. You'll fill in this string next. (You treat the
string as a list of characters.)

At ❹ and the next line, you compute the left and right x-coordinates of
each tile, and at ❺, you correct the x-coordinate for the last tile for the same
reasons you corrected the y-coordinate. Use image.crop() at ❻ to extract the
image tile and then pass that tile to the getAverageL() function ❼, defined
in "Computing the Average Brightness" on page 93, to get the average
brightness of the tile. At ❾, you scale down the average brightness value
from [0, 255] to [0, 9] (the range of values for the default 10-level grayscale
ramp). You then use gscale2 (the stored ramp string) as a lookup table for

the relevant ASCII value. The line at ❽ is similar, except that it's used only when the command line flag is set to use the ramp with 70 levels. Finally, you append the looked-up ASCII value, gsval, to the text row at ❿, and the code loops until all rows are processed.

Command Line Options

Next, define some command line options for the program. This code uses the built-in argparse class:

```
    parser = argparse.ArgumentParser(description="descStr")
    # add expected arguments
❶  parser.add_argument('--file', dest='imgFile', required=True)
❷  parser.add_argument('--scale', dest='scale', required=False)
❸  parser.add_argument('--out', dest='outFile', required=False)
❹  parser.add_argument('--cols', dest='cols', required=False)
❺  parser.add_argument('--morelevels', dest='moreLevels', action='store_true')
```

At ❶, you include options to specify the image file to input (the only required argument) and to set the vertical scale factor ❷, the output filename ❸, and the number of text columns in the ASCII output ❹. At ❺, you add a --morelevels option so the user can select the grayscale ramp with more levels.

Writing the ASCII Art Strings to a Text File

Finally, take the generated list of ASCII character strings and write those strings to a text file:

```
    # open a new text file
❶  f = open(outFile, 'w')
    # write each string in the list to the new file
❷  for row in aimg:
        f.write(row + '\n')
    # clean up
❸  f.close()
```

At ❶, you use the built-in open() method to open a new text file for writing. Then you iterate through each string in the list and write it to the file at ❷. At ❸, you close the file object to release system resources.

The Complete Code

Here is the complete ASCII art program. You can also download the code for this project from *https://github.com/electronut/pp/blob/master/ascii/ascii.py*.

```
import sys, random, argparse
import numpy as np
import math
```

```python
from PIL import Image

# grayscale level values from:
# http://paulbourke.net/dataformats/asciiart/

# 70 levels of gray
gscale1 = "$@B%8&WM#*oahkbdpqwmZO0QLCJUYXzcvunxrjft/\|()1{}[]?-_+~<>i!lI;:,\"^
`'.  "
# 10 levels of gray
gscale2 = '@%#*+=-:.  '

def getAverageL(image):
    """
    Given PIL Image, return average value of grayscale value
    """
    # get image as numpy array
    im = np.array(image)
    # get the dimensions
    w,h = im.shape
    # get the average
    return np.average(im.reshape(w*h))

def covertImageToAscii(fileName, cols, scale, moreLevels):
    """
    Given Image and dimensions (rows, cols), returns an m*n list of Images
    """
    # declare globals
    global gscale1, gscale2
    # open image and convert to grayscale
    image = Image.open(fileName).convert('L')
    # store the image dimensions
    W, H = image.size[0], image.size[1]
    print("input image dims: %d x %d" % (W, H))
    # compute tile width
    w = W/cols
    # compute tile height based on the aspect ratio and scale of the font
    h = w/scale
    # compute number of rows to use in the final grid
    rows = int(H/h)

    print("cols: %d, rows: %d" % (cols, rows))
    print("tile dims: %d x %d" % (w, h))

    # check if image size is too small
    if cols > W or rows > H:
        print("Image too small for specified cols!")
        exit(0)

    # an ASCII image is a list of character strings
    aimg = []
    # generate the list of tile dimensions
    for j in range(rows):
        y1 = int(j*h)
        y2 = int((j+1)*h)
```

```python
            # correct the last tile
            if j == rows-1:
                y2 = H
            # append an empty string
            aimg.append("")
            for i in range(cols):
                # crop the image to fit the tile
                x1 = int(i*w)
                x2 = int((i+1)*w)
                # correct the last tile
                if i == cols-1:
                    x2 = W
                # crop the image to extract the tile into another Image object
                img = image.crop((x1, y1, x2, y2))
                # get the average luminance
                avg = int(getAverageL(img))
                # look up the ASCII character for grayscale value (avg)
                if moreLevels:
                    gsval = gscale1[int((avg*69)/255)]
                else:
                    gsval = gscale2[int((avg*9)/255)]
                # append the ASCII character to the string
                aimg[j] += gsval

    # return text image
    return aimg

# main() function
def main():
    # create parser
    descStr = "This program converts an image into ASCII art."
    parser = argparse.ArgumentParser(description=descStr)
    # add expected arguments
    parser.add_argument('--file', dest='imgFile', required=True)
    parser.add_argument('--scale', dest='scale', required=False)
    parser.add_argument('--out', dest='outFile', required=False)
    parser.add_argument('--cols', dest='cols', required=False)
    parser.add_argument('--morelevels', dest='moreLevels', action='store_true')

    # parse arguments
    args = parser.parse_args()

    imgFile = args.imgFile
    # set output file
    outFile = 'out.txt'
    if args.outFile:
        outFile = args.outFile
    # set scale default as 0.43, which suits a Courier font
    scale = 0.43
    if args.scale:
        scale = float(args.scale)
    # set cols
    cols = 80
    if args.cols:
        cols = int(args.cols)
```

```
        print('generating ASCII art...')
        # convert image to ASCII text
        aimg = covertImageToAscii(imgFile, cols, scale, args.moreLevels)

        # open a new text file
        f = open(outFile, 'w')
        # write each string in the list to the new file
        for row in aimg:
            f.write(row + '\n')
        # clean up
        f.close()
        print("ASCII art written to %s" % outFile)

# call main
if __name__ == '__main__':
    main()
```

Running the ASCII Art Generator

To run your finished program, enter a command like the following one, replacing data/robot.jpg with the relative path to the image file you want to use.

```
$ python ascii.py --file data/robot.jpg --cols 100
```

Figure 6-3 shows the ASCII art that results from sending the image *robot.jpg* (at the left).

Figure 6-3: Sample run of ascii.py

Now you are all set to create your own ASCII art!

Summary

In this project, you learned how to generate ASCII art from any input image. You also learned how to convert an image to grayscale by computing average brightness values and how to replace part of an image with a character based on the grayscale value. Have fun creating your own ASCII art!

Experiments!

Here are some ideas for exploring ASCII art further.

1. Run the program with the command line option --scale 1.0. How does the resulting image look? Experiment with different values for scale. Copy the output to a text editor and try setting the text to different (fixed-width) fonts to see how doing so affects the appearance of the final image.

2. Add the command line option --invert to the program to invert the ASCII art input values so that black appears white, and vice versa. (Hint: try subtracting the tile brightness value from 255 during lookup.)

3. In this project, you created lookup tables for grayscale values based on two-character hard-coded ramps. Implement a command line option to pass in a different character ramp to create the ASCII art, like so:

```
python3 ascii.py --map "@$%^`."
```

A ramp like the previous one should create the ASCII output using the given six-character ramp, where @ maps to a brightness value of 0 and . maps to a value of 255.

7

PHOTOMOSAICS

When I was in the sixth grade, I saw a picture like the one shown in Figure 7-1 but couldn't quite figure out what it was. After squinting at it for a while, I eventually figured it out. (Turn the book upside down, and view it from across the room. I won't tell anyone.)

A *photomosaic* is an image split into a grid of rectangles, with each replaced by another image that matches the *target* (the image you ultimately want to appear in the photomosaic). In other words, if you look at a photomosaic from a distance, you see the target image; but if you come closer, you will see that the image actually consists of many smaller images.

The puzzle works because of how the human eye functions. The low-resolution, blocky image shown in Figure 7-1 is hard to recognize up close, but when seen from a distance, you know what it represents because you perceive less detail, which makes the edges smooth. A photomosaic works according to a similar principle. From a distance, the image looks normal, but up close, the secret is revealed—each "block" is a unique image!

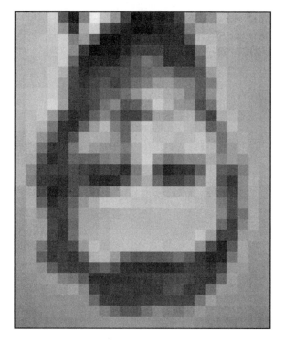

Figure 7-1: A puzzling image

In this project, you'll learn how to create photomosaics using Python. You'll divide a target image into a grid of smaller images and replace each block in the grid with a suitable image to create a photomosaic of the original image. You'll be able to specify the grid dimensions and choose whether input images can be reused in the mosaic.

In this project, you'll learn how to do the following:

- Create images using the Python Imaging Library (PIL).
- Compute the average RGB value of an image.
- Crop images.
- Replace part of an image by pasting in another image.
- Compare RGB values using a measurement of average distance.

How It Works

To create a photomosaic, begin with a blocky, low-resolution version of the target image (because the number of tile images would be too great in a high-resolution image). The resolution of this image will determine the dimensions $M \times N$ (where M is the number of rows and N is the number of columns) of the mosaic. Next, replace each tile in the original image according to this methodology:

1. Read the tile images, which will replace the tiles in the original image.
2. Read the target image and split it into an $M \times N$ grid of tiles.

3. For each tile, find the best match from the input images.

4. Create the final mosaic by arranging the selected input images in an *M*×*N* grid.

Splitting the Target Image

Begin by splitting the target image into an *M*×*N* grid according to the scheme shown in Figure 7-2.

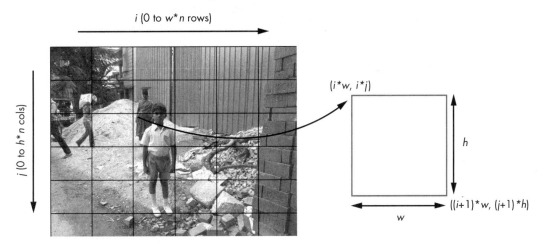

Figure 7-2: Splitting the target image

The image in Figure 7-2 shows how you can split the original image into a grid of tiles. The x-axis represents the grid columns, and the y-axis represents the grid rows.

Now let's look at how to calculate the coordinates for a single tile from this grid. The tile with index (i, j) has a top-left corner coordinate of $(i*w, i*j)$ and a bottom-right corner coordinate of $((i+1)*w, (j+1)*h)$, where w and h stand for the width and height of a tile, respectively. These can be used with the PIL to crop and create a tile from this image.

Averaging Color Values

Every pixel in an image has a color that can be represented by its red, green, and blue values. In this case, you are using 8-bit images, so each of these components has an 8-bit value in the range [0, 255]. Given an image with a total of N pixels, the average RGB is calculated as follows:

$$(r,g,b)_{\text{avg}} = \left(\frac{(r_1 + r_2 + \cdots + r_N)}{N}, \frac{(g_1 + g_2 + \cdots + g_N)}{N}, \frac{(b_1 + b_2 + \cdots + b_N)}{N} \right)$$

Note that the average RGB is also a triplet, not a scalar or single number, because the averages are calculated separately for each color component. You calculate the average RGB to match the tiles with the target image.

Matching Images

For each tile in the target image, you need to find a matching image from the images in the input folder specified by the user. To determine whether two images match, use the average RGB values. The closest match is the image with the closest average RGB value.

The simplest way to do this is to calculate the distance between the RGB values in a pixel to find the best match among the input images. You can use the following distance calculation for 3D points from geometry:

$$D_{1,2} = \sqrt{\left(r_1 - r_2\right)^2 + \left(g_1 - g_2\right)^2 + \left(b_1 - b_2\right)^2}$$

Here you compute the distance between the points (r_1, g_1, b_1) and (r_2, g_2, b_2). Given a target average RGB value and a list of average RGB values from the input images, you can use a linear search and the distance calculation for 3D points to find the closest matching image.

Requirements

For this project, you'll use Pillow to read in the images, access their underlying data, and create and modify the images. You'll also use numpy to manipulate image data.

The Code

You'll begin by reading in the tile images that you'll use to create the photomosaic. Next, you'll compute the average RGB value of the images, and then split the target into a grid of images and find the best matches for tiles. Finally, you'll assemble the image tiles to create the final photomosaic. To see the complete project code, skip ahead to "The Complete Code" on page 110.

Reading in the Tile Images

First, read in the input images from the given folder. Here's how to do that:

```
def getImages(imageDir):
    """
    given a directory of images, return a list of Images
    """
❶    files = os.listdir(imageDir)
     images = []
     for file in files:
❷        filePath = os.path.abspath(os.path.join(imageDir, file))
         try:
             # explicit load so we don't run into resource crunch
❸            fp = open(filePath, "rb")
             im = Image.open(fp)
             images.append(im)
```

```
                    # force loading the image data from file
❹                   im.load()
                    # close the file
❺                   fp.close()
               except:
                    # skip
                    print("Invalid image: %s" % (filePath,))
          return images
```

At ❶, you use os.listdir() to gather the files in the *imageDir* directory in a list. Next, you iterate through each file in the list and load it into a PIL Image object.

At ❷, you use os.path.abspath() and os.path.join() to get the complete filename of the image. This idiom is commonly used in Python to ensure that your code will work with both relative paths (for example, *foo\bar*) and absolute paths (*c:\foo\bar*), as well as across operating systems with different directory-naming conventions (\ in Windows versus / in Linux).

To load the files into PIL Image objects, you could pass each filename to the Image.open() method, but if your photomosaic folder had hundreds or even thousands of images, doing so would be highly resource intensive. Instead, you can use Python to open each tile image and pass the file handle *fp* into PIL using Image.open(). Once the image has been loaded, close the file handle and release the system resources.

At ❸, you open the image file using open(). In the lines that follow, you pass the handle to Image.open() and store the resulting image, im, in an array.

You call Image.load() at ❹ to force load the image data inside im because open() is a lazy operation. It identifies the image but doesn't actually read all the image data until you try to use the image.

At ❺, you close the file handle to release system resources.

Calculating the Average Color Value of the Input Images

Once you've read in the input images, you need to calculate their average color value, as well as the value for each tile in the target. Create a method getAverageRGB() to compute both values.

```
def getAverageRGB(image):
    """
    return the average color value as (r, g, b) for each input image
    """
    # get each tile image as a numpy array
❶  im = np.array(image)
    # get the shape of each input image
❷  w,h,d = im.shape
    # get the average RGB value
❸  return tuple(np.average(im.reshape(w*h, d), axis=0))
```

At ❶, you use numpy to convert each Image object into a data array. The numpy array returned has the shape (w, h, d), where w is the weight of the image, h is the height, and d is the depth, which, in this case, is three units (one each for R, G, and B) for RGB images. You store the shape tuple at ❷ and then compute the average RGB value by reshaping this array into a more convenient form with shape (w*h, d) so that you can compute the average using numpy.average() ❸.

Splitting the Target Image into a Grid

Now you need to split the target image into an *M*×*N* grid of smaller images. Let's create a method to do that.

```
def splitImage(image, size):
    """
    given the image and dimensions (rows, cols), return an m*n list of images
    """
❶  W, H = image.size[0], image.size[1]
❷  m, n = size
❸  w, h = int(W/n), int(H/m)
    # image list
    imgs = []
    # generate a list of dimensions
    for j in range(m):
        for i in range(n):
            # append cropped image
❹          imgs.append(image.crop((i*w, j*h, (i+1)*w, (j+1)*h)))
    return imgs
```

First, you gather the dimensions of the target image at ❶ and the grid size at ❷. At ❸, you calculate the dimensions of each tile in the target image using basic division.

Now you need to iterate through the grid dimensions and cut out and store each tile as a separate image. At ❹, image.crop() crops out a portion of the image using the upper-left image coordinates and the dimensions of the cropped image as arguments (as discussed in "Splitting the Target Image" on page 103).

Finding the Best Match for a Tile

Now let's find the best match for a tile from the folder of input images. You create a utility method, getBestMatchIndex(), as follows:

```
def getBestMatchIndex(input_avg, avgs):
    """
    return index of the best image match based on average RGB value distance
    """

    # input image average
    avg = input_avg

    # get the closest RGB value to input, based on RGB distance
    index = 0
❶  min_index = 0
❷  min_dist = float("inf")
❸  for val in avgs:
```

```
❹          dist = ((val[0] - avg[0])*(val[0] - avg[0]) +
                    (val[1] - avg[1])*(val[1] - avg[1]) +
                    (val[2] - avg[2])*(val[2] - avg[2]))
❺          if dist < min_dist:
                min_dist = dist
                min_index = index
            index += 1

    return min_index
```

You are trying to find the closest match for the average RGB value, input_avg, from the list avgs. The latter is a list of average RGB values from the tile images.

To find the best match, you compare the average RGB values of the input images. At ❶ and ❷, you initialize the closest match index to 0 and the minimum distance to infinity. This test will always pass the first time since any distance will be less than infinity. At ❸, you loop through the values in the list of averages and start computing distances at ❹ using the standard formula. (You compare squares of distance to reduce computation time.) If the computed distance is less than the stored minimum distance min_dist, it is replaced with the new minimum distance at ❺. At the end of the iteration, you have the index of the average RGB value from the avgs list that is closest to input_avg. Now you can use this index to select the matching tile image from the list of tile images.

Creating an Image Grid

You need one more utility method before moving on to photomosaic creation. The createImageGrid() method will create a grid of images of size $M{\times}N$. This image grid is the final photomosiac image, created from the list of selected tile images.

```
def createImageGrid(images, dims):
    """
    given a list of images and a grid size (m, n), create a grid of images
    """
❶   m, n = dims

    # sanity check
    assert m*n == len(images)

    # get the maximum height and width of the images
    # don't assume they're all equal
❷   width = max([img.size[0] for img in images])
    height = max([img.size[1] for img in images])

    # create the target image
❸   grid_img = Image.new('RGB', (n*width, m*height))

    # paste the tile images into the image grid
    for index in range(len(images)):
❹       row = int(index/n)
```

```
❺          col = index - n*row
❻          grid_img.paste(images[index], (col*width, row*height))

       return grid_img
```

At ❶, you gather the dimensions of the grid and then use assert to see whether the number of images supplied to createImageGrid() matches the grid size. (The assert method checks assumptions in your code, especially during development and testing.) Now you have a list of tile images based on the closest RGB match, which you'll use to create an image grid representing the photomosaic. Some of the selected images may not fill a tile exactly because of differences in their sizes, but that won't be a problem because you'll fill the tile with a black background first.

At ❷ and in the following line, you compute the maximum width and height of the tile images. (You haven't made any assumptions regarding the size of the selected input images; the code will work whether they're the same or different.) If the input images won't completely fill a tile, the spaces between the tiles will show as the background color, which is black by default.

At ❸, you create an empty Image sized to fit all images in the grid; you'll paste the tile images into this. Then you fill the image grid. At ❻, you loop through the selected images and paste them into the appropriate grid using the Image.paste() method. The first argument to Image.paste() is the Image object to be pasted, and the second is the top-left coordinate. Now you need to figure out in which row and column to paste a tile image into the image grid. To do so, you express the image index in terms of rows and columns. The index of a tile in the image grid is given by $N*row + col$, where N is the number of cells along the width and (*row*, *col*) is the coordinate in this grid; at ❹, you give the row from the previous formula and at ❺ the column.

Creating the Photomosaic

Now that you have all the required utilities, let's write the main function that creates the photomosaic.

```
def createPhotomosaic(target_image, input_images, grid_size, reuse_images=True):
    """
    creates a photomosaic given target and input images
    """

    print('splitting input image...')
    # split the target image into tiles
❶  target_images = splitImage(target_image, grid_size)

    print('finding image matches...')
    # for each tile, pick one matching input image
    output_images = []
    # for user feedback
    count = 0
❷  batch_size = int(len(target_images)/10)
```

```
        # calculate the average of the input image
        avgs = []
        for img in input_images:
❸           avgs.append(getAverageRGB(img))

        for img in target_images:
            # compute the average RGB value of the image
❹           avg = getAverageRGB(img)
            # find the matching index of closest RGB value
            # from a list of average RGB values
❺           match_index = getBestMatchIndex(avg, avgs)
❻           output_images.append(input_images[match_index])
            # user feedback
❼           if count > 0 and batch_size > 10 and count % batch_size is 0:
                print('processed %d of %d...' %(count, len(target_images)))
            count += 1
            # remove the selected image from input if flag set
❽           if not reuse_images:
                input_images.remove(match)

        print('creating mosaic...')
        # create photomosaic image from tiles
❾       mosaic_image = createImageGrid(output_images, grid_size)

        # display the mosaic
        return mosaic_image
```

The createPhotomosaic() method takes as input the target, the list of input images, the size of the generated photomosaic, and a flag that indicates whether an image can be reused. At ❶, it splits the target into a grid. Once the image is split, you find matches for each tile from the images in the input folder. (Because this process can be lengthy, you provide feedback to users to let them know that the program is still working.)

At ❷, you set batch_size to one-tenth the total number of tile images. This variable will be used to update the user in the code at ❼. (The choice of one-tenth is arbitrary and simply a way for the program to say "I'm still alive." Each time the program processes a tenth of the images, it prints a message indicating that it's still running.)

At ❸, you compute the average RGB value for each image in the input folder and store that value in the list avgs. Then you start iterating through each tile in the target image grid. For each tile, you calculate the average RGB value ❹; then, at ❺, you search for the closest match to this value in the list of averages for the input images. The result is returned as an index, which you use at ❻ to retrieve the Image object and store it in a list.

At ❼, for every batch_size number of images processed, you print a message to the user. At ❽, if the reuse_images flag is set to False, you remove the selected input image from the list so that it won't be reused in another tile. (This works best when you have a wide range of input images to choose from.) Finally, at ❾, you combine the images to create the final photomosaic.

Adding the Command Line Options

The main() method of the program supports these command line options:

```
# parse arguments
parser = argparse.ArgumentParser(description='Creates a photomosaic from
                                 input images')
# add arguments
parser.add_argument('--target-image', dest='target_image', required=True)
parser.add_argument('--input-folder', dest='input_folder', required=True)
parser.add_argument('--grid-size', nargs=2, dest='grid_size', required=True)
parser.add_argument('--output-file', dest='outfile', required=False)
```

This code contains three required command line parameters: the name of the target, the name of the input folder of images, and the grid size. The fourth parameter is for the optional filename. If the filename is omitted, the photomosaic will be written to a file named *mosaic.png*.

Controlling the Size of the Photomosaic

One last issue to address is the size of the photomosaic. If you were to blindly paste the input images together based on matching tiles in the target, you could end up with a huge photomosaic that is much bigger than the target. To avoid this, resize the input images to match the size of each tile in the grid. (This has the added benefit of speeding up the average RGB computation since you're using smaller images.) The main() method also handles this:

```
        print('resizing images...')
        # for given grid size, compute the maximum width and height of tiles
❶       dims = (int(target_image.size[0]/grid_size[1]),
               int(target_image.size[1]/grid_size[0]))
        print("max tile dims: %s" % (dims,))
        # resize
        for img in input_images:
❷           img.thumbnail(dims)
```

You compute the target dimensions at ❶ based on the specified grid size; then, at ❷, you use the PIL Image.thumbnail() method to resize the images to fit those dimensions.

The Complete Code

You can find the complete code for the project at *https://github.com/electronut/pp/tree/master/photomosaic/photomosaic.py*.

```
import sys, os, random, argparse
from PIL import Image
import imghdr
import numpy as np
```

```python
def getAverageRGB(image):
    """
    return the average color value as (r, g, b) for each input image
    """
    # get each tile image as a numpy array
    im = np.array(image)
    # get the shape of each input image
    w,h,d = im.shape
    # get the average RGB value
    return tuple(np.average(im.reshape(w*h, d), axis=0))

def splitImage(image, size):
    """
    given the image and dimensions (rows, cols), returns an m*n list of images
    """
    W, H = image.size[0], image.size[1]
    m, n = size
    w, h = int(W/n), int(H/m)
    # image list
    imgs = []
    # generate a list of dimensions
    for j in range(m):
        for i in range(n):
            # append cropped image
            imgs.append(image.crop((i*w, j*h, (i+1)*w, (j+1)*h)))
    return imgs

def getImages(imageDir):
    """
    given a directory of images, return a list of Images
    """
    files = os.listdir(imageDir)
    images = []
    for file in files:
        filePath = os.path.abspath(os.path.join(imageDir, file))
        try:
            # explicit load so we don't run into a resource crunch
            fp = open(filePath, "rb")
            im = Image.open(fp)
            images.append(im)
            # force loading image data from file
            im.load()
            # close the file
            fp.close()
        except:
            # skip
            print("Invalid image: %s" % (filePath,))
    return images

def getImageFilenames(imageDir):
    """
    given a directory of images, return a list of image filenames
    """
    files = os.listdir(imageDir)
    filenames = []
```

```
        for file in files:
            filePath = os.path.abspath(os.path.join(imageDir, file))
            try:
                imgType = imghdr.what(filePath)
                if imgType:
                    filenames.append(filePath)
            except:
                # skip
                print("Invalid image: %s" % (filePath,))
        return filenames

def getBestMatchIndex(input_avg, avgs):
    """
    return index of the best image match based on average RGB value distance
    """

    # input image average
    avg = input_avg

    # get the closest RGB value to input, based on RGB distance
    index = 0
    min_index = 0
    min_dist = float("inf")
    for val in avgs:
        dist = ((val[0] - avg[0])*(val[0] - avg[0]) +
                (val[1] - avg[1])*(val[1] - avg[1]) +
                (val[2] - avg[2])*(val[2] - avg[2]))
        if dist < min_dist:
            min_dist = dist
            min_index = index
        index += 1

    return min_index


def createImageGrid(images, dims):
    """
    given a list of images and a grid size (m, n), create a grid of images
    """
    m, n = dims

    # sanity check
    assert m*n == len(images)

    # get the maximum height and width of the images
    # don't assume they're all equal
    width = max([img.size[0] for img in images])
    height = max([img.size[1] for img in images])

    # create the target image
    grid_img = Image.new('RGB', (n*width, m*height))

    # paste the tile images into the image grid
    for index in range(len(images)):
        row = int(index/n)
```

```
            col = index - n*row
            grid_img.paste(images[index], (col*width, row*height))

    return grid_img


def createPhotomosaic(target_image, input_images, grid_size, reuse_images=True):
    """

    creates photomosaic given target and input images
    """

    print('splitting input image...')
    # split the target image into tiles
    target_images = splitImage(target_image, grid_size)

    print('finding image matches...')
    # for each tile, pick one matching input image
    output_images = []
    # for user feedback
    count = 0
    batch_size = int(len(target_images)/10)

    # calculate the average of the input image
    avgs = []
    for img in input_images:
        avgs.append(getAverageRGB(img))

    for img in target_images:
        # compute the average RGB value of the image
        avg = getAverageRGB(img)
        # find the matching index of closest RGB value
        # from a list of average RGB values
        match_index = getBestMatchIndex(avg, avgs)
        output_images.append(input_images[match_index])
        # user feedback
        if count > 0 and batch_size > 10 and count % batch_size is 0:
            print('processed %d of %d...' %(count, len(target_images)))
        count += 1
        # remove the selected image from input if flag set
        if not reuse_images:
            input_images.remove(match)

    print('creating mosaic...')
    # create photomosaic image from tiles
    mosaic_image = createImageGrid(output_images, grid_size)

    # display the mosaic
    return mosaic_image

# gather our code in a main() function
def main():
    # command line arguments are in sys.argv[1], sys.argv[2], ...
    # sys.argv[0] is the script name itself and can be ignored
```

```
# parse arguments
parser = argparse.ArgumentParser(description='Creates a photomosaic from
                                 input images')
# add arguments
parser.add_argument('--target-image', dest='target_image', required=True)
parser.add_argument('--input-folder', dest='input_folder', required=True)
parser.add_argument('--grid-size', nargs=2, dest='grid_size', required=True)
parser.add_argument('--output-file', dest='outfile', required=False)

args = parser.parse_args()

###### INPUTS ######

# target image
target_image = Image.open(args.target_image)

# input images
print('reading input folder...')
input_images = getImages(args.input_folder)

# check if any valid input images found
if input_images == []:
    print('No input images found in %s. Exiting.' % (args.input_folder, ))
    exit()

# shuffle list to get a more varied output?
random.shuffle(input_images)

# size of the grid
grid_size = (int(args.grid_size[0]), int(args.grid_size[1]))

# output
output_filename = 'mosaic.png'
if args.outfile:
    output_filename = args.outfile

# reuse any image in input
reuse_images = True

# resize the input to fit the original image size?
resize_input = True

##### END INPUTS #####

print('starting photomosaic creation...')

# if images can't be reused, ensure m*n <= num_of_images
if not reuse_images:
    if grid_size[0]*grid_size[1] > len(input_images):
        print('grid size less than number of images')
        exit()
```

```
# resizing input
if resize_input:
    print('resizing images...')
    # for given grid size, compute the maximum width and height of tiles
    dims = (int(target_image.size[0]/grid_size[1]),
            int(target_image.size[1]/grid_size[0]))
    print("max tile dims: %s" % (dims,))
    # resize
    for img in input_images:
        img.thumbnail(dims)


# create photomosaic
mosaic_image = createPhotomosaic(target_image, input_images, grid_size,
                                 reuse_images)


# write out mosaic
mosaic_image.save(output_filename, 'PNG')

print("saved output to %s" % (output_filename,))
print('done.')

# standard boilerplate to call the main() function
# to begin the program
if __name__ == '__main__':
    main()
```

Running the Photomosaic Generator

Here is a sample run of the program:

```
$ python photomosaic.py --target-image test-data/cherai.jpg --input-folder
test-data/set6/ --grid-size 128 128
reading input folder...
starting photomosaic creation...
resizing images...
max tile dims: (23, 15)
splitting input image...
finding image matches...
processed 1638 of 16384 ...
processed 3276 of 16384 ...
processed 4914 of 16384 ...
creating mosaic...
saved output to mosaic.png
done.
```

Figure 7-3(a) shows the target image, and Figure 7-3(b) shows the photomosaic. You can see a close-up of the photomosaic in Figure 7-3(c).

Figure 7-3: Photomosaic sample run

Summary

In this project, you learned how to create a photomosaic, given a target image and a collection of input images. When viewed from a distance, the photomosaic looks like the original image, but up close, you can see the individual images that make up the mosaic.

Experiments!

Here are some ways to further explore photomosaics.

1. Write a program that creates a blocky version of any image, similar to Figure 7-1.

2. With the code in this chapter, you created the photomosaic by pasting the matched images without any gaps in between. A more artistic presentation might include a uniform gap of a few pixels around each tile image. How would you create the gap? (Hint: factor in the gaps when computing the final image dimensions and when doing the paste in createImageGrid().)

3. Most of the time in the program is spent finding the best match for a tile from the input folder. To speed up the program, getBestMatchIndex() needs to run faster. Your implementation of this method was a simple linear search through the list of averages (treated as three-dimensional points). This task falls under the general problem of a *nearest neighbor search*. One particularly effective way to find the closest point is a *k-d tree search*. The scipy library has a convenient class called scipy.spatial .KDTree, which lets you create a *k*-d and query it for the nearest point matches. Try replacing the linear search with a *k*-d tree using SciPy. (See *http://docs.scipy.org/doc/scipy/reference/generated/scipy.spatial.KDTree .html*.)

8

AUTOSTEREOGRAMS

Stare at Figure 8-1 for a minute. Do you see anything other than random dots? Figure 8-1 is an *autostereogram*, a two-dimensional image that creates the illusion of three dimensions. Autostereograms usually consist of repeating patterns that resolve into three dimensions on closer inspection. If you can't see any sort of image, don't worry; it took me a while and a bit of experimentation before I could. (If you aren't having any luck with the version printed in this book, try the color version here: *https://github.com/electronut/pp/images/*. The footnote to the caption reveals what you should see.)

In this project, you'll use Python to create an autostereogram. Here are some of the concepts covered in this project:

- Linear spacing and depth perception
- Depth maps
- Creating and editing images using `Pillow`
- Drawing into images using `Pillow`

Figure 8-1: A puzzling image that might gnaw at you[1]

The autostereograms you'll generate in this project are designed for "wall-eyed" viewing. The best way to see them is to focus your eyes on a point behind the image (such as a wall). Almost magically, once you perceive something in the patterns, your eyes should automatically bring it into focus, and when the three-dimensional image "locks in," you will have a hard time shaking it off. (If you're still having trouble viewing the image, see Gene Levin's article "How to View Stereograms and Viewing Practice"[2] for help.)

How It Works

An autostereogram works by changing the linear spacing between patterns in an image, thereby creating the illusion of depth. When you look at repeating patterns in an autostereogram, your brain can interpret the spacing as depth information, especially if there are multiple patterns with different spacing.

Perceiving Depth in an Autostereogram

When your eyes converge at an imaginary point behind the image, your brain matches the points seen with your left eye with a different group seen by your right eye, and you see these points lying on a plane behind the image. The perceived distance to this plane depends on the amount of spacing in the pattern. For example, Figure 8-2 shows three rows of As. The As are equidistant within each row, but their horizontal spacing increases from top to bottom.

---

1. The hidden image is a shark.

2. *http://colorstereo.com/texts_.txt/practice.htm*

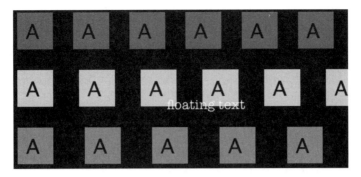

Figure 8-2: Linear spacing and depth perception

When this image is viewed "wall-eyed," the top row in Figure 8-2 should appear to be behind the paper, the middle row should look like it's a little behind the first row, and the bottom row should appear farthest from your eye. The text that says *floating text* should appear to "float" on top of these rows.

Why does your brain interpret the spacing between these patterns as depth? Normally, when you look at a distant object, your eyes work together to focus and converge at the same point, with both eyes rotating inward to point directly at the object. But when viewing a "wall-eyed" autostereogram, focus and convergence happen at different locations. Your eyes focus on the autostereogram, but your brain sees the repeated patterns as coming from the same virtual (imaginary) object, and your eyes converge on a point behind the image, as shown in Figure 8-3. This combination of decoupled focus and convergence allows you to see depth in an autostereogram.

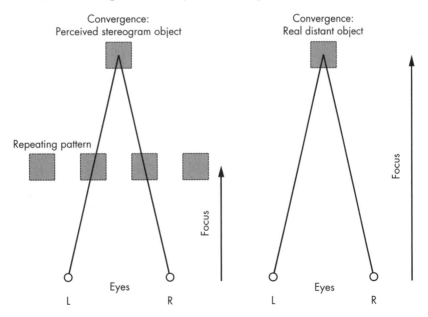

Figure 8-3: Seeing depth in autostereograms

The perceived depth of the autostereogram depends on the horizontal spacing of pixels. Because the first row in Figure 8-2 has the closest spacing, it appears in front of the other rows. However, if the spacing of the points were varied in the image, your brain would perceive each point at a different depth, and you could see a virtual three-dimensional image appear.

Depth Maps

A *depth map* is an image where the value of each pixel represents a depth value, which is the distance from the eye to the part of the object represented by that pixel. Depth maps are often shown as a grayscale image with light areas for nearby points and darker areas for points farther away, as shown in Figure 8-4.

Figure 8-4: A depth map

Notice that the nose of the shark, the lightest part of the image, seems closest to you. The darker area toward the tail seems farthest away.

Because the depth map represents the depth or distance from the center of each pixel to the eye, you can use it to get the depth value associated with a pixel location in the image. You know that horizontal shifts are perceived as depth in images. So if you shift a pixel in a (patterned) image proportionally to the corresponding pixel's depth value, you would create a depth perception for that pixel consistent with the depth map. If you do this for all pixels, you will end up encoding the entire depth map into the image, creating an autostereogram.

Depth maps store depth values for each pixel, and the resolution of the value depends on the number of bits used to represent it. Because you will be using common 8-bit images in this chapter, depth values will be in the range [0, 255].

By the way, the image in Figure 8-4 is the same depth map used to create the first autostereogram shown in Figure 8-1. You will soon learn how to do this yourself.

The code for this project will follow these steps:

1. Read in a depth map.
2. Read in a tile image or create a "random dot" tile.
3. Create a new image by repeating the tile. The dimensions of this image should match those of the depth map.
4. For each pixel in the new image, shift the pixel to the right by an amount proportional to the depth value associated with the pixel.
5. Write the autostereogram to a file.

Requirements

In this project, you'll use Pillow to read in images, access their underlying data, and create and modify images.

The Code

To create an autostereogram from an input depth map image, you'll first generate an intermediate image by repeating a given tile image. Next you'll create a tile image filled with random dots. You'll then go through the core code that creates an autostereogram by shifting an input image using information from a supplied depth map image. To see the complete project, skip ahead to "The Complete Code" on page 125.

Repeating a Given Tile

Let's start by using the createTiledImage() method to tile a graphics file and create a new image with the dimensions specified by the tuple dims of the form (*width*, *height*).

```
# tile a graphics file to create an intermediate image of a set size
def createTiledImage(tile, dims):
    # create the new image
❶   img = Image.new('RGB', dims)
    W, H = dims
    w, h = tile.size
    # calculate the number of tiles needed
❷   cols = int(W/w) + 1
❸   rows = int(H/h) + 1
    # paste the tiles into the image
    for i in range(rows):
        for j in range(cols):
❹           img.paste(tile, (j*w, i*h))
    # output the image
    return img
```

At ❶, you create a new Python Imaging Library (PIL) `Image` object using the supplied dimensions (`dims`). The dimensions of the new image are given as the tuple `dims` of the form (*width, height*). Next, store the width and height of both the tile and the output files. At ❷, you determine the number of columns, and at ❸, you determine the number of rows you need to have in the intermediate image by dividing the final image dimension by those of the tile. Add 1 to each measurement to make sure that the last tile on the right is not missed when the output image dimension is not an exact integer multiple of the tile dimension. Without this precaution, the right side of the image might be cut off. Then, at ❹, loop through the rows and columns and fill them with tiles. Determine the location of the top-left corner of the tile by multiplying (j*w, i*h) so it aligns with the rows and columns. Once complete, the method returns an `Image` object of the specified dimensions, tiled with the input image tile.

Creating a Tile from Random Circles

If the user doesn't provide a tile image, create a tile with random circles using the `createRandomTile()` method.

```
     # create an image tile filled with random circles
     def createRandomTile(dims):
         # create image
❶        img = Image.new('RGB', dims)
❷        draw = ImageDraw.Draw(img)
         # set the radius of a random circle to 1% of
         # width or height, whichever is smaller
❸        r = int(min(*dims)/100)
         # number of circles
❹        n = 1000
         # draw random circles
         for i in range(n):
             # -r makes sure that the circles stay inside and aren't cut off
             # at the edges of the image so that they'll look better when tiled
❺            x, y = random.randint(0, dims[0]-r), random.randint(0, dims[1]-r)
❻            fill = (random.randint(0, 255), random.randint(0, 255),
                     random.randint(0, 255))
❼            draw.ellipse((x-r, y-r, x+r, y+r), fill)
         return img
```

At ❶, you create a new `Image` with the dimensions given by `dim`. Use `ImageDraw.Draw()` ❷ to draw circles inside the image with an arbitrarily chosen radius of 1/100th of either the width or the height of the image, whichever is smaller ❸. (The Python * operator unpacks the width and height values in the `dims` tuple so that it can be passed into the `min()` method.)

At ❹, set the number of circles to draw to 1000. Then calculate the x- and y-coordinates of each circle by calling `random.randint()` to get random integers in the range [0, *width*-r] and [0, *height*-r] ❺. The -r makes sure the generated circles stay inside the image rectangle of dimensions width × height. Without the -r, you could end up drawing a circle right at the edge of the image, which means it would be partly cut off. If you tiled such an image to create the autostereogram, the result wouldn't look good because the circles at the edge between two tiles would have no spacing between them.

To create a random circle, first draw the outline and then fill in a color. At ❻, you select a color for the fill by randomly choosing RGB values from the range [0, 255]. Finally, at ❼, you use the ellipse() method in draw to draw each of your circles. The first argument to this method is the bounding box of the circle, which is given by the top-left and bottom-right corners as (x-r, y-r) and (x+r, y+r), respectively, where (x, y) is the center of the circle and r is its radius.

Let's test this method in the Python interpreter.

```
>>> import autos
>>> img = autos.createRandomTile((256, 256))
>>> img.save('out.png')
>>> exit()
```

Figure 8-5 shows the output from the test.

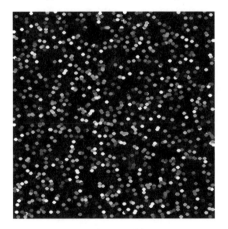

Figure 8-5: Sample run of createRandomTile()

As you can see in Figure 8-5, you have created a tile image with random dots. You'll use this to create the autostereogram.

Creating Autostereograms

Now let's create some autostereograms. The createAutostereogram() method does most of the work. Here it is:

```
def createAutostereogram(dmap, tile):
    # convert the depth map to a single channel if needed
❶   if dmap.mode is not 'L':
        dmap = dmap.convert('L')
```

```
          # if no image is specified for a tile, create a random circles tile
❷         if not tile:
              tile = createRandomTile((100, 100))
          # create an image by tiling
❸         img = createTiledImage(tile, dmap.size)
          # create a shifted image using depth map values
❹         sImg = img.copy()
          # get access to image pixels by loading the Image object first
❺         pixD = dmap.load()
          pixS = sImg.load()
          # shift pixels horizontally based on depth map
❻         cols, rows = sImg.size
          for j in range(rows):
              for i in range(cols):
❼                 xshift = pixD[i, j]/10
❽                 xpos = i - tile.size[0] + xshift
❾                 if xpos > 0 and xpos < cols:
❿                     pixS[i, j] = pixS[xpos, j]
          # display the shifted image
          return sImg
```

At ❶, you perform a sanity check to ensure that the depth map and the image have the same dimensions. If the user doesn't supply an image for the tile, you create a random circle tile at ❷. At ❸, you create a tile that matches the size of the supplied depth map image. You then make a copy of this tiled image at ❹.

At ❺, you use the Image.Load() method, which loads image data into memory. This method allows accessing image pixels as a two-dimensional array in the form [i, j]. At ❻, you store the image dimensions as a number of rows and columns, treating the image as a grid of individual pixels.

The core of the autostereogram creation algorithm lies in the way you shift the pixels in the tiled image according to the information gathered from the depth map. To do this, iterate through the tiled image and process each pixel. At ❼, you look up the value of the shift associated with a pixel from the depth map pixD. You then divide this depth value by 10 because you are using 8-bit depth maps here, which means the depth varies from 0 to 255. If you divide these values by 10, you get depth values in the approximate range of 0 to 25. Since the depth map input image dimensions are usually in the hundreds of pixels, these shift values work fine. (Play around by changing the value you divide by to see how it affects the final image.)

At ❽, you calculate the new x position of the pixel by filling the autostereogram with the tiles. The value of a pixel keeps repeating every w pixels and is expressed by the formula $a_i = a_i + w$, where a_i is the color of a given pixel at index i along the x-axis. (Because you're considering rows, not columns, of pixels, you ignore the y-direction.)

To create a perception of depth, make the spacing, or *repeat interval*, proportional to the depth map value for that pixel. So in the final autostereogram image, every pixel is shifted by delta_i compared to the previous (periodic) appearance of the same pixel. You can express this as $b_i = b_{i-w+\delta_i}$.

Here, b_i represents the color value of a given pixel at index i for the final autostereogram image. This is exactly what you are doing at ❽. Pixels with a depth map value of 0 (black) are not shifted and are perceived as the background.

At ❿, you replace each pixel with its shifted value. At ❾, check to make sure you're not trying to access a pixel that's not in the image, which can happen at the image's edges because of the shift.

Command Line Options

Now let's look at main() method of the program, where we provide some command line options.

```
# create a parser
parser = argparse.ArgumentParser(description="Autosterograms...")
# add expected arguments
parser.add_argument('--depth', dest='dmFile', required=True)
parser.add_argument('--tile', dest='tileFile', required=False)
parser.add_argument('--out', dest='outFile', required=False)
# parse args
args = parser.parse_args()
# set the output file
outFile = 'as.png'
if args.outFile:
    outFile = args.outFile
# set tile
tileFile = False
if args.tileFile:
    tileFile = Image.open(args.tileFile)
```

At ❶, as with previous projects, you define the command line options for the program using argparse. The one required argument is the depth map file, and the two optional arguments are the tile filename and the name of the output file. If a tile image is not specified, the program will generate a tile of random circles. If the output filename is not specified, the output is written to an autostereogram file named *as.png*.

The Complete Code

Here is the complete autostereogram program. You can also download this code from *https://github.com/electronut/pp/blob/master/autos/autos.py*.

```
import sys, random, argparse
from PIL import Image, ImageDraw

# create spacing/depth example
def createSpacingDepthExample():
    tiles = [Image.open('test/a.png'), Image.open('test/b.png'),
            Image.open('test/c.png')]
    img = Image.new('RGB', (600, 400), (0, 0, 0))
    spacing = [10, 20, 40]
```

```python
    for j, tile in enumerate(tiles):
        for i in range(8):
            img.paste(tile, (10 + i*(100 + j*10), 10 + j*100))
    img.save('sdepth.png')

# create an image filled with random circles
def createRandomTile(dims):
    # create image
    img = Image.new('RGB', dims)
    draw = ImageDraw.Draw(img)
    # set the radius of a random circle to 1% of
    # width or height, whichever is smaller
    r = int(min(*dims)/100)
    # number of circles
    n = 1000
    # draw random circles
    for i in range(n):
        # -r makes sure that the circles stay inside and aren't cut off
        # at the edges of the image so that they'll look better when tiled
        x, y = random.randint(0, dims[0]-r), random.randint(0, dims[1]-r)
        fill = (random.randint(0, 255), random.randint(0, 255),
                random.randint(0, 255))
        draw.ellipse((x-r, y-r, x+r, y+r), fill)
    # return image
    return img

# tile a graphics file to create an intermediate image of a set size
def createTiledImage(tile, dims):
    # create the new image
    img = Image.new('RGB', dims)
    W, H = dims
    w, h = tile.size
    # calculate the number of tiles needed
    cols = int(W/w) + 1
    rows = int(H/h) + 1
    # paste the tiles into the image
    for i in range(rows):
        for j in range(cols):
            img.paste(tile, (j*w, i*h))
    # output the image
    return img

# create a depth map for testing
def createDepthMap(dims):
    dmap = Image.new('L', dims)
    dmap.paste(10, (200, 25, 300, 125))
    dmap.paste(30, (200, 150, 300, 250))
    dmap.paste(20, (200, 275, 300, 375))
    return dmap

# given a depth map image and an input image,
# create a new image with pixels shifted according to depth
def createDepthShiftedImage(dmap, img):
    # size check
    assert dmap.size == img.size
```

```
        # create shifted image
        sImg = img.copy()
        # get pixel access
        pixD = dmap.load()
        pixS = sImg.load()
        # shift pixels output based on depth map
        cols, rows = sImg.size
        for j in range(rows):
            for i in range(cols):
                xshift = pixD[i, j]/10
                xpos = i - 140 + xshift
                if xpos > 0 and xpos < cols:
                    pixS[i, j] = pixS[xpos, j]
        # return shifted image
        return sImg


# given a depth map (image) and an input image,
# create a new image with pixels shifted according to depth
def createAutostereogram(dmap, tile):
    # convert the depth map to a single channel if needed
    if dmap.mode is not 'L':
        dmap = dmap.convert('L')
    # if no image is specified for a tile, create a random circles tile
    if not tile:
        tile = createRandomTile((100, 100))
    # create an image by tiling
    img = createTiledImage(tile, dmap.size)
    # create a shifted image using depth map values
    sImg = img.copy()
    # get access to image pixels by loading the Image object first
    pixD = dmap.load()
    pixS = sImg.load()
    # shift pixels horizontally based on depth map
    cols, rows = sImg.size
    for j in range(rows):
        for i in range(cols):
            xshift = pixD[i, j]/10
            xpos = i - tile.size[0] + xshift
            if xpos > 0 and xpos < cols:
                pixS[i, j] = pixS[xpos, j]
    # return shifted image
    return sImg

# main() function
def main():
    # use sys.argv if needed
    print('creating autostereogram...')
    # create parser
    parser = argparse.ArgumentParser(description="Autosterograms...")
    # add expected arguments
    parser.add_argument('--depth', dest='dmFile', required=True)
    parser.add_argument('--tile', dest='tileFile', required=False)
    parser.add_argument('--out', dest='outFile', required=False)
    # parse args
    args = parser.parse_args()
```

```
# set the output file
outFile = 'as.png'
if args.outFile:
    outFile = args.outFile
# set tile
tileFile = False
if args.tileFile:
    tileFile = Image.open(args.tileFile)
# open depth map
dmImg = Image.open(args.dmFile)
# create stereogram
asImg = createAutostereogram(dmImg, tileFile)
# write output
asImg.save(outFile)

# call main
if __name__ == '__main__':
    main()
```

Running the Autostereogram Generator

Now let's run the program using a depth map of a stool (*stool-depth.png*).

```
$ python3 autos.py --depth data/stool-depth.png
```

Figure 8-6 shows the depth map image on the left and the generated
autostereogram on the right. Because you haven't supplied a graphic for the
tile, this autostereogram is created using random tiles.

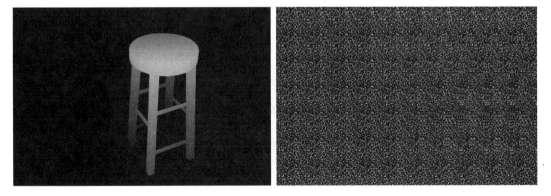

Figure 8-6: Sample run of autos.py

Now let's give a tile image as input. Use the *stool-depth.png* depth map as
you did earlier, but this time, supply the image *escher-tile.jpg*[3] for the tiles.

```
$ python3 autos.py --depth data/stool-depth.png -tile data/escher-tile.jpg
```

---

3. *http://calculus-geometry.hubpages.com/hub/Free-M-C-Escher-Tessellation-Background-Patterns
-Tiling-Lizard-Background/*

Figure 8-7 shows the output.

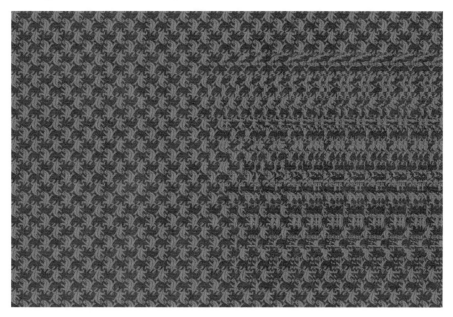

Figure 8-7: Sample run of autos.py using tiles

Summary

In this project, you learned how to create autostereograms. Given a depth map image, you can now create either a random dot autostereogram or one tiled with an image you supply.

Experiments!

Here are some ways to further explore autostereograms.

1. Write code to create an image similar to Figure 8-2 that demonstrates how changes in the linear spacing in an image can create illusions of depth. (Hint: use image tiles and the Image.paste() method.)

2. Add a command line option to the program to specify the scale to be applied to the depth map values. (Remember that the code divides the depth map value by 10.) How does changing the value affect the autostereogram?

3. Learn to create your own depth maps from three-dimensional models using a tool like SketchUp (*http://sketchup.com/*) or access the many ready-made SketchUp models online. Use SketchUp's Fog option to create your depth maps. If you need help, check out this YouTube video: *https://www.youtube.com/watch?v=fDzNJYi6Bok/*.

PART IV

ENTER 3D

"In One Dimensions, did not a moving Point produce a Line with two terminal points?
In two Dimensions, did not a moving Line produce a Square with four terminal points?
In Three Dimensions, did not a moving Square produce—did not the eyes of mine behold it—
that blessed being, a Cube, with eight terminal points?"
— Edwin A. Abbott, *Flatland: A Romance of Many Dimensions*

9

UNDERSTANDING OPENGL

In this project, you'll create a simple program that displays a texture-mapped square using OpenGL and GLFW. OpenGL adds a software interface to your graphics processing unit (GPU), and GLFW is a windowing toolkit. You'll also learn how to use the C-like OpenGL Shading Language (GLSL) to write *shaders*—code that executes in the GPU. Shaders bring immense flexibility to computations in OpenGL. I'll show you how to use GLSL shaders to transform and color geometry as you create a rotating, textured polygon (as shown in Figure 9-1).

GPUs are optimized to perform the same operations on huge amounts of data repeatedly, in parallel, which makes them much faster than central processing units (CPUs) for this purpose. In addition to rendering computer graphics, they're also being used for general-purpose computing, and specialized languages now let you use your GPU hardware for this purpose. You'll leverage the GPU, OpenGL, and shaders in this project.

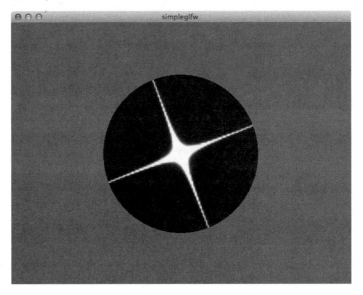

Figure 9-1: The final image for the project in this chapter: a rotating polygon with a star image. This square polygon boundary is clipped to a black circle using a shader.

Python is an excellent "glue" language. There are a vast number of Python *bindings* available for libraries written in other languages, such as C, that allow you to use these libraries in Python. In this chapter and in Chapters 10 and 11, you'll use PyOpenGL, the Python binding to OpenGL, to create computer graphics.

OpenGL is a *state machine*, kind of like an electrical switch, with two states: ON and OFF. When you switch from one state to the other, the switch remains in that new state. However, OpenGL is more complex than a simple electrical switch; it's more like a switchboard with numerous switches and dials. Once you change the state of a particular setting, it remains OFF unless you turn it ON. When you bind an OpenGL call to a particular object, subsequent related OpenGL calls will be directed toward the bound object until it is unbound.

Here are some of the concepts introduced in this project:

- Using the GLFW windowing library for OpenGL
- Using GLSL to write vertex and fragment shaders
- Performing texture mapping
- Using 3D transformations

First, let's take a look at how OpenGL works.

Old-School OpenGL

In most computer graphics systems, drawing is done by sending vertices through a series of interconnected functional blocks that form a pipeline.

Recently, the OpenGL application programming interface (API) transitioned from a fixed-function graphics pipeline to a programmable graphics pipeline. You'll focus on modern OpenGL, but because you'll find numerous "old-school" OpenGL examples on the Web, I'll give you a taste of what the API used to look like so you'll have a better sense of what has changed.

For example, the following simple old-school OpenGL program draws a yellow rectangle on the screen:

```python
import sys
from OpenGL.GLUT import *
from OpenGL.GL import *

def display():
    glClear (GL_COLOR_BUFFER_BIT|GL_DEPTH_BUFFER_BIT)
    glColor3f (1.0, 1.0, 0.0)
    glBegin(GL_QUADS)
    glVertex3f (-0.5, -0.5, 0.0)
    glVertex3f (0.5, -0.5, 0.0)
    glVertex3f (0.5, 0.5, 0.0)
    glVertex3f (-0.5, 0.5, 0.0)
    glEnd()
    glFlush();

glutInit(sys.argv)
glutInitDisplayMode(GLUT_SINGLE|GLUT_RGB)
glutInitWindowSize(400, 400)
glutCreateWindow("oldgl")
glutDisplayFunc(display)
glutMainLoop()
```

Figure 9-2 shows the result.

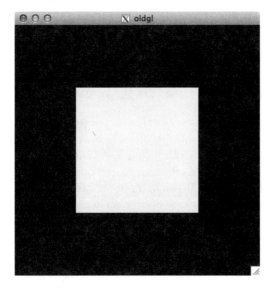

Figure 9-2: Output from a simple old-school OpenGL program

Using old-school OpenGL, you would specify individual vertices for the 3D primitive (a GL_QUAD, or rectangle, in this case), but then each vertex needs to be sent to the GPU separately, which is inefficient. This old-school model of programming doesn't scale well and is really slow when your geometry becomes complex. It also offers only limited control over how the vertices and pixels on the screen are transformed. (As you will see in this project, you can use the new programmable pipeline paradigm to overcome these limitations.)

Modern OpenGL: The 3D Graphics Pipeline

To give you a sense of how modern OpenGL works at a high level, let's make a triangle appear on the screen through a sequence of operations commonly known as the *3D graphics pipeline*. Figure 9-3 shows a simplified representation of the OpenGL 3D graphics pipeline.

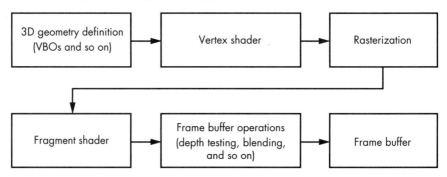

Figure 9-3: The (simplified) OpenGL graphics pipeline

In the first step, you define the 3D geometry by defining the vertices of the triangle in 3D space and specifying the colors associated with each vertex. Next, you transform these vertices: the first transformation places the vertices in 3D space, and the second projects the 3D coordinates onto 2D space. The color values for the corresponding vertices are also calculated in this step based on factors such as lighting, typically in code called the *vertex shader.*

Next, the geometry is *rasterized* (converted from geometric objects to pixels), and for each pixel, another block of code called the *fragment shader* is executed. Just as the vertex shader operates on 3D vertices, the fragment shader operates on the 2D pixels after rasterization.

Finally, the pixel passes through a series of frame buffer operations, where it undergoes *depth buffer testing* (checking whether one fragment obscures another), *blending* (mixing two fragments with transparency), and other operations that combine its current color with what is already on the frame buffer at that location. These changes end up on the final frame buffer, which is typically displayed on the screen.

Geometric Primitives

Because OpenGL is a low-level graphics library, you can't ask it directly to draw a cube or a sphere, though libraries built on top of it can do such tasks for you. OpenGL understands only low-level geometric primitives such as points, lines, and triangles.

Modern OpenGL supports only the primitive types GL_POINTS, GL_LINES, GL_LINE_STRIP, GL_LINE_LOOP, GL_TRIANGLES, GL_TRIANGLE_STRIP, and GL_TRIANGLE_FAN. Figure 9-4 shows how the vertices for the primitives are organized. Each vertex shown is a 3D coordinate such as (x, y, z).

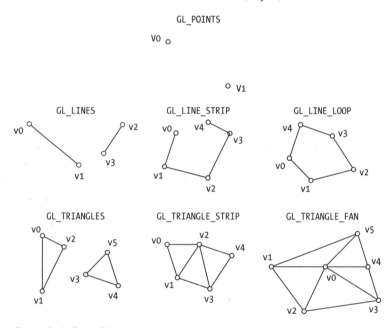

Figure 9-4: OpenGL primitives

To draw a sphere in OpenGL, first define the geometry of the sphere mathematically and compute its 3D vertices. Then, assemble the vertices into basic geometric primitives; for example, you could group each set of three vertices into a triangle. You can then render these vertices using OpenGL.

3D Transformations

You can't learn computer graphics without learning about 3D transformations. Conceptually, these are quite simple to understand. You have an object—what can you do with it? You can move it, stretch (or squash) it, or rotate it. You can do other things to it too, but these three tasks are the operations or transformations most commonly performed on an object: translation, scale, and rotation. In addition to these commonly used transformations, you'll use a perspective projection to map the 3D objects onto the 2D plane of the screen. These transformations are all applied on the coordinates of the object you are trying to transform.

While you're probably familiar with 3D coordinates in the form (x, y, z), in 3D computer graphics you use coordinates in the form (x, y, z, w), called *homogeneous coordinates*. (These coordinates come from a branch of mathematics called *projective geometry*, which is beyond the scope of this book.)

Homogenous coordinates allow you to express these common 3D transformations as 4×4 matrices. But for purposes of these OpenGL projects, all you need to know is that the homogenous coordinate (x, y, z, w) is equivalent to the 3D coordinate $(x/w, y/w, z/w, 1.0)$. A 3D point $(1.0, 2.0, 3.0)$ can be expressed in homogeneous coordinates as $(1.0, 2.0, 3.0, 1.0)$.

Here is an example of a 3D transformation using a translation matrix. See how the matrix multiplication translates a point $(x, y, z, 1.0)$ to $(x + tx, y + ty, z + tz, 1.0)$.

$$\begin{bmatrix} 1 & 0 & 0 & t_x \\ 0 & 1 & 0 & t_y \\ 0 & 0 & 1 & t_z \\ 0 & 0 & 0 & 1 \end{bmatrix} \times \begin{bmatrix} x \\ y \\ z \\ 1 \end{bmatrix} = \begin{bmatrix} x + t_x \\ y + t_y \\ z + t_z \\ 1 \end{bmatrix}$$

Two terms that you will encounter often in OpenGL are *modelview* and *projection* transformations. With the advent of customizable shaders in modern OpenGL, modelviews and projections are just generic transformations. Historically, in old-school versions of OpenGL, the modelview transformations were applied to your 3D model to position it in space, and the projection transformations were used to map the 3D coordinates onto a 2D surface for display, as you'll see in a moment. Modelview transformations are user-defined transformations that let you position your 3D objects, and projection transformations are projective transformations that map 3D onto 2D.

The two most commonly used 3D graphic projective transformations are *orthographic* and *perspective*, but here you'll use only perspective projections, which are defined by a *field of view* (the extent to which the eye can see), a *near plane* (the plane closest to the eye), a *far plane* (the plane farthest from the eye), and an *aspect ratio* (the ratio of the width to the height of the near plane). Together, these parameters constitute a camera model for a projection that determines how the 3D figure will be mapped onto a 2D screen, as shown in Figure 9-5. The truncated pyramid shown in the figure is the *view frustum*. The *eye* is the 3D location where you place the camera. (For orthographic projection, the eye will be at infinity, and the pyramid will become a rectangular cuboid.)

Once the perspective projection is complete and before rasterization, the graphics primitives are clipped (or cut out) against the near and far planes, as shown in Figure 9-5. The near and far planes are chosen such that the 3D objects you want to appear onscreen lie inside the view frustum; otherwise, they will be clipped away.

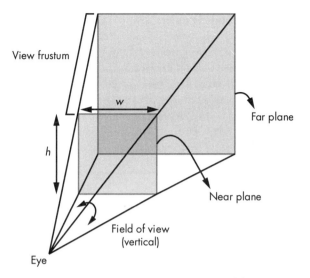

Figure 9-5: Perspective projection camera model

Shaders

You've seen how shaders fit into the modern OpenGL programmable graphics pipeline. Now let's look at a simple pair of vertex and fragment shaders to get a sense of how GLSL works.

A Vertex Shader

Here is a simple vertex shader:

```
❶ #version 330 core

❷ in vec3 aVert;

❸ uniform mat4 uMVMatrix;
❹ uniform mat4 uPMatrix;

❺ out vec4 vCol;

   void main() {
       // apply transformations
❻     gl_Position = uPMatrix * uMVMatrix * vec4(aVert, 1.0);
       // set color
❼     vCol = vec4(1.0, 0.0, 0.0, 1.0);
   }
```

At ❶, you set the version of GLSL used in the shader to version 3.3. Then, you define an input named aVert of type vec3 (a 3D vector) for the vertex shader using the keyword in ❷. At ❸ and ❹, you define two variables of type mat4 (4×4 matrices), which correspond to the modelview and projection matrices, respectively. The uniform prefix to these variables indicates that they do not change during execution of the vertex shader for a given rendering call on a set of vertices. You use the out prefix at ❺ to define the output of the vertex shader, which is a color variable of type vec4 (a 4D vector to store red, green, blue, and alpha channels).

Now you come to the main() function, where the vertex shader program starts. The value of gl_Position is computed at ❻ by transforming the input aVert using the uniform matrices passed in. The GLSL variable gl_Position is used to store the transformed vertices. At ❼, you set the output color from the vertex shader to red with no transparency by using the value (1, 0, 0, 1). You'll use this as input in the next shader in the pipeline.

A Fragment Shader

Now let's look at a simple fragment shader:

```
❶ #version 330 core

❷ in vec4 vCol;

❸ out vec4 fragColor;

  void main() {
      // use vertex color
❹     fragColor = vCol;
  }
```

After setting the version of GLSL used in the shader at ❶, you set vCol at ❷ as the input to the fragment shader. This variable, vCol, was set as output from the vertex shader. (Remember, the vertex shader executes for every vertex in the 3D scene, whereas the fragment shader executes for every pixel on the screen.)

During rasterization (which occurs between the vertex and fragment shaders), OpenGL converts the transformed vertices to pixels, and the color of the pixels lying between the vertices is calculated by interpolating the color values at the vertices.

You set up an output color variable fragColor at ❸, and at ❹, the interpolated color is set as the output. By default, and in most cases, the intended output of the fragment shader is the screen, and the color you set ends up there (unless it's affected by operations such as depth testing that occur in the final stage of the graphics pipeline).

For the GPU to execute the shader code, it needs to be compiled and linked to instructions that the hardware understands. OpenGL provides ways to do this and reports detailed compiler and linker errors that will help you develop the shader code.

The compilation process also generates a table of locations or indices for the variables declared in your shaders that you'll use to connect variables in your Python code with those in the shader.

Vertex Buffers

Vertex buffers are an important mechanism used by OpenGL shaders. Modern graphics hardware and OpenGL are designed to work with large amounts of 3D geometry. Consequently, several mechanisms are built into OpenGL to help transfer data from the program to the GPU. A typical setup to draw 3D geometry in a program will do the following:

1. Define arrays of coordinates, colors, and other attributes for each vertex of the 3D geometry.
2. Create a Vertex Array Object (VAO) and bind to it.
3. Create Vertex Buffer Objects (VBOs) for each attribute, defined on a per-vertex basis.
4. Bind to the VBO and set the buffer data using the predefined arrays.
5. Specify the data and location of vertex attributes to be used in the shader.
6. Enable the vertex attributes.
7. Render the data.

After you define the 3D geometry in terms of vertices, you create and bind to a vertex array object. VAOs are a convenient way to group geometry as multiple arrays of coordinates, colors, and so on. Then, for each attribute of each vertex, you create a vertex buffer object and set your 3D data into it. The VBO stores the vertex data in the GPU memory. Now, all that's left is to connect the buffer data so you can access it from your shaders. You do this through calls that use the location of the variables employed in the shader.

Texture Mapping

Next let's look at texture mapping, an important computer graphics technique that you'll use in this chapter. *Texture mapping* is a way to give a scene a realistic feel with the help of a 2D picture of a 3D object (like the backdrop in a play). A texture is usually read from an image file and is stretched to drape over a geometric region by mapping the 2D coordinates (in the range [0, 1]) onto the 3D coordinates of the polygons. For example, Figure 9-6 shows an image draped onto one face of a cube. (I used GL_TRIANGLE_STRIP primitives to draw the cube faces, and the ordering of the vertices is indicated by the lines on the face.)

In Figure 9-6, the (0, 0) corner of the texture is mapped to the bottom-left vertex of the cube face. Similarly, you can see how the other corners of the texture are mapped, with the net effect that the texture is "pasted" onto this cube face. The geometry of the cube face itself is defined as a triangle strip, and the vertices zigzag from the bottom to the top left and from the bottom to the top right. Textures are extremely powerful and versatile computer graphics tools, as you'll see in Chapter 11.

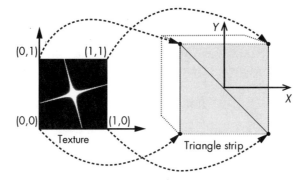

Figure 9-6: Texture mapping

Displaying OpenGL

Now let's talk about how to get OpenGL to draw stuff on the screen. The entity that stores all the OpenGL state information is called the *OpenGL context*. Contexts have a viewable, window-like area where the OpenGL drawings go, and you can have multiple contexts per process or run of an application, but only one context per thread can be current at a time. (Fortunately, the window toolkit will take care of most of the context handling.)

For your OpenGL output to appear in a window onscreen, you need the help of the operating system. For these projects, you'll use GLFW, a lightweight cross-platform C library that lets you create and manage OpenGL contexts, display the 3D graphics in a window, and handle user input like mouse clicks and keyboard presses. (Appendix A covers the installation details for this library.)

Because you're writing code in Python and not C, you'll also use a Python binding to GLFW (*glfw.py*, available in the *common* directory in the book's code repository), which lets you access all the GLFW features using Python.

Requirements

We'll use PyOpenGL, a popular Python binding for OpenGL, for rendering and numpy arrays to represent 3D coordinates and transformation matrices.

The Code

Let's build a simple Python application using OpenGL. To see the complete project code, skip ahead to "The Complete Code" on page 151.

Creating an OpenGL Window

The first order of business is to set up GLFW so you have an OpenGL window to render into. I've created a class called RenderWindow for this purpose.

Here is the initialization code for this class:

```
class RenderWindow:
    """GLFW Rendering window class"""
    def __init__(self):

        # save current working directory
        cwd = os.getcwd()

        # initialize glfw
❶       glfw.glfwInit()

        # restore cwd
        os.chdir(cwd)

        # version hints
❷       glfw.glfwWindowHint(glfw.GLFW_CONTEXT_VERSION_MAJOR, 3)
        glfw.glfwWindowHint(glfw.GLFW_CONTEXT_VERSION_MINOR, 3)
        glfw.glfwWindowHint(glfw.GLFW_OPENGL_FORWARD_COMPAT, GL_TRUE)
        glfw.glfwWindowHint(glfw.GLFW_OPENGL_PROFILE,
                            glfw.GLFW_OPENGL_CORE_PROFILE)

        # make a window
        self.width, self.height = 640, 480
        self.aspect = self.width/float(self.height)
❸       self.win = glfw.glfwCreateWindow(self.width, self.height,
                                         b'simpleglfw')

        # make the context current
❹       glfw.glfwMakeContextCurrent(self.win)
```

You initialize the GLFW library at ❶. Then, starting at ❷, you set
the OpenGL version to the OpenGL 3.3 core profile. At ❸, you create an
OpenGL-capable window with the dimensions 640×480. Finally, at ❹, you
make the context current, and you're ready to make OpenGL calls.

Next, you make some initialization calls.

```
        # initialize GL
❶       glViewport(0, 0, self.width, self.height)
❷       glEnable(GL_DEPTH_TEST)
❸       glClearColor(0.5, 0.5, 0.5, 1.0)
```

At ❶, you set the viewport or screen dimensions (width and height)
where OpenGL will render your 3D scene. At ❷, turn on depth testing with
GL_DEPTH_TEST. At ❸, you set the color the background should become when
glClear() is issued during rendering to 50 percent gray with an alpha setting
of 1.0. (Alpha is a measure of the transparency of a pixel.)

Setting Callbacks

Next you register some event callbacks for user interface events within the
GLFW window so you can respond to mouse clicks and keypresses.

```
# set window callbacks
glfw.glfwSetMouseButtonCallback(self.win, self.onMouseButton)
glfw.glfwSetKeyCallback(self.win, self.onKeyboard)
glfw.glfwSetWindowSizeCallback(self.win, self.onSize)
```

This code sets callbacks for mouse button presses, keyboard presses, and window resizing, respectively. Every time one of these events happens, the function registered as a callback is executed.

The Keyboard Callback

Let's look at the keyboard callback:

```
    def onKeyboard(self, win, key, scancode, action, mods):
        #print 'keyboard: ', win, key, scancode, action, mods
❶      if action == glfw.GLFW_PRESS:
            # ESC to quit
            if key == glfw.GLFW_KEY_ESCAPE:
❷              self.exitNow = True
            else:
                # toggle cut
❸              self.scene.showCircle = not self.scene.showCircle
```

The onKeyboard() callback is called every time a keyboard event happens. The arguments to the function arrive filled with useful information such as what type of event occurred (key-up versus key-down, for example) and which key was pressed. The code glfw.GLFW_PRESS says to look only for key-down, or PRESS, events ❶. At ❷, you set an exit flag if the ESC key is pressed. If any other key is pressed, you toggle a showCircle Boolean that will be passed into the fragment shader ❸.

The Window-Resizing Event

Here is the handler for the window-resizing event:

```
    def onSize(self, win, width, height):
        #print 'onsize: ', win, width, height
        self.width = width
        self.height = height
        self.aspect = width/float(height)
❶      glViewport(0, 0, self.width, self.height)
```

Every time the window size changes, you call glViewport() to reset the dimensions for the graphics to ensure that the 3D scene is drawn correctly on the screen ❶. You also store the dimensions in width and height and store the aspect ratio for the changed window in aspect.

The Main Loop

Now you come to the main loop of the program. (GLFW does not provide a default program loop.)

```
      def run(self):
          # initializer timer
❶        glfw.glfwSetTime(0)
         t = 0.0
❷        while not glfw.glfwWindowShouldClose(self.win) and not self.exitNow:
             # update every x seconds
❸           currT = glfw.glfwGetTime()
            if currT - t > 0.1:
                # update time
                t = currT
                # clear
❹              glClear(GL_COLOR_BUFFER_BIT | GL_DEPTH_BUFFER_BIT)

                # build projection matrix
❺              pMatrix = glutils.perspective(45.0, self.aspect, 0.1, 100.0)

❻              mvMatrix = glutils.lookAt([0.0, 0.0, -2.0], [0.0, 0.0, 0.0],
                                          [0.0, 1.0, 0.0])
                # render
❼              self.scene.render(pMatrix, mvMatrix)
                # step
❽              self.scene.step()

❾              glfw.glfwSwapBuffers(self.win)
                # poll for and process events
❿              glfw.glfwPollEvents()
         # end
         glfw.glfwTerminate()
```

In the main loop, glfw.glfwSetTime ()resets the GLFW timer to 0 ❶. You'll use this timer to redraw the graphics at regular intervals. A while loop starts at ❷ and exits only if the window is closed or exitNow is set to True. When the loop exits, glfw.glfwTerminate() is called to shut down GLFW cleanly.

Inside the loop, glfw.glfwGetTime() gets the current timer value ❸, which you use to calculate the elapsed time since the last drawing. By setting a desired interval here (in this case, to 0.1 seconds or 100 milliseconds), you can adjust the rendering frame rate.

Next, at ❹, glClear() clears the depth and color buffers and replaces them with the set background color to get ready for the next frame. At ❺, you compute the projection matrix using the perspective() method defined in *glutils.py* (you'll take a closer look at this in the next section). Here, you ask for a 45-degree field of view and a near/far plane distance of 0.1/100.0. Then, you set the modelview matrix at ❻ using the lookAt() method defined in *glutils.py*. Set the eye position at (0, 0, –2), looking at the origin (0, 0, 0) with an "up" vector of (0, 1, 0). Then, call the render() method on the scene object at ❼, passing in these matrices, and at ❽, call scene.step() so it can update the variables necessary for the time step. At ❾, glfwSwapBuffers() is called, which swaps the back and front buffers, thus displaying your updated 3D graphic. The GLFW PollEvents() call at ❿ checks for any UI events and returns control to the while loop.

The Scene Class

Now let's look at the Scene class, which is responsible for initializing and drawing the 3D geometry.

```
class Scene:
    """ OpenGL 3D scene class"""
    # initialization
    def __init__(self):
        # create shader
❶       self.program = glutils.loadShaders(strVS, strFS)

❷       glUseProgram(self.program)
```

In the Scene class constructor, you first compile and load the shaders. For this, I've used the utility method loadShaders() ❶ defined in *glutils.py*, which provides a convenient wrapper around the series of OpenGL calls required to load the shaders from the string, compile them, and link them into an OpenGL program object. Because OpenGL is a state machine, you need to set the code to use a particular "program object" (because a project could have multiple programs) using the glUseProgram() call at ❷.

Now connect the variables in the Python code with those in the shaders.

```
        self.pMatrixUniform = glGetUniformLocation(self.program, b'uPMatrix')
        self.mvMatrixUniform = glGetUniformLocation(self.program, b'uMVMatrix')
        # texture
        self.tex2D = glGetUniformLocation(self.program, b'tex2D')
```

This code uses the glGetUniformLocation() method to retrieve the locations of the variables uPMatrix, uMVMatrix, and tex2D defined inside the vertex and fragment shaders. These locations can then be used to set the values for the shader variables.

Defining the 3D Geometry

Let's first define the 3D geometry for the square.

```
    # define triangle strip vertices
❶  vertexData = numpy.array(
        [-0.5, -0.5, 0.0,
         0.5, -0.5, 0.0,
         -0.5, 0.5, 0.0,
         0.5, 0.5, 0.0], numpy.float32)

    # set up vertex array object (VAO)
❷  self.vao = glGenVertexArrays(1)
    glBindVertexArray(self.vao)
    # vertices
❸  self.vertexBuffer = glGenBuffers(1)
    glBindBuffer(GL_ARRAY_BUFFER, self.vertexBuffer)
    # set buffer data
❹  glBufferData(GL_ARRAY_BUFFER, 4*len(vertexData), vertexData,
                GL_STATIC_DRAW)
    # enable vertex array
❺  glEnableVertexAttribArray(0)
    # set buffer data pointer
❻  glVertexAttribPointer(0, 3, GL_FLOAT, GL_FALSE, 0, None)
    # unbind VAO
❼  glBindVertexArray(0)
```

At ❶, you define the array of vertices of the triangle strip used to draw the square. Think of a square of side 1.0 centered at the origin. The bottom-left vertex of this square has the coordinates (−0.5, −0.5, 0.0); the next vertex (the bottom-right one) has the coordinates (0.5, −0.5, 0.0); and so on. The order of the coordinates is that of a GL_TRIANGLE_STRIP. At ❷, you create a VAO. Once you bind to this VAO, all upcoming calls will be bound to it. At ❸, you create a VBO to manage the rendering of the vertex data. Once the buffer is bound, the line at ❹ sets the buffer data from the vertices you have defined.

Now you need to enable the shaders to access this data, and you do this at ❺; glEnableVertexAttribArray() is called with an index of 0 because that is the location you have set in the vertex shader for the vertex data variable. At ❻, glVertexAttribPointer() sets the location and data format of the vertex attribute array. The index of the attribute is 0, the number of components is 3 (you use 3D vertices), and the data type of the vertex is GL_FLOAT. You unbind the VAO at ❼ so other related calls don't interfere with it. In OpenGL, it's best practice to reset states when you are done. OpenGL is a state machine, so if you leave things in a mess, they will remain that way.

The following code loads the image as an OpenGL texture:

```
    # texture
    self.texId = glutils.loadTexture('star.png')
```

The texture ID returned will be used later in rendering.

Next we'll update variables in the Scene object to make the square rotate on the screen:

```
# step
def step(self):
    # increment angle
❶    self.t = (self.t + 1) % 360
    # set shader angle in radians
❷    glUniform1f(glGetUniformLocation(self.program, 'uTheta'),
                math.radians(self.t))
```

At ❶, you increment the angle variable t and use the modulus operator (%) to keep this value within [0, 360]. You then use the glUniform1f() method at ❷ to set this value in the shader program. As before, you use glGetUniformLocation() to get the location of the uTheta angle variable from the shader, and the Python math.radians() method to convert the angle from degrees to radians.

Now let's look at the main rendering code:

```
# render
def render(self, pMatrix, mvMatrix):
    # use shader
❶    glUseProgram(self.program)

    # set projection matrix
❷    glUniformMatrix4fv(self.pMatrixUniform, 1, GL_FALSE, pMatrix)

    # set modelview matrix
    glUniformMatrix4fv(self.mvMatrixUniform, 1, GL_FALSE, mvMatrix)

    # show circle?
❸    glUniform1i(glGetUniformLocation(self.program, b'showCircle'),
                self.showCircle)

    # enable texture
❹    glActiveTexture(GL_TEXTURE0)
❺    glBindTexture(GL_TEXTURE_2D, self.texId)
❻    glUniform1i(self.tex2D, 0)

    # bind VAO
❼    glBindVertexArray(self.vao)
    # draw
❽    glDrawArrays(GL_TRIANGLE_STRIP, 0, 4)
    # unbind VAO
❾    glBindVertexArray(0)
```

At ❶, set up the rendering to use the shader program. Then, starting at ❷, set the computed projection and modelview matrices in the shader using the glUniformMatrix4fv() method. You use glUniform1i() at ❸ to set the current value of the showCircle variable in the fragment shader. OpenGL has a concept of multiple texture units, and glActiveTexture() ❹ activates texture unit 0 (the default). At ❺, you bind the texture ID you generated earlier to activate it for rendering. The `sampler2D` variable in the fragment shader is set to texture unit 0 at ❻. At ❼, you bind to the VAO you created previously. Now you see the benefit of using VAOs: you don't need to repeat a whole bunch of vertex buffer–related calls before the actual drawing. At ❽, `glDrawArrays()` is called to render the bound vertex buffers. The primitive type is a triangle strip, and there are four vertices to be rendered. You unbind the VAO at ❾, which is always a good coding practice.

Defining the GLSL Shaders

Now let's look at the most exciting part of the project—the GLSL shaders. This is the vertex shader:

```
#version 330 core

❶ layout(location = 0) in vec3 aVert;

❷ uniform mat4 uMVMatrix;
  uniform mat4 uPMatrix;
  uniform float uTheta;

❸ out vec2 vTexCoord;

  void main() {
      // rotational transform
❹    mat4 rot = mat4(
                  vec4(cos(uTheta), sin(uTheta), 0.0, 0.0),
                  vec4(-sin(uTheta), cos(uTheta), 0.0, 0.0),
                  vec4(0.0, 0.0, 1.0, 0.0),
                  vec4(0.0, 0.0, 0.0, 1.0)
                  );
      // transform vertex
❺    gl_Position = uPMatrix * uMVMatrix * rot * vec4(aVert, 1.0);
      // set texture coordinate
❻    vTexCoord = aVert.xy + vec2(0.5, 0.5);
  }
```

At ❶, you use the `layout` keyword to set explicitly the location of the vertex attribute aVert—to 0, in this case. Starting at ❷, declare `uniform` variables: projection and modelview matrices and the rotation angle. These will be set from the Python code. At ❸, you set a 2D vector vTexCoord as an output from this shader. This will be available as an input to the fragment shader. In the `main()` method in the shader, set up a rotation matrix at ❹, which rotates around the z-axis by a given angle. You compute gl_Position at ❺ using a concatenation of projection, modelview, and rotation matrices. At ❻, you set up a 2D vector as a texture coordinate. You may recall that you defined the triangle strip for a square centered at the origin with side 1.0. Because texture coordinates are in the range [0, 1], you can generate these from the vertex coordinates by adding (0.5, 0.5) to the x- and y-values. This also demonstrates the power and immense flexibility of shaders for your computations. Texture coordinates and other variables are not sacrosanct; you can set them to just about anything.

Now let's look at the fragment shader:

```
#version 330 core

❶ in vec4 vCol;
   in vec2 vTexCoord;

❷ uniform sampler2D tex2D;
❸ uniform bool showCircle;

❹ out vec4 fragColor;

   void main() {
       if (showCircle) {
           // discard fragment outside circle
❺         if (distance(vTexCoord, vec2(0.5, 0.5)) > 0.5) {
               discard;
           }
           else {
❻             fragColor = texture(tex2D, vTexCoord);
           }
       }
           else {
❼             fragColor = texture(tex2D, vTexCoord);
           }
   }
```

Starting at ❶, you define inputs to the fragment shader—the same color and texture coordinate variables you set as output in the vertex shader. Recall that the fragment shader operates on a per-pixel basis, so the values set for these variables are those for the current pixel, interpolated across the polygon. You declare a sampler2D variable at ❷, which is linked to a particular texture unit and is used to look up the texture value. At ❸, declare a Boolean uniform flag showCircle, which is set from the Python code, and at ❹, declare fragColor as the output from the fragment shader. By default, this goes to the screen (after final frame buffer operations such as depth testing and blending).

If the showCircle flag is not set, at ❼, you use the GLSL texture() method to look up the texture color value using the texture coordinate and the sampler. In effect, you are just texturing the triangle strip using the star image. But if the showCircle flag is true, at ❺, use the GLSL built-in method distance to check how far the current pixel is from the center of the polygon. It uses the (interpolated) texture coordinates for this purpose, which are passed in by the vertex shader. If the distance is greater than a certain threshold (0.5 in this case), it calls the GLSL discard method, which drops the current pixel. If the distance is less than the threshold, you set the appropriate color from the texture ❻. Basically, what this does is ignore pixels that are outside a circle with a radius of 0.5 centered at the midpoint of the square, thus cutting the polygon into a circle when showCircle is set.

The Complete Code

The complete code for our simple OpenGL application resides in two files: *simpleglfw.py*, which has the code shown here and can be found at *https://github.com/electronut/pp/tree/master/simplegl/*, and *glutils.py*, which includes some helper methods to make life easier and can be found in the *common* directory.

```python
import OpenGL
from OpenGL.GL import *

import numpy, math, sys, os
import glutils

import glfw

strVS = """
#version 330 core

layout(location = 0) in vec3 aVert;

uniform mat4 uMVMatrix;
uniform mat4 uPMatrix;
uniform float uTheta;

out vec2 vTexCoord;

void main() {
    // rotational transform
    mat4 rot =  mat4(
                vec4(cos(uTheta), sin(uTheta), 0.0, 0.0),
                vec4(-sin(uTheta), cos(uTheta), 0.0, 0.0),
                vec4(0.0, 0.0, 1.0, 0.0),
                vec4(0.0, 0.0, 0.0, 1.0)
                );
    // transform vertex
    gl_Position = uPMatrix * uMVMatrix * rot * vec4(aVert, 1.0);
    // set texture coordinate
    vTexCoord = aVert.xy + vec2(0.5, 0.5);
}
"""
strFS = """
#version 330 core

in vec2 vTexCoord;

uniform sampler2D tex2D;
uniform bool showCircle;

out vec4 fragColor;

void main() {
    if (showCircle) {
```

```
            // discard fragment outside circle
            if (distance(vTexCoord, vec2(0.5, 0.5)) > 0.5) {
                discard;
            }
            else {
                fragColor = texture(tex2D, vTexCoord);
            }
        }
        else {
            fragColor = texture(tex2D, vTexCoord);
        }
    }
    """


class Scene:
    """ OpenGL 3D scene class"""
    # initialization
    def __init__(self):
        # create shader
        self.program = glutils.loadShaders(strVS, strFS)

        glUseProgram(self.program)

        self.pMatrixUniform = glGetUniformLocation(self.program, b'uPMatrix')
        self.mvMatrixUniform = glGetUniformLocation(self.program, b'uMVMatrix')
        # texture
        self.tex2D = glGetUniformLocation(self.program, b'tex2D')

        # define triange strip vertices
        vertexData = numpy.array(
            [-0.5, -0.5, 0.0,
              0.5, -0.5, 0.0,
             -0.5, 0.5, 0.0,
              0.5, 0.5, 0.0], numpy.float32)

        # set up vertex array object (VAO)
        self.vao = glGenVertexArrays(1)
        glBindVertexArray(self.vao)
        # vertices
        self.vertexBuffer = glGenBuffers(1)
        glBindBuffer(GL_ARRAY_BUFFER, self.vertexBuffer)
        # set buffer data
        glBufferData(GL_ARRAY_BUFFER, 4*len(vertexData), vertexData,
                     GL_STATIC_DRAW)
        # enable vertex array
        glEnableVertexAttribArray(0)
        # set buffer data pointer
        glVertexAttribPointer(0, 3, GL_FLOAT, GL_FALSE, 0, None)
        # unbind VAO
        glBindVertexArray(0)

        # time
        self.t = 0
```

```python
        # texture
        self.texId = glutils.loadTexture('star.png')

        # show circle?
        self.showCircle = False

    # step
    def step(self):
        # increment angle
        self.t = (self.t + 1) % 360
        # set shader angle in radians
        glUniform1f(glGetUniformLocation(self.program, 'uTheta'),
                    math.radians(self.t))

    # render
    def render(self, pMatrix, mvMatrix):
        # use shader
        glUseProgram(self.program)

        # set projection matrix
        glUniformMatrix4fv(self.pMatrixUniform, 1, GL_FALSE, pMatrix)

        # set modelview matrix
        glUniformMatrix4fv(self.mvMatrixUniform, 1, GL_FALSE, mvMatrix)

        # show circle?
        glUniform1i(glGetUniformLocation(self.program, b'showCircle'),
                    self.showCircle)

        # enable texture
        glActiveTexture(GL_TEXTURE0)
        glBindTexture(GL_TEXTURE_2D, self.texId)
        glUniform1i(self.tex2D, 0)

        # bind VAO
        glBindVertexArray(self.vao)
        # draw
        glDrawArrays(GL_TRIANGLE_STRIP, 0, 4)
        # unbind VAO
        glBindVertexArray(0)


class RenderWindow:
    """GLFW Rendering window class"""
    def __init__(self):

        # save current working directory
        cwd = os.getcwd()

        # initialize glfw - this changes cwd
        glfw.glfwInit()

        # restore cwd
        os.chdir(cwd)
```

```
        # version hints
        glfw.glfwWindowHint(glfw.GLFW_CONTEXT_VERSION_MAJOR, 3)
        glfw.glfwWindowHint(glfw.GLFW_CONTEXT_VERSION_MINOR, 3)
        glfw.glfwWindowHint(glfw.GLFW_OPENGL_FORWARD_COMPAT, GL_TRUE)
        glfw.glfwWindowHint(glfw.GLFW_OPENGL_PROFILE,
                            glfw.GLFW_OPENGL_CORE_PROFILE)

        # make a window
        self.width, self.height = 640, 480
        self.aspect = self.width/float(self.height)
        self.win = glfw.glfwCreateWindow(self.width, self.height,
                                         b'simpleglfw')
        # make context current
        glfw.glfwMakeContextCurrent(self.win)

        # initialize GL
        glViewport(0, 0, self.width, self.height)
        glEnable(GL_DEPTH_TEST)
        glClearColor(0.5, 0.5, 0.5, 1.0)

        # set window callbacks
        glfw.glfwSetMouseButtonCallback(self.win, self.onMouseButton)
        glfw.glfwSetKeyCallback(self.win, self.onKeyboard)
        glfw.glfwSetWindowSizeCallback(self.win, self.onSize)

        # create 3D
        self.scene = Scene()

        # exit flag
        self.exitNow = False


    def onMouseButton(self, win, button, action, mods):
        #print 'mouse button: ', win, button, action, mods
        pass

    def onKeyboard(self, win, key, scancode, action, mods):
        #print 'keyboard: ', win, key, scancode, action, mods
        if action == glfw.GLFW_PRESS:
            # ESC to quit
            if key == glfw.GLFW_KEY_ESCAPE:
                self.exitNow = True
            else:
                # toggle cut
                self.scene.showCircle = not self.scene.showCircle

    def onSize(self, win, width, height):
        #print 'onsize: ', win, width, height
        self.width = width
        self.height = height
        self.aspect = width/float(height)
        glViewport(0, 0, self.width, self.height)
```

```python
    def run(self):
        # initializer timer
        glfw.glfwSetTime(0)
        t = 0.0
        while not glfw.glfwWindowShouldClose(self.win) and not self.exitNow:
            # update every x seconds
            currT = glfw.glfwGetTime()
            if currT - t > 0.1:
                # update time
                t = currT
                # clear
                glClear(GL_COLOR_BUFFER_BIT | GL_DEPTH_BUFFER_BIT)

                # build projection matrix
                pMatrix = glutils.perspective(45.0, self.aspect, 0.1, 100.0)

                mvMatrix = glutils.lookAt([0.0, 0.0, -2.0], [0.0, 0.0, 0.0],
                                          [0.0, 1.0, 0.0])
                # render
                self.scene.render(pMatrix, mvMatrix)
                # step
                self.scene.step()

                glfw.glfwSwapBuffers(self.win)
                # poll for and process events
                glfw.glfwPollEvents()
        # end
        glfw.glfwTerminate()

    def step(self):
        # clear
        glClear(GL_COLOR_BUFFER_BIT | GL_DEPTH_BUFFER_BIT)

        # build projection matrix
        pMatrix = glutils.perspective(45.0, self.aspect, 0.1, 100.0)

        mvMatrix = glutils.lookAt([0.0, 0.0, -2.0], [0.0, 0.0, 0.0],
                                  [0.0, 1.0, 0.0])
        # render
        self.scene.render(pMatrix, mvMatrix)
        # step
        self.scene.step()

        glfw.SwapBuffers(self.win)
        # poll for and process events
        glfw.PollEvents()

# main() function
def main():
    print("Starting simpleglfw. "
          "Press any key to toggle cut. Press ESC to quit.")
    rw = RenderWindow()
    rw.run()
```

```
# call main
if __name__ == '__main__':
    main()
```

Running the OpenGL Application

Here is a sample run of the project:

```
$python simpleglfw.py
```

The output will be the same as shown in Figure 9-1.

Now let's take a quick look at some of the utility methods defined in *glutils.py*. This one loads an image into an OpenGL texture:

```
def loadTexture(filename):
    """load OpenGL 2D texture from given image file"""
❶  img = Image.open(filename)
❷  imgData = numpy.array(list(img.getdata()), np.int8)
❸  texture = glGenTextures(1)
❹  glBindTexture(GL_TEXTURE_2D, texture)
❺  glPixelStorei(GL_UNPACK_ALIGNMENT, 1)
❻  glTexParameterf(GL_TEXTURE_2D, GL_TEXTURE_WRAP_S, GL_CLAMP_TO_EDGE)
   glTexParameterf(GL_TEXTURE_2D, GL_TEXTURE_WRAP_T, GL_CLAMP_TO_EDGE)
❼  glTexParameterf(GL_TEXTURE_2D, GL_TEXTURE_MAG_FILTER, GL_LINEAR)
   glTexParameterf(GL_TEXTURE_2D, GL_TEXTURE_MIN_FILTER, GL_LINEAR)
❽  glTexImage2D(GL_TEXTURE_2D, 0, GL_RGBA, img.size[0], img.size[1],
               0, GL_RGBA, GL_UNSIGNED_BYTE, imgData)
    return texture
```

The loadTexture() function uses the Python Imaging Library (PIL) Image module at ❶ to read the image file. Then it gets the data out of the Image object onto an 8-bit numpy array at ❷. It creates an OpenGL texture object at ❸, which is a prerequisite to doing anything with textures in OpenGL. At ❹, you perform the now familiar binding to the texture object so all further texture-related settings apply to this object. At ❺, you set the unpacking alignment of data to 1, which means the image data will be considered to be 1-byte or 8-bit data by the hardware. Starting at ❻, you tell OpenGL what to do with the texture at the edges. In this case, it says to just clamp the texture color to the edge of the geometry. (In specifying texture coordinates, the convention is to use the letters S and T for the axes instead of x and y.) At ❼ and the following line, you specify the kind of interpolation to be used when the texture is stretched or compressed to map onto a polygon. In this case, *linear filtering* is specified. At ❽, you set the image data in the bound texture. At this point, the image data is transferred to graphics memory, and the texture is ready for use.

Summary

Congratulations on completing your first program using Python and OpenGL. You have begun your journey into the fascinating world of 3D graphics programming.

Experiments!

Here are some ideas for modifying this project.

1. The vertex shader in this project rotates the square around the z-axis (0, 0, 1). Can you make it rotate around the axis (1, 1, 0)? You can do this in two ways: first, by modifying the rotation matrix in the shader, and second, by computing this matrix in the Python code and passing it as a *uniform* into the shader. Try both!

2. In the project, the texture coordinates are generated inside the vertex shader and passed to the fragment shader. This is a trick, and it works only because of the convenient values chosen for the vertices of the triangle strip. Pass the texture coordinates as a separate attribute into the vertex shader, similar to how the vertices are passed in. Now, can you make the star texture *tile* across the triangle strip? Instead of displaying a single star, you want to produce a 4×4 grid of stars on the square. (Hint: use texture coordinates greater than 1.0 and set GL_TEXTURE_WRAP_S/T parameters in glTexParameterf() to GL_REPEAT.)

3. By changing just your fragment shader, can you make your square look like Figure 9-7? (Hint: use the GLSL sin() function.)

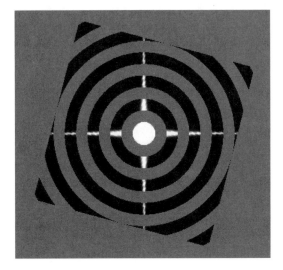

Figure 9-7: Using the fragment shader to block out concentric circles

10

PARTICLE SYSTEMS

In the world of computer graphics, a *particle system* is a technique that uses many small graphical primitives (such as lines, points, triangles, and polygons) to represent objects such as smoke, fire, or even hair, which don't have clear geometric shapes and hence are difficult to model using standard techniques.

For example, how would you create an explosion on your computer (without using lighter fluid, that is)? Imagine the explosion originating from a point in space and growing outward as a rapidly expanding, complex, three-dimensional entity that changes shape and color over time. Trying to model this mathematically is daunting to say the least.

But now think of the explosion as consisting of a bunch of tiny particles, each with an associated position and color. At the start of the explosion, the particles are bunched up at a single point in space. As time passes, they move outward and change color according to certain mathematical rules, allowing you to create an animation of the explosion by drawing all particles at regular intervals. By using a good mathematical model, a large number of particles, and rendering techniques such as transparency and billboarding, you can create realistic-looking effects, as shown in Figure 10-1.

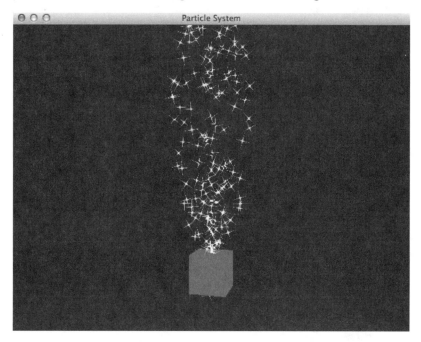

Figure 10-1: Sample run of the completed project

In this project, you'll formulate a mathematical model for the motion of particles as a function of time and use shaders on the graphics processing unit (GPU) for computation. Then, you'll devise a rendering scheme to draw these particles in a convincing way using a technique called *billboarding*, which makes a two-dimensional image look three-dimensional by keeping it constantly facing the viewer. You'll also use OpenGL shaders to make the particles spin and to animate the scene. You'll be able to turn the various effects on or off for comparison by using keypresses.

The mathematical model will set the initial position and velocity of each particle and determine how the particles move over time. You'll create sparks from square images by making the black region of each texture transparent, and you'll keep each spark facing the viewer to make them look three-dimensional. You'll animate the particles so that their positions are updated at regular intervals and their brightness fades over time.

Here are some of the concepts you will explore:

- Developing a mathematical model for a fountain particle system
- Using GPU shaders for computation

- Using textures and billboarding to imitate complex 3D objects
- Using OpenGL rendering features such as blending, depth masks, and alpha channels to draw semitransparent objects
- Using a camera model to draw 3D perspective views

How It Works

To create the animation, you need a mathematical model. You'll form a fountain of sparks by moving a number of particles originating from a fixed point through a parabolic trajectory over time, as shown in Figure 10-2. This is the fountain particle system.

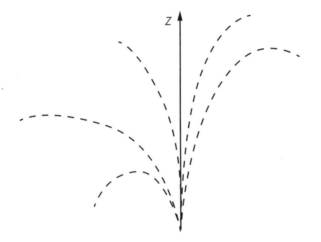

Figure 10-2: The trajectory of five example sparks in the fountain particle system

Your particle system should have these features:

- The particles should emerge from a fixed point, and their motion should follow the shape of a parabola.
- The particles should be able to travel a predefined distance with respect to the vertical axis (z-axis or height) of the fountain.
- Particles closer to the center of the fountain's vertical axis should have larger initial velocities than those farther from the center.
- To produce a more realistic effect, the particles should not all be ejected at the same time.
- The brightness of the particles should fade over their lifetime.

Modeling the Motion of a Particle

Let's assume that the particle system consists of N particles. The equation for motion of the ith particle is as follows:

$$P_t^i = P_0 + V_0^i t + \frac{1}{2} a t^2$$

Here, P_t is the position at any given time, t. P_0 is the initial position of the particle, V_0 is the initial velocity of the particle, and a is the acceleration. Think of a as the force of gravity in your system, making the particles arc downward.

These parameters are all three-dimensional vectors that can be expressed as three-dimensional coordinates. For instance, the value of acceleration you'll use is $(0, 0, -9.8)$, which is the acceleration of Earth's gravity in the z direction (height) in meters per second squared.

Setting a Maximum Spread

To make the fountain look realistic, the particles should fly out at different angles with respect to the z-axis of the cone. But you also want to set a maximum spread so the initial velocity of each particle is within a certain range, funneling the particles into a fountain shape. To accomplish that, you'll fix the maximum angle of velocity at 20 degrees with respect to the vertical axis, as shown in Figure 10-3.

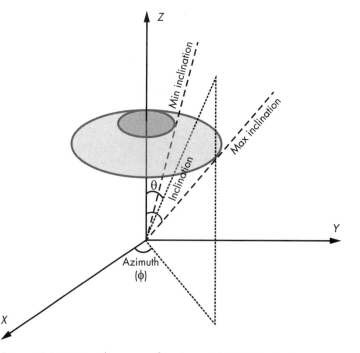

Figure 10-3: Limiting the range of each particle's initial velocity. Each particle is assigned a velocity within the shaded circle.

In Figure 10-3, the azimuth, ϕ, is the angle of the velocity vector to the x-axis. The inclination, θ, is the angle made by the velocity vector to the z-axis. The range of inclination chosen is such that the velocity vector lies within the light gray shaded area in the figure.

The velocity directions should be chosen at random from the part of the hemisphere enclosed within the large circle. These directions intersect points on a sphere with a radius of one unit, so you can use the spherical coordinate system to compute them. In addition, you want the magnitude of the velocity to decrease as the angle from the axis increases. Keeping this in mind, the initial velocity of a particle is as follows:

$$V_0^i = \left(1 - \alpha^2\right)V$$

Here, α is the ratio of the angle of inclination of the particle to the maximum angle (in this case, 20 degrees). As a result, the velocity decreases (quadratically) as this ratio moves toward 1.0. The velocity, V, is a point on the unit sphere and is as follows:

$$V = \left(\cos(\theta)\sin(\phi), \sin(\theta)\sin(\phi), \cos(\phi)\right)$$

You choose a random inclination in the range of [0, 20] degrees and a random azimuth in the range of [0, 360] degrees:

$$\theta = random\left([0, 20]\right), \phi = random\left([0, 360]\right)$$

This equation points the particle at a random spot in the region within the circle in Figure 10-3. (Note that in this program, all angle calculations need to be done in radians, not degrees.)

You also want to ensure the particles don't all start at the same time. (See "Experiments!" on page 189 to find out why.) To do this, you compute a time lag for each particle, which you use later in the computation of the particle's position. The lag for the ith particle is computed as follows:

$$t_{lag}^i = 0.05i$$

What about the arbitrary numerical constants in these equations? Why use 0.05 for the lag time, for example, or 20 degrees for the maximum angle? The answer is experimentation. The important thing is to make a basic model and then tweak these constants to get the best visual effect. Change these parameters in your program to see how different values influence the results.

Rendering the Particles

One simple way to render the particles is to draw them as points. OpenGL has a GL_POINTS primitive that is essentially a dot on the screen; you can control the pixel size and color of the dot. But you want the particles to look like little sparks and to spin around as they shoot up.

Drawing sparks from scratch is too complicated, so you'll take a picture of a spark and paste it as a texture onto a rectangle (also called a *quad*). Each particle in the fountain will be drawn as a textured triangular image of a spark. But that leaves you with two problems. First, you don't want square sparks because that would look fake. Second, the quads will be aligned incorrectly if you look at the fountain from other angles.

Using OpenGL Blending to Create More Realistic Sparks

To create more realistic-looking sparks, you'll use *OpenGL blending*. You combine the incoming fragment (after execution of the fragment shader) with the content already in the frame buffer. The alpha channel is usually involved in this operation.

For example, say you're drawing two polygons onscreen and you want to blend them together. You can use alpha blending to do the trick, which works like placing two transparent sheets on top of each other. The alpha channel represents the opacity of the pixel, which is a measure of how transparent it is. In addition to the *red*, *green*, and *blue* components that represent the color of a pixel, you can also store an *alpha* value, and the resulting color scheme is called *RGBA*. For a 32-bit RGBA color scheme, the alpha value is in the range [0, 255], with 0 being fully transparent and 255 fully opaque. The alpha channel by itself doesn't do anything. Only when you use the alpha value to change the final RGB value of a pixel are various transparency effects created.

OpenGL gives you several ways to tailor your blending equations. For your fountain particles, you'll use the texture shown in Figure 10-4, but you want the black regions of the texture to disappear so you see just the sparks.

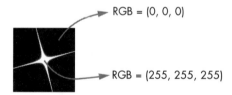

Figure 10-4: The spark texture, labeled with RGB values: (0, 0, 0) for black and (255, 255, 255) for white

You can make the black regions disappear by enabling OpenGL blending and multiplying the alpha value of a fragment by the texture color. For the black regions, the RGB color value is (0, 0, 0), and if you multiply this by an alpha value, you get 0. As a result, during blending, the opacity of the black regions in the final image is set to 0 and you see only the background color, effectively cutting off the black regions in the spark texture. (The alpha value is set in the fragment shader, as you'll see in "Creating the Fragment Shader" on page 171.)

Instead of setting the alpha value in the shader, you could control the transparency by using the alpha channel in the texture image and setting different alpha values for the black-and-white regions. It's much simpler to use the alpha value in the shader to create a texture with a black background and then make all black regions transparent than it is to apply different transparency values to specific regions using the alpha channel in the texture.

Using Billboarding

For the second problem (quads being incorrectly aligned when you look at the fountain from other angles), you'll use billboarding. Instead of drawing a complex three-dimensional object, you'll position a two-dimensional picture such that you always view it head-on (perpendicular to the view direction) as a kind of billboard. For example, if you were developing a three-dimensional game with a landscape of trees in the background, you could replace the landscape with a textured polygon billboard. As long as the player doesn't get too close, the fake "picture tree" looks realistic.

Now let's look at the math behind positioning a polygon so it always faces the view direction. Figure 10-5 shows how you can turn a textured quad into a billboard.

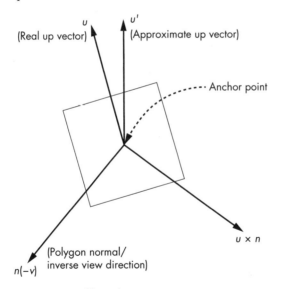

Figure 10-5: Billboarding

The alignment happens with respect to an anchor point on the quad. In this case, you've chosen the center of the quad. To align the quad, you need a set of three orthogonal vectors to create a minicoordinate system. The first vector of interest is n, which represents the *normal* vector of the quad. The normal vector extends perpendicular to the plane of the quad, which means the direction you set for the normal vector is the direction the quad will be facing. You want the quad to face the view direction, v, so the n vector needs to align itself with this vector but in the opposite direction. Because the view direction faces into the screen, the normal vector of the quad should point in the opposite direction—out of the screen.

This means you want direction $n = -v$. Now, choose a vector u, which is an approximate up vector for the final orientation of the quad. You choose u as (0, 0, 1) because the z-direction points "up." (I say this vector is approximate because although you know the normal vector of the quad ahead of time, you don't know the camera orientation yet.) Then you calculate the third vector, r, where $r = u \times n$ (the cross product of the two vectors). Now you have two orthogonal vectors, n and r, both in the plane of the quad. You get the third one by taking the cross product of these two. Thus, you have a new up vector of $u' = n \times r = n \times (u \times n)$. You need a new up vector to ensure these three vectors are orthogonal, or perpendicular to each other. Finally, these vectors all need to be normalized to a length equal to one unit during calculation to create an orthonormal coordinate system (where all vectors are unit length and orthogonal). Once you have these three vectors, you can use a rotation matrix for an arbitrary orientation from 3D graphics theory. The rotation matrix R rotates the orthonormal coordinate system positioned at the origin onto the coordinate system formed by the vectors r, u', and n:

$$R = \begin{pmatrix} r_x & u'_x & n_x & 0 \\ r_y & u'_y & n_y & 0 \\ r_z & u'_z & n_z & 0 \\ 0 & 0 & 0 & 1 \end{pmatrix}$$

Applying this rotation matrix aligns your textured quad correctly toward the view direction, making it a billboard.

Animating the Sparks

To animate the fountain of sparks, draw the positions of the particle system at regular time intervals by updating both the rendering and the time, using the GLFW library.

Requirements

We'll use PyOpenGL, a popular Python binding for OpenGL, for rendering and numpy arrays to represent 3D coordinates and transformation matrices.

The Code for the Particle System

Let's begin by defining the 3D geometry of the particles used in the fountain. You'll then look at how to create a time lag between particles in the animation, how to set initial velocities for the particles, and how the

OpenGL vertex and fragment shaders are used in the program. Lastly, you'll look at how to put all of this together to render the particle system. For the full project code, skip ahead to "The Complete Particle System Code" on page 174.

The code for the fountain is encapsulated in a class called ParticleSystem, which creates the particle system, sets up the OpenGL shaders, renders the system using OpenGL, and restarts the animation every five seconds.

Defining the Particle Geometry

First, define the geometry of the particles by creating a Vertex Array Object (VAO) to manage the subsequent vertex attribute arrays.

```
# create Vertex Array Object (VAO)
self.vao = glGenVertexArrays(1)
# bind VAO
glBindVertexArray(self.vao)
```

Each particle is a square, whose vertices and texture coordinates are defined as follows:

```
            # vertices
            s = 0.2
❶          quadV = [
                -s, s, 0.0,
                -s, -s, 0.0,
                s, s, 0.0,
                s, -s, 0.0,
                s, s, 0.0,
                -s, -s, 0.0
                ]
❷          vertexData = numpy.array(numP*quadV, numpy.float32)
❸          self.vertexBuffer = glGenBuffers(1)
❹          glBindBuffer(GL_ARRAY_BUFFER, self.vertexBuffer)
❺          glBufferData(GL_ARRAY_BUFFER, 4*len(vertexData), vertexData,
                        GL_STATIC_DRAW)

            # texture coordinates
❻          quadT = [
                0.0, 1.0,
                0.0, 0.0,
                1.0, 1.0,
                1.0, 0.0,
                1.0, 1.0,
                0.0, 0.0
                ]
            tcData = numpy.array(numP*quadT, numpy.float32)
            self.tcBuffer = glGenBuffers(1)
            glBindBuffer(GL_ARRAY_BUFFER, self.tcBuffer)
            glBufferData(GL_ARRAY_BUFFER, 4*len(tcData), tcData, GL_STATIC_DRAW)
```

At ❶, you define the vertices of the square, with sides centered around the origin and measuring 0.2 in length. The vertex ordering is the same as for a couple of GL_TRIANGLES. You then create a numpy array at ❷ by repeating these vertices numP times—one quad for each particle in the system. (All the geometry you are drawing is put into one big array.)

Next, you put these vertices into a vertex buffer object, as you did in Chapter 9. The VBO is created at ❸ and bound at ❹; then at ❺, the bound buffer is filled with the vertex data. The 4*len(vertexData) code specifies that 4 bytes are needed for each element in the vertexData array.

Finally, you define the texture coordinates of the quad at ❻, and the lines of code that follow set up the associated VBO.

Defining the Time-Lag Array for the Particles

Next, define the time-lag array for the particles. You want the time lag to be the same for each set of four vertices, which represent a square-shaped particle, as you can see in the following code:

```
        # time lags
❶       timeData = numpy.repeat(0.005*numpy.arange(numP, dtype=numpy.float32),
                          4)
        self.timeBuffer = glGenBuffers(1)
        glBindBuffer(GL_ARRAY_BUFFER, self.timeBuffer)
        glBufferData(GL_ARRAY_BUFFER, 4*len(timeData), timeData,
                    GL_STATIC_DRAW)
```

At ❶, numpy.arange() creates an array of increasing values of the form $[0, 1, \ldots, numP_{-1}]$. Multiplying this array by 0.005 and using numpy.repeat() with an argument of 4 produces an array of the form [0.0, 0.0, 0.0, 0.0, 0.005, 0.005, 0.005, 0.005, ...]. The code that follows sets up the VBO.

Setting the Initial Particle Velocities

You create the initial velocities of the particles next. The goal is to create a spread of random velocities within a certain maximum angular displacement from the vertical axis. Here's the code:

```
        # velocites
        velocities = []
        # cone angle
❶       coneAngle = math.radians(20.0)
        # set up particle velocities
        for i in range(numP):
            # inclination
❷           angleRatio = random.random()
            a = angleRatio*coneAngle
            # azimuth
❸           t = random.random()*(2.0*math.pi)
            # get velocity on sphere
❹           vx = math.sin(a)*math.cos(t)
            vy = math.sin(a)*math.sin(t)
            vz = math.cos(a)
```

```
              # speed decreases with angle
❺             speed = 15.0*(1.0 - angleRatio*angleRatio)
              # add a set of calculated velocities
❻             velocities += 6*[speed*vx, speed*vy, speed*vz]
          # set up velocity vertex buffer
          self.velBuffer = glGenBuffers(1)
          glBindBuffer(GL_ARRAY_BUFFER, self.velBuffer)
❼         velData = numpy.array(velocities, numpy.float32)
          glBufferData(GL_ARRAY_BUFFER, 4*len(velData), velData, GL_STATIC_DRAW)
```

At ❶, you define the cone angle used to restrict the trajectory of the
fountain particles. (Notice the conversion from degrees to radians using
the built-in `math.radians()` method.) Next, you calculate a velocity for
each particle using the formulas discussed in "Modeling the Motion of a
Particle" on page 162.

At ❷, you compute a random fraction of the maximum inclination
angle, which the lines that follow use to compute the current inclination.
Next, at ❸, you calculate the azimuth, and because `random.random()` returns
a value in [0, 1], you multiply the azimuth by `2.0*math.pi` to get a random
angle from 0 to 2π radians.

Starting at ❹, you compute the velocity vector on the unit sphere using
the spherical coordinate formula. At ❺, use the angle ratio from ❷ to
calculate a velocity inversely proportional to the vertical angle. Calculate the
particle's final velocity at ❻ and repeat this value for all six vertices of the
two triangles. At ❼, you create a `numpy` array from the Python list, and you're
ready to create a VBO for velocities. Finally, you enable all vertex attributes and set the data format for the vertex buffers. (Because this process is similar to what you did in Chapter 9, I'll skip the discussion here and
move on to the vertex shader.)

Creating the Vertex Shader

The vertex shader computes the trajectory of the particle system by processing individual vertices. Here's its code:

```
#version 330 core

in vec3 aVel;
in vec3 aVert;
in float aTime0;
in vec2 aTexCoord;

uniform mat4 uMVMatrix;
uniform mat4 uPMatrix;
uniform mat4 bMatrix;
uniform float uTime;
uniform float uLifeTime;
uniform vec4 uColor;
uniform vec3 uPos;

out vec4 vCol;
out vec2 vTexCoord;
```

The vertex shader is executed for every vertex of the quad, for all quads in the particle system. It first defines some variables in attribute arrays, which represent the array you put into the VBOs; then *uniform* variables that remain constant while the shader is executed; and finally *out* quantities, which are set in the vertex shader and passed to the fragment shader for interpolation.

Now let's look at the shader's main() function:

```
void main() {
    // set position
❶    float dt = uTime - aTime0;
❷    float alpha = clamp(1.0 - 2.0*dt/uLifeTime, 0.0, 1.0);
❸    if(dt < 0.0 || dt > uLifeTime || alpha < 0.01) {
        // out of sight!
        gl_Position = vec4(0.0, 0.0, -1000.0, 1.0);
    }
    else {
        // calculate new position
❹        vec3 accel = vec3(0.0, 0.0, -9.8);
        // apply a twist
        float PI = 3.14159265358979323846264;
❺        float theta = mod(100.0*length(aVel)*dt, 360.0)*PI/180.0;
❻        mat4 rot = mat4(vec4(cos(theta), sin(theta), 0.0, 0.0),
                vec4(-sin(theta), cos(theta), 0.0, 0.0),
                vec4(0.0, 0.0, 1.0, 0.0),
                vec4(0.0, 0.0, 0.0, 1.0));
        // apply billboard matrix
❼        vec4 pos2 = bMatrix*rot*vec4(aVert, 1.0);
        // calculate position
❽        vec3 newPos = pos2.xyz + uPos + aVel*dt + 0.5*accel*dt*dt;
        // apply transformations
❾        gl_Position = uPMatrix * uMVMatrix * vec4(newPos, 1.0);
    }
    // set color
❿    vCol = vec4(uColor.rgb, alpha);
    // set texture coordinates
    vTexCoord = aTexCoord;
}
```

At ❶, you calculate the current elapsed time for a particular particle, which is the difference between the current time step and the time lag for that particle. Then you calculate an alpha value for the vertex at ❷, which decreases as a function of elapsed time and has the particles fade over time. You use the clamp() method in GLSL to restrict the values to the range [0, 1].

To make the particles disappear once their lifetime is over, you put them outside your OpenGL view frustum, where they are clipped away. At ❸, you see whether a particle's lifetime is up (as set in the constructor of the particle system) or whether its alpha has dropped below a certain value, in which case the final position is set to a value outside your view.

You set particle acceleration to 9.8 m/s² at ❹, the rate of acceleration due to Earth's gravity. To make the particles spin quickly as they fly out of the fountain with their higher initial velocity, use the mod() method (similar to the Python modulus operator, %), and at ❺, restrict the angle values to the range [0, 360]. At ❻, apply this calculated angle as a rotation around the z-axis of the quad according to the formula for the transformation matrix for rotation by an angle θ around the z-axis as follows:

$$
R_{\theta, z} = \begin{pmatrix}
\cos(\theta) & \sin(\theta) & 0.0 & 0.0 \\
-\sin(\theta) & \cos(\theta) & 0.0 & 0.0 \\
0.0 & 0.0 & 1.0 & 0.0 \\
0.0 & 0.0 & 0.0 & 1.0
\end{pmatrix}
$$

At ❼, you apply two transformations to the particle's vertices: the spin rotation just computed and the rotation for the billboarding using bMatrix. Calculate the current position of the vertex at ❽ using the equation of motion discussed earlier. (The uPos in this line simply lets you position the origin of the fountain wherever you want.)

At ❾, you apply the modelview and projection matrices to the particle position. Finally, at ❿ and in the following line, set the colors and texture coordinates to pass to the fragment shader for interpolation. (Note that you set the alpha of the vertex based on the computation at ❷.)

Creating the Fragment Shader

Now let's look at the fragment shader, which sets the color of the pixels.

```
#version 330 core

uniform sampler2D uSampler;
in vec4 vCol;
in vec2 vTexCoord;
out vec4 fragColor;

void main() {
    // get the texture color
    vec4 texCol = texture2D(uSampler, vec2(vTexCoord.s, vTexCoord.t));
    // multiply texture color by set vertex color; use the vertex color alpha
    fragColor = vec4(texCol.rgb*vCol.rgb, vCol.a);
}
```

At ❶, you use the GLSL texture2D() method to look up the base texture color (the color you look up from the image used as texture) for the spark image using the texture coordinates passed in from the vertex shader. Then, you multiply this texture color value by the color of the spark fountain and set the resulting color to the output variable fragColor ❷. The fountain color is set randomly by the restart() method of ParticleSystem each time a particle system is restarted. The alpha is set based on the calculation done in the vertex shader and is used for blending during rendering.

Rendering

The code follows these steps to render the fountain particle system:

1. Enables the vertex/fragment program
2. Sets the modelview and projection matrices
3. Computes and sets the billboard matrix based on the current camera view
4. Sets uniform variables for position, time, lifetime, and color
5. Enables vertex attribute arrays for vertices, texture coordinates, time lags, and velocities
6. Enables texturing and binding to the particle spark texture
7. Disables depth buffer writing
8. Enables OpenGL blending
9. Draws the geometry

Let's take a look at code snippets that implement some of these steps.

Computing the Rotation Matrix for Billboarding

This code computes the rotation matrix for billboarding:

```
        N = camera.eye - camera.center
❶       N /= numpy.linalg.norm(N)
        U = camera.up
        U /= numpy.linalg.norm(U)
        R = numpy.cross(U, N)
        U2 = numpy.cross(N, R)
❷       bMatrix = numpy.array([R[0], U2[0], N[0], 0.0,
                               R[1], U2[1], N[1], 0.0,
                               R[2], U2[2], N[2], 0.0,
                               0.0, 0.0, 0.0, 1.0], numpy.float32)
❸       glUniformMatrix4fv(self.bMatrixU, 1, GL_TRUE, bMatrix)
```

You already looked at the theory behind formulating a rotation matrix that will keep a quad "billboarded," or aligned toward the view. (This is required so that the fountain particles always face your viewing direction.) At ❶, you use numpy.linalg.norm() to normalize the vectors. (This makes the magnitude of the vector equal to 1.) At ❷, you assemble the rotation matrix as a numpy array and then set it in the program at ❸.

The Main Rendering Code

The main rendering code uses alpha blending to give transparency to the particle system. This technique is commonly used in OpenGL to render semitransparent objects.

```
        # enable texture
❶       glActiveTexture(GL_TEXTURE0)
```

```
❷        glBindTexture(GL_TEXTURE_2D, self.texid)
❸        glUniform1i(self.samplerU, 0)

         # turn depth mask off
         if self.disableDepthMask:
❹            glDepthMask(GL_FALSE)

         # enable blending
         if self.enableBlend:
❺            glBlendFunc(GL_SRC_ALPHA, GL_ONE)
❻            glEnable(GL_BLEND)

         # bind VAO
❼        glBindVertexArray(self.vao)
         # draw
❽        glDrawArrays(GL_TRIANGLES, 0, 6*self.numP)
```

At ❶, you set the first OpenGL texture unit, (GL_TEXTURE0), active. You have only one texture unit, but because multiple texture units can be active at the same time in an OpenGL context, it's good programming practice to call each explicitly. At ❷, you activate the texture object that you created using the spark image with glutils.loadTexture() in the constructor of ParticleSystem.

Textures are accessed from within shaders using samplers, and at ❸, you set the sampler variable to use the first texture unit, GL_TEXTURE0. You then use OpenGL blending to cut out the black pixels in the texture, but these "invisible" pixels still have a depth value associated with them and can obscure parts of other particles that are behind them. To avoid this, disable writing to the depth buffer at ❹.

NOTE   *Strictly speaking, this is the wrong way to draw because if you mix these semitransparent objects with opaque objects, they will not be depth tested properly. The correct way to render such a scene is to first draw the opaque objects and then enable blending, sort the semitransparent objects in depth from back to front, and draw them last. But because you have so many moving particles, this simple approximation is acceptable, and in the end, it looks fine, which is what you care about.*

At ❺, you set up the OpenGL blending function to use the alpha in the source pixels coming from the fragment shader, and at ❻, you enable OpenGL blending. Then, bind to the created VAO at ❼, which enables all the vertex attributes you've set up, and draw the bound vertex buffer objects on the screen at ❽.

The Camera Class

Finally, the Camera class sets up the OpenGL viewing parameters:

```
# a simple camera class
class Camera:
    """helper class for viewing"""
❶    def __init__(self, eye, center, up):
```

```
            self.r = 10.0
            self.theta = 0
            self.eye = numpy.array(eye, numpy.float32)
            self.center = numpy.array(center, numpy.float32)
            self.up = numpy.array(up, numpy.float32)

       def rotate(self):
            """rotate eye by one step"""
❷          self.theta = (self.theta + 1) % 360
            # recalculate eye
❸          self.eye = self.center + numpy.array([
                   self.r*math.cos(math.radians(self.theta)),
                   self.r*math.sin(math.radians(self.theta)),
                   0.0], numpy.float32)
```

Three-dimensional perspective view is typically characterized by three parameters: an eye position, an up vector, and a direction vector. The `Camera` class groups these parameters and provides a convenient way to rotate the view for every time step.

The constructor at ❶ sets the initial values of the camera object. When the rotate() method is called, you increment the rotation angle ❷ and calculate the new eye position and direction after the rotation ❸.

NOTE *The point (r cos(θ), r sin(θ)) represents a point on a circle of radius r centered at the origin, and θ is the angle that the line from the origin to the point makes with the x-axis. The translation using* center *ensures this works even if your center of rotation is not at the origin.*

The Complete Particle System Code

This is the complete code for the particle system. You can also find it as *ps.py* at *https://github.com/electronut/pp/tree/master/particle-system/*.

```
import sys, random, math
import OpenGL
from OpenGL.GL import *
import numpy
import glutils

strVS = """
#version 330 core

in vec3 aVel;
in vec3 aVert;
in float aTime0;
in vec2 aTexCoord;

uniform mat4 uMVMatrix;
uniform mat4 uPMatrix;
uniform mat4 bMatrix;
uniform float uTime;
```

```
uniform float uLifeTime;
uniform vec4 uColor;
uniform vec3 uPos;

out vec4 vCol;
out vec2 vTexCoord;

void main() {
    // set position
    float dt = uTime - aTime0;
    float alpha = clamp(1.0 - 2.0*dt/uLifeTime, 0.0, 1.0);
    if(dt < 0.0 || dt > uLifeTime || alpha < 0.01) {
        // out of sight!
        gl_Position = vec4(0.0, 0.0, -1000.0, 1.0);
    }
    else {
        // calculate new position
        vec3 accel = vec3(0.0, 0.0, -9.8);
        // apply a twist
        float PI = 3.14159265358979323846264;
        float theta = mod(100.0*length(aVel)*dt, 360.0)*PI/180.0;
        mat4 rot =  mat4(vec4(cos(theta), sin(theta), 0.0, 0.0),
                    vec4(-sin(theta), cos(theta), 0.0, 0.0),
                    vec4(0.0, 0.0, 1.0, 0.0),
                    vec4(0.0, 0.0, 0.0, 1.0));
        // apply billboard matrix
        vec4 pos2 =  bMatrix*rot*vec4(aVert, 1.0);
        // calculate position
        vec3 newPos = pos2.xyz + uPos + aVel*dt + 0.5*accel*dt*dt;
        // apply transformations
        gl_Position = uPMatrix * uMVMatrix * vec4(newPos, 1.0);
    }
    // set color
    vCol = vec4(uColor.rgb, alpha);
    // set tex coords
    vTexCoord = aTexCoord;
}
"""


strFS = """
#version 330 core

uniform sampler2D uSampler;
in vec4 vCol;
in vec2 vTexCoord;
out vec4 fragColor;

void main() {
    // get texture color
    vec4 texCol = texture(uSampler, vec2(vTexCoord.s, vTexCoord.t));
    // multiply by set vertex color; use the vertex color alpha
    fragColor = vec4(texCol.rgb*vCol.rgb, vCol.a);
}
"""
```

```python
# a simple camera class
class Camera:
    """helper class for viewing"""
    def __init__(self, eye, center, up):
        self.r = 10.0
        self.theta = 0
        self.eye = numpy.array(eye, numpy.float32)
        self.center = numpy.array(center, numpy.float32)
        self.up = numpy.array(up, numpy.float32)

    def rotate(self):
        """rotate eye by one step"""
        self.theta = (self.theta + 1) % 360
        # recalculate eye
        self.eye = self.center + numpy.array([
                self.r*math.cos(math.radians(self.theta)),
                self.r*math.sin(math.radians(self.theta)),
                0.0], numpy.float32)

# particle system class
class ParticleSystem:

    # initialization
    def __init__(self, numP):
        # number of particles
        self.numP = numP
        # time variable
        self.t = 0.0
        self.lifeTime = 5.0
        self.startPos = numpy.array([0.0, 0.0, 0.5])
        # load texture
        self.texid = glutils.loadTexture('star.png')
        # create shader
        self.program = glutils.loadShaders(strVS, strFS)
        glUseProgram(self.program)

        # set sampler
        texLoc = glGetUniformLocation(self.program, b"uTex")
        glUniform1i(texLoc, 0)

        # uniforms
        self.timeU = glGetUniformLocation(self.program, b"uTime")
        self.lifeTimeU = glGetUniformLocation(self.program, b"uLifeTime")
        self.pMatrixUniform = glGetUniformLocation(self.program, b'uPMatrix')
        self.mvMatrixUniform = glGetUniformLocation(self.program, b"uMVMatrix")
        self.bMatrixU = glGetUniformLocation(self.program, b"bMatrix")
        self.colorU = glGetUniformLocation(self.program, b"uColor")
        self.samplerU = glGetUniformLocation(self.program, b"uSampler")
        self.posU = glGetUniformLocation(self.program, b"uPos")

        # attributes
        self.vertIndex = glGetAttribLocation(self.program, b"aVert")
        self.texIndex = glGetAttribLocation(self.program, b"aTexCoord")
        self.time0Index = glGetAttribLocation(self.program, b"aTime0")
        self.velIndex = glGetAttribLocation(self.program, b"aVel")
```

```python
        # render flags
        self.enableBillboard = True
        self.disableDepthMask = True
        self.enableBlend = True

        # which texture to use
        self.useStarTexture = True
        # restart - first time
        self.restart(numP)

# step
def step(self):
    # increment time
    self.t += 0.01

# restart particle system
def restart(self, numP):
    # set number of particles
    self.numP = numP

    # time variables
    self.t = 0.0
    self.lifeTime = 5.0

    # color
    self.col0 = numpy.array([random.random(), random.random(),
                             random.random(), 1.0])

    # create Vertex Arrays Object (VAO)
    self.vao = glGenVertexArrays(1)
    # bind VAO
    glBindVertexArray(self.vao)

    # create attribute arrays and vertex buffers:

    # vertices
    s = 0.2
    quadV = [
        -s, s, 0.0,
        -s, -s, 0.0,
        s, s, 0.0,
        s, -s, 0.0,
        s, s, 0.0,
        -s, -s, 0.0
        ]
    vertexData = numpy.array(numP*quadV, numpy.float32)
    self.vertexBuffer = glGenBuffers(1)
    glBindBuffer(GL_ARRAY_BUFFER, self.vertexBuffer)
    glBufferData(GL_ARRAY_BUFFER, 4*len(vertexData), vertexData,
                 GL_STATIC_DRAW)

    # texture coordinates
    quadT = [
        0.0, 1.0,
        0.0, 0.0,
```

```
                1.0, 1.0,
                1.0, 0.0,
                1.0, 1.0,
                0.0, 0.0
                ]
    tcData = numpy.array(numP*quadT, numpy.float32)
    self.tcBuffer = glGenBuffers(1)
    glBindBuffer(GL_ARRAY_BUFFER, self.tcBuffer)
    glBufferData(GL_ARRAY_BUFFER, 4*len(tcData), tcData, GL_STATIC_DRAW)

    # time lags
    timeData = numpy.repeat(0.005*numpy.arange(numP, dtype=numpy.float32),
                            4)
    self.timeBuffer = glGenBuffers(1)
    glBindBuffer(GL_ARRAY_BUFFER, self.timeBuffer)
    glBufferData(GL_ARRAY_BUFFER, 4*len(timeData), timeData,
                 GL_STATIC_DRAW)

    # velocites
    velocities = []
    # cone angle
    coneAngle = math.radians(20.0)
    # set up particle velocities
    for i in range(numP):
        # inclination
        angleRatio = random.random()
        a = angleRatio*coneAngle
        # azimuth
        t = random.random()*(2.0*math.pi)
        # get veocity on sphere
        vx = math.sin(a)*math.cos(t)
        vy = math.sin(a)*math.sin(t)
        vz = math.cos(a)
        # speed decreases with angle
        speed = 15.0*(1.0 - angleRatio*angleRatio)
        # add a set of calculated velocities
        velocities += 6*[speed*vx, speed*vy, speed*vz]
    # set up velocity vertex buffer
    self.velBuffer = glGenBuffers(1)
    glBindBuffer(GL_ARRAY_BUFFER, self.velBuffer)
    velData = numpy.array(velocities, numpy.float32)
    glBufferData(GL_ARRAY_BUFFER, 4*len(velData), velData, GL_STATIC_DRAW)

    # enable arrays
    glEnableVertexAttribArray(self.vertIndex)
    glEnableVertexAttribArray(self.texIndex)
    glEnableVertexAttribArray(self.time0Index)
    glEnableVertexAttribArray(self.velIndex)

    # set buffers
    glBindBuffer(GL_ARRAY_BUFFER, self.vertexBuffer)
    glVertexAttribPointer(self.vertIndex, 3, GL_FLOAT, GL_FALSE, 0, None)

    glBindBuffer(GL_ARRAY_BUFFER, self.tcBuffer)
    glVertexAttribPointer(self.texIndex, 2, GL_FLOAT, GL_FALSE, 0, None)
```

```
        glBindBuffer(GL_ARRAY_BUFFER, self.velBuffer)
        glVertexAttribPointer(self.velIndex, 3, GL_FLOAT, GL_FALSE, 0, None)

        glBindBuffer(GL_ARRAY_BUFFER, self.timeBuffer)
        glVertexAttribPointer(self.timeOIndex, 1, GL_FLOAT, GL_FALSE, 0, None)

        # unbind VAO
        glBindVertexArray(0)

    # render the particle system
    def render(self, pMatrix, mvMatrix, camera):
        # use shader
        glUseProgram(self.program)

        # set projection matrix
        glUniformMatrix4fv(self.pMatrixUniform, 1, GL_FALSE, pMatrix)
        # set modelview matrix
        glUniformMatrix4fv(self.mvMatrixUniform, 1, GL_FALSE, mvMatrix)
        # set up a billboard matrix to keep quad aligned to view direction
        if self.enableBillboard:
            N = camera.eye - camera.center
            N /= numpy.linalg.norm(N)
            U = camera.up
            U /= numpy.linalg.norm(U)
            R = numpy.cross(U, N)
            U2 = numpy.cross(N, R)
            bMatrix = numpy.array([R[0], U2[0], N[0], 0.0,
                                   R[1], U2[1], N[1], 0.0,
                                   R[2], U2[2], N[2], 0.0,
                                   0.0,  0.0,  0.0,  1.0], numpy.float32)
            glUniformMatrix4fv(self.bMatrixU, 1, GL_TRUE, bMatrix)
        else:
            # identity matrix
            bMatrix = numpy.array([1.0, 0.0, 0.0, 0.0,
                                   0.0, 1.0, 0.0, 0.0,
                                   0.0, 0.0, 1.0, 0.0,
                                   0.0, 0.0, 0.0, 1.0], numpy.float32)
            glUniformMatrix4fv(self.bMatrixU, 1, GL_FALSE, bMatrix)

        # set start position
        glUniform3fv(self.posU, 1, self.startPos)
        # set time
        glUniform1f(self.timeU, self.t)
        #set lifetime
        glUniform1f(self.lifeTimeU, self.lifeTime)
        # set color
        glUniform4fv(self.colorU, 1, self.col0)

        # enable texture
        glActiveTexture(GL_TEXTURE0)
        glBindTexture(GL_TEXTURE_2D, self.texid)
        glUniform1i(self.samplerU, 0)
```

```
# turn depth mask off
if self.disableDepthMask:
    glDepthMask(GL_FALSE)

# enable blending
if self.enableBlend:
    glBlendFunc(GL_SRC_ALPHA, GL_ONE)
    glEnable(GL_BLEND)

# bind VAO
glBindVertexArray(self.vao)
# draw
glDrawArrays(GL_TRIANGLES, 0, 6*self.numP)
# unbind VAO
glBindVertexArray(0)

# disable blend
if self.enableBlend:
    glDisable(GL_BLEND)

# turn depth mask on
if self.disableDepthMask:
    glDepthMask(GL_TRUE)

# disable texture
glBindTexture(GL_TEXTURE_2D, 0)
```

That's all the code for the spark fountain, but let's also draw a red box to represent the source of the fountain particle system.

The Box Code

To keep the viewer's attention focused on the fountain, just draw a red cube without any lighting.

```
import sys, random, math
import OpenGL
from OpenGL.GL import *
import numpy
import glutils

strVS = """
#version 330 core

in vec3 aVert;
uniform mat4 uMVMatrix;
uniform mat4 uPMatrix;
out vec4 vCol;

void main() {
    // apply transformations
    gl_Position = uPMatrix * uMVMatrix * vec4(aVert, 1.0);
```

```
    // set color
    vCol = vec4(0.8, 0.0, 0.0, 1.0);
}
"""

strFS = """
#version 330 core

in vec4 vCol;
out vec4 fragColor;

void main() {
    // use vertex color
    fragColor = vCol;
}
"""


class Box:
    def __init__(self, side):
        self.side = side

        # load shaders
        self.program = glutils.loadShaders(strVS, strFS)
        glUseProgram(self.program)

        s = side/2.0
        vertices = [
            -s, s, -s,
            -s, -s, -s,
            s, s, -s,
            s, -s, -s,
            s, s, -s,
            -s, -s, -s,

            -s, s, s,
            -s, -s, s,
            s, s, s,
            s, -s, s,
            s, s, s,
            -s, -s, s,

            -s, -s, s,
            -s, -s, -s,
            s, -s, s,
            s, -s, -s,
            s, -s, s,
            -s, -s, -s,

            -s, s, s,
            -s, s, -s,
            s, s, s,
            s, s, -s,
            s, s, s,
            -s, s, -s,
```

```
                -s, -s, s,
                -s, -s, -s,
                -s, s, s,
                -s, s, -s,
                -s, s, s,
                -s, -s, -s,

                s, -s, s,
                s, -s,-s,
                s, s, s,
                s, s, -s,
                s, s, s,
                s, -s,-s
                ]

        # set up vertex array object (VAO)
        self.vao = glGenVertexArrays(1)
        glBindVertexArray(self.vao)
        # set up VBOs
        vertexData = numpy.array(vertices, numpy.float32)
        self.vertexBuffer = glGenBuffers(1)
        glBindBuffer(GL_ARRAY_BUFFER, self.vertexBuffer)
        glBufferData(GL_ARRAY_BUFFER, 4*len(vertexData), vertexData,
                     GL_STATIC_DRAW)
        #enable arrays
        self.vertIndex = glGetAttribLocation(self.program, "aVert")
        glEnableVertexAttribArray(self.vertIndex)
        # set buffers
        glBindBuffer(GL_ARRAY_BUFFER, self.vertexBuffer)
        glVertexAttribPointer(self.vertIndex, 3, GL_FLOAT, GL_FALSE, 0, None)
        # unbind VAO
        glBindVertexArray(0)

    def render(self, pMatrix, mvMatrix):

        # use shader
        glUseProgram(self.program)

        # set projection matrix
        glUniformMatrix4fv(glGetUniformLocation(self.program, 'uPMatrix'),
                           1, GL_FALSE, pMatrix)

        # set modelview matrix
        glUniformMatrix4fv(glGetUniformLocation(self.program, 'uMVMatrix'),
                           1, GL_FALSE, mvMatrix)

        # bind VAO
        glBindVertexArray(self.vao)
        # draw
        glDrawArrays(GL_TRIANGLES, 0, 36)
        # unbind VAO
        glBindVertexArray(0)
```

The code for the box uses simple vertex and fragment shaders to draw a cube. The concepts used here are identical to what we discussed earlier in this chapter and in Chapter 9.

The Code for the Main Program

The main source file for the project, *psmain.py*, sets up the GLFW window, handles keyboard events, and creates the particle system. Skip ahead to "The Complete Main Program Code" on page 186 if you'd like to see the full program code.

```
class PSMaker:
    """GLFW Rendering window class for Particle System"""
    def __init__(self):
❶       self.camera = Camera([15.0, 0.0, 2.5],
                             [0.0, 0.0, 2.5],
                             [0.0, 0.0, 1.0])
        self.aspect = 1.0
        self.numP = 300
        self.t = 0
        # flag to rotate camera view
        self.rotate = True

        # save current working directory
        cwd = os.getcwd()

        # initialize glfw; this changes cwd
❷       glfw.glfwInit()

        # restore cwd
        os.chdir(cwd)

        # version hints
        glfw.glfwWindowHint(glfw.GLFW_CONTEXT_VERSION_MAJOR, 3)
        glfw.glfwWindowHint(glfw.GLFW_CONTEXT_VERSION_MINOR, 3)
        glfw.glfwWindowHint(glfw.GLFW_OPENGL_FORWARD_COMPAT, GL_TRUE)
        glfw.glfwWindowHint(glfw.GLFW_OPENGL_PROFILE,
                            glfw.GLFW_OPENGL_CORE_PROFILE)

        # make a window
        self.width, self.height = 640, 480
        self.aspect = self.width/float(self.height)
        self.win = glfw.glfwCreateWindow(self.width, self.height,
                                         b"Particle System")

        # make context current
        glfw.glfwMakeContextCurrent(self.win)

        # initialize GL
        glViewport(0, 0, self.width, self.height)
        glEnable(GL_DEPTH_TEST)
        glClearColor(0.2, 0.2, 0.2,1.0)
```

```
              # set window callbacks
              glfw.glfwSetMouseButtonCallback(self.win, self.onMouseButton)
              glfw.glfwSetKeyCallback(self.win, self.onKeyboard)
              glfw.glfwSetWindowSizeCallback(self.win, self.onSize)

              # create 3D
❸            self.psys = ParticleSystem(self.numP)
❹            self.box = Box(1.0)

              # exit flag
❺            self.exitNow = False
```

The class PSMaker creates the particle system, handles the GLFW window, and manages the rendering of the fountain and the box that represents its source. At ❶, you create a Camera object, which you use to set up the viewing parameters in OpenGL. The code block beginning at ❷ sets up the GLFW window; at ❸, you create the ParticleSystem object, and at ❹, you create the Box object. At ❺, an exit flag is used in the main GLFW render loop, which you'll look at next.

Updating the Particles at Each Step

You create the animation by updating a time variable in your main program loop, which in turn updates the time variable in the vertex shader. The next frame is computed and rendered using this new time value, thus updating the position of the particles. The shader computes the new orientation of the particles, also making them spin. In addition, the shader computes the alpha values as a function of this time variable, which is used in the final rendering to make the sparks fade out.

The step() method updates the particle system for each time step.

```
          def step(self):
              # increment time
❶            self.t += 10
❷            self.psys.step()
              # rotate eye
              if self.rotate:
❸                self.camera.rotate()
              # restart every 5 seconds
              if not int(self.t) % 5000:
❹                self.psys.restart(self.numP)
```

At ❶, you increment the time variable, which tracks elapsed time in milliseconds. The code at ❷ calls the step() method in ParticleSystem so it can update itself. If the flag is set, the camera is rotated at ❸. Every five seconds (5,000 milliseconds), the particle system is restarted ❹.

The Keyboard Handler

Now let's look at the keyboard handler for the GLFW window.

❶
```
def onKeyboard(self, win, key, scancode, action, mods):
    #print 'keyboard: ', win, key, scancode, action, mods
    if action == glfw.GLFW_PRESS:
        # ESC to quit
        if key == glfw.GLFW_KEY_ESCAPE:
            self.exitNow = True
        elif key == glfw.GLFW_KEY_R:
            self.rotate = not self.rotate
        elif key == glfw.GLFW_KEY_B:
            # toggle billboarding
            self.psys.enableBillboard = not self.psys.enableBillboard
        elif key == glfw.GLFW_KEY_D:
            # toggle depth mask
            self.psys.disableDepthMask = not self.psys.disableDepthMask
        elif key == glfw.GLFW_KEY_T:
            # toggle transparency
            self.psys.enableBlend = not self.psys.enableBlend
```

The keyboard handler at ❶ is mainly there to make it easy for you to see what happens when you turn off the various rendering tricks that you employed to draw the particle system. This code lets you toggle rotation, billboarding, the depth mask, and transparency.

Managing the Main Program Loop

You have to manage your own main program loop when using GLFW. Here's the loop you use in this program:

```
def run(self):
    # initializer timer
    glfw.SetTime(0)
    t = 0.0
```
❶
```
    while not glfw.glfwWindowShouldClose(self.win) and not self.exitNow:
        # update every x seconds
```
❷
```
        currT = glfw.glfwGetTime()
        if currT - t > 0.01:
            # update time
            t = currT

            # clear
            glClear(GL_COLOR_BUFFER_BIT | GL_DEPTH_BUFFER_BIT)

            # render
            pMatrix = glutils.perspective(100.0, self.aspect, 0.1, 100.0)
            # modelview matrix
            mvMatrix = glutils.lookAt(self.camera.eye, self.camera.center,
                                      self.camera.up)
```

```
                    # draw nontransparent object first
❸                   self.box.render(pMatrix, mvMatrix)

                    # render
❹                   self.psys.render(pMatrix, mvMatrix, self.camera)

                    # step
❺                   self.step()

                    glfw.glfwSwapBuffers(self.win)
                    # poll for and process events
                    glfw.glfwPollEvents()
            # end
            glfw.glfwTerminate()
```

This code is almost identical to the loop you used in Chapter 9. At ❶, the while loop exits if either the exit flag is set or the GLFW window closes. At ❷ and in the following line, you use the GLFW timer to render only when a certain amount of time (0.1 seconds) has elapsed, thus controlling the frame rate of the rendering. You draw the box at ❸ and the particle system at ❹. (The order of rendering is important: transparent objects are always drawn last so they can be blended and depth buffered correctly with respect to the opaque objects in a scene.) At ❺, you update the particle system for the current time step.

The Complete Main Program Code

Here is the complete code for *psmain.py*. You can also find this code at *https://github.com/electronut/pp/tree/master/particle-system/*.

```
import sys, os, math, numpy
import OpenGL
from OpenGL.GL import *
import numpy
from ps import ParticleSystem, Camera
from box import Box
import glutils
import glfw

class PSMaker:
    """GLFW Rendering window class for Particle System"""
    def __init__(self):
        self.camera = Camera([15.0, 0.0, 2.5],
                             [0.0, 0.0, 2.5],
                             [0.0, 0.0, 1.0])
        self.aspect = 1.0
        self.numP = 300
        self.t = 0
        # flag to rotate camera view
        self.rotate = True
```

```python
        # save current working directory
        cwd = os.getcwd()

        # initialize glfw; this changes cwd
        glfw.glfwInit()

        # restore cwd
        os.chdir(cwd)

        # version hints
        glfw.glfwWindowHint(glfw.GLFW_CONTEXT_VERSION_MAJOR, 3)
        glfw.glfwWindowHint(glfw.GLFW_CONTEXT_VERSION_MINOR, 3)
        glfw.glfwWindowHint(glfw.GLFW_OPENGL_FORWARD_COMPAT, GL_TRUE)
        glfw.glfwWindowHint(glfw.GLFW_OPENGL_PROFILE,
                            glfw.GLFW_OPENGL_CORE_PROFILE)

        # make a window
        self.width, self.height = 640, 480
        self.aspect = self.width/float(self.height)
        self.win = glfw.glfwCreateWindow(self.width, self.height,
                                         b"Particle System")
        # make context current
        glfw.glfwMakeContextCurrent(self.win)

        # initialize GL
        glViewport(0, 0, self.width, self.height)
        glEnable(GL_DEPTH_TEST)
        glClearColor(0.2, 0.2, 0.2,1.0)

        # set window callbacks
        glfw.glfwSetMouseButtonCallback(self.win, self.onMouseButton)
        glfw.glfwSetKeyCallback(self.win, self.onKeyboard)
        glfw.glfwSetWindowSizeCallback(self.win, self.onSize)

        # create 3D
        self.psys = ParticleSystem(self.numP)
        self.box = Box(1.0)

        # exit flag
        self.exitNow = False


    def onMouseButton(self, win, button, action, mods):
        #print 'mouse button: ', win, button, action, mods
        pass

    def onKeyboard(self, win, key, scancode, action, mods):
        #print 'keyboard: ', win, key, scancode, action, mods
        if action == glfw.GLFW_PRESS:
            # ESC to quit
            if key == glfw.GLFW_KEY_ESCAPE:
                self.exitNow = True
            elif key == glfw.GLFW_KEY_R:
                self.rotate = not self.rotate
```

```
            elif key == glfw.GLFW_KEY_B:
                # toggle billboarding
                self.psys.enableBillboard = not self.psys.enableBillboard
            elif key == glfw.GLFW_KEY_D:
                # toggle depth mask
                self.psys.disableDepthMask = not self.psys.disableDepthMask
            elif key == glfw.GLFW_KEY_T:
                # toggle transparency
                self.psys.enableBlend = not self.psys.enableBlend

    def onSize(self, win, width, height):
        #print 'onsize: ', win, width, height
        self.width = width
        self.height = height
        self.aspect = width/float(height)
        glViewport(0, 0, self.width, self.height)

    def step(self):
        # increment time
        self.t += 10
        self.psys.step()
        # rotate eye
        if self.rotate:
            self.camera.rotate()
        # restart every 5 seconds
        if not int(self.t) % 5000:
            self.psys.restart(self.numP)

    def run(self):
        # initializer timer
        glfw.glfwSetTime(0)
        t = 0.0
        while not glfw.glfwWindowShouldClose(self.win) and not self.exitNow:
            # update every x seconds
            currT = glfw.glfwGetTime()
            if currT - t > 0.01:
                # update time
                t = currT

                # clear
                glClear(GL_COLOR_BUFFER_BIT | GL_DEPTH_BUFFER_BIT)

                # render
                pMatrix = glutils.perspective(100.0, self.aspect, 0.1, 100.0)
                # modelview matrix
                mvMatrix = glutils.lookAt(self.camera.eye, self.camera.center,
                                          self.camera.up)

                # draw nontransparent object first
                self.box.render(pMatrix, mvMatrix)

                # render
                self.psys.render(pMatrix, mvMatrix, self.camera)
```

```
            # step
            self.step()

            glfw.glfwSwapBuffers(self.win)
            # poll for and process events
            glfw.glfwPollEvents()
        # end
        glfw.glfwTerminate()

# main() function
def main():
    # use sys.argv if needed
    print('starting particle system...')
    prog = PSMaker()
    prog.run()

# call main
if __name__ == '__main__':
    main()
```

Running the Program

To run the project, enter the following:

```
$ python3 psmain.py
```

Figure 10-1 at the beginning of this chapter shows the output.

Summary

In this chapter, you created a fountain particle system using Python and OpenGL. You learned to create a mathematical model for the particle system, set up shader programs, and use some OpenGL tricks to render the particles in a realistic-looking way.

Experiments!

Here are some ideas for more ways to experiment with particle system animation:

1. See what happens if you don't have a time lag between the ejection of each particle.
2. Make the particles in the fountain grow in size as they shoot up. (Hint: scale the quad vertices in the vertex shader.)
3. As written, this code has each particle follow a perfect parabolic arc as it's ejected from the fountain. Add some randomness to the path of the particles. (Hint: research the noise() method in GLSL, which you can use in the vertex shader.)

4. The particles in the fountain take a parabolic path, rising and then falling because of gravitational effects. Can you make them bounce off the floor when they fall? You may need to increase the lifetime of the particles to accomplish this. (Hint: the floor is at $z = 0.0$. In the vertex shader, reverse the z-component of the velocities as the points come close to the floor.)

11

VOLUME RENDERING

MRI and CT scans are diagnostic processes that create *volumetric* data that consists of a set of 2D images showing cross sections through a 3D volume. *Volume rendering* is a computer graphics technique used to construct 3D images from this type of volumetric data. Although volume rendering is commonly used to analyze medical scans, it can also be used to create 3D scientific visualizations in academic disciplines such as geology, archeology, and molecular biology.

The data captured by MRI and CT scans typically follows the form of a 3D grid of $N_x \times N_y \times N_z$, or N_z 2D "slices," where each slice is an image of size $N_x \times N_y$. Volume-rendering algorithms are used to display the collected slice data with some type of transparency, and various techniques are used to accentuate the parts of the rendered volume that are of interest.

In this project, you'll look at a volume-rendering algorithm called *volume ray casting*, which takes full advantage of the graphics-processing unit (GPU) to perform computations using OpenGL Shading Language

(GLSL) shaders. Your code executes for every pixel onscreen and leverages the GPU, which is designed to do parallel computations efficiently. You'll use a folder of 2D images consisting of slices from a 3D data set to construct a volume-rendered image using the volume ray casting algorithm. You'll also implement a method to show 2D slices of the data in the *x*, *y*, and *z* directions so users can scroll through the slices using the arrow keys. Keyboard commands will let the user toggle between the 3D rendering and the 2D slices.

Here are some of the topics covered in this project:

- Using GLSL for GPU computations
- Creating vertex and fragment shaders
- Representing 3D volumetric data and using the volume ray casting algorithm
- Using numpy arrays for 3D transformation matrices

How It Works

There are various ways to render a 3D data set. In this project, you'll use the volume ray casting method, which is an *image-based* rendering technique used to generate the final image from the 2D slice, pixel by pixel. In contrast, typical 3D rendering methods are *object based*: they begin with a 3D object representation and then apply transformations to generate the pixels in the projected 2D image.

In the volume ray casting method that you'll use in this project, for each pixel in the output image, a ray is shot into the discrete 3D volumetric data set, which is typically represented as a cuboid. As the ray passes through the volume, the data is sampled at regular intervals, and the samples are combined, or *composited*, to compute the color value or intensity of the final image. (You might think of this process as similar to stacking a bunch of transparencies on top of each other and holding them up against a bright light to see a blend of all the sheets.)

While volume ray casting rendering implementations typically use techniques such as applying gradients to improve the appearance of the final render, filtering to isolate 3D features, and using spatial optimization techniques to improve speed, you'll just implement the basic ray casting algorithm and composite the final image by x-ray casting. (My implementation is largely based on the seminal paper on this topic by Kruger and Westermann, published in 2003.[1])

---

1. J. Kruger and R. Westermann, "Acceleration Techniques for GPU-based Volume Rendering," IEEE Visualization, 2003.

Data Format

For this project, you'll use medical data from 3D scans from the Stanford Volume Data Archive.[2] This archive offers a few excellent 3D medical data sets (both CT and MRI) of TIFF images, one for each 2D cross section of the volume. You'll read a folder of these images into an OpenGL 3D texture; this is sort of like stacking a set of 2D images to form a cuboid, as shown in Figure 11-1.

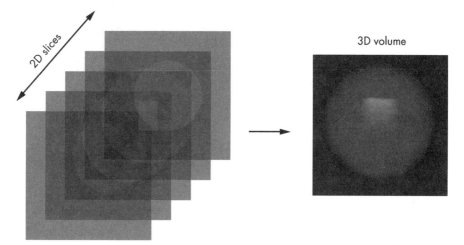

Figure 11-1: Building 3D volumetric data from 2D slices

Recall from Chapter 9 that a 2D texture in OpenGL is addressed with a 2D coordinate (s, t). Similarly, a 3D texture is addressed using a 3D texture coordinate of the form (s, t, p). As you will see, storing the volumetric data as a 3D texture allows you to access the data quickly and provides you with interpolated values required by your ray casting scheme.

Generating Rays

Your goal in this project is to generate a perspective projection of the 3D volumetric data, as shown in Figure 11-2.

Figure 11-2 shows the OpenGL view frustum as discussed in Chapter 9. Specifically, it shows how a ray from the eye enters this frustum at the near plane, passes through the cubic volume (which contains the volumetric data), and exits from the rear at the far plane.

---

2. *http://graphics.stanford.edu/data/voldata/*

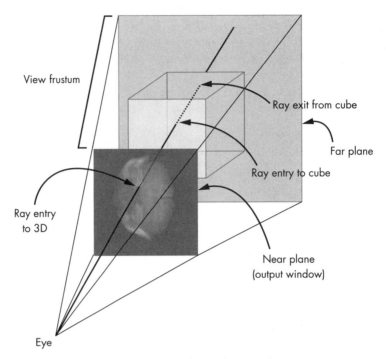

Figure 11-2: Perspective projection of 3D volumetric data

To implement ray casting, you need to generate rays that go into the volume. For each pixel in the output window shown in Figure 11-2, you generate a vector *R* that goes into the volume you consider a unit cube (which I'll refer to as the *color cube*) defined between the coordinates (0, 0, 0) and (1, 1, 1). You color each point inside this cube with the RGB values equal to the 3D coordinates of the cube. The origin is colored (0, 0, 0), or black; the (1, 0, 0) corner is red; and the point on the cube diagonally opposite the origin is colored (1, 1, 1), or white. Figure 11-3 shows this cube.

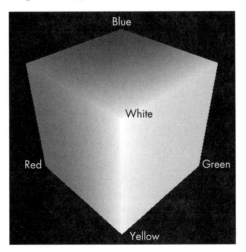

Figure 11-3: A color cube

In OpenGL, a color can be represented as a strip of 8-bit unsigned values (r, g, b), where r, g, *and* b *are in the range [0, 255]. It can also be represented as a 32-bit floating-point value (r, g, b), where* r, g, *and* b *are in the range [0.0, 1.0]. These representations are equivalent. For example, the red color (255, 0, 0) in the former is the same as (1.0, 0.0, 0.0) in the latter.*

To draw the cube, first draw its six faces using the OpenGL primitive GL_TRIANGLES. Then color each vertex and use the interpolation provided by OpenGL when it rasterizes polygons to take care of the colors between each vertex. For example, Figure 11-4(a) shows the three front-faces of the cube. The back-faces of the cube are drawn in Figure 11-4(b) by setting OpenGL to cull front-faces.

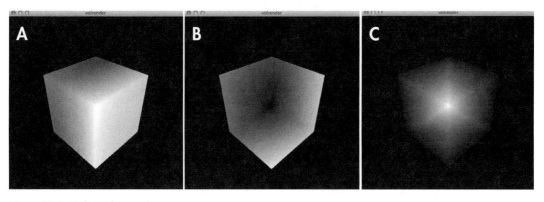

Figure 11-4: Color cube used to compute rays

If you subtract the colors in Figure 11-4(a) from Figure 11-4(b) by subtracting $(r, g, b)_{front}$ from $(r, g, b)_{back}$, you actually compute a sect of vectors that go from the front to the back of the cube because each color (r, g, b) on this cube is the same as the 3D coordinate. Figure 11-4(c) shows the result. (Negative values have been flipped to positive for the purposes of this illustration because negative numbers cannot be displayed as colors directly.) Reading the color value (r, g, b) of a pixel, as shown in Figure 11-4(c), gives the (rx, ry, rz) coordinates for the ray passing into the volume at that point.

Once you have the casting rays, you render them into an image or 2D texture for later use with OpenGL's frame buffer object (FBO) feature. After this texture is generated, you can access it inside the shaders that you'll use to implement the ray casting algorithm.

Ray Casting in the GPU

To implement the ray casting algorithm, you first draw the back-faces of the color cube into an FBO. Next, the front-faces are drawn on the screen. The bulk of the ray casting algorithm happens in the fragment shader for this second rendering, which runs for each pixel in the output. The ray is computed by subtracting the front-face color of the incoming fragment from the back-face color of the color cube, which is read in from a texture. The computed ray is then used to accumulate and compute the final pixel value using the 3D volumetric texture data, available within the shader.

Showing 2D Slices

In addition to the 3D rendering, you show 2D slices of the data by extracting the 2D cross section from the 3D data perpendicular to the x-, y-, or z-axis and applying that as a texture on a quad. Because you store the volume as a 3D texture, you can easily get the required data by specifying the texture coordinates (*s*, *t*, *p*). OpenGL's built-in texture interpolation gives you the texture values anywhere inside the 3D texture.

Displaying the OpenGL Window

As in your other OpenGL projects, this project uses the GLFW library to display the OpenGL window. You'll use handlers for drawing, for resizing the window, and for keyboard events. You'll use keyboard events to toggle between volume and slice rendering, as well as for rotating and slicing through the 3D data.

Requirements

We'll use PyOpenGL, a popular Python binding for OpenGL, for rendering. We'll also use numpy arrays to represent 3D coordinates and transformation matrices.

An Overview of the Project Code

You'll begin by generating a 3D texture from the volumetric data read in from the file. Next you'll look at a color cube technique for generating rays from the eye that point into the volume, which is a key concept in implementing the volume ray casting algorithm. You'll look at how to define the cube geometry as well as how to draw the back- and front-faces of this cube. You'll then explore the volume ray casting algorithm and the associated vertex and fragment shaders. Finally, you'll learn how to implement 2D slicing of the volumetric data.

This project has seven Python files:

glutils.py   Contains the utility methods for OpenGL shaders, transformations, and so on

makedata.py   Contains utility methods for creating volumetric data for testing

raycast.py   Implements the `RayCastRender` class for ray casting

raycube.py   Implements the `RayCube` class for use in `RayCastRender`

slicerender.py   Implements the `SliceRender` class for 2D slicing of volumetric data

volreader.py   Contains the utility method to read volumetric data into the OpenGL 3D texture

volrender.py   Contains the main methods that create the GLFW window and the renderers

We'll cover all but two of these files in this chapter. The *makedata.py* file lives with the other project files for this chapter at *https://github.com/ electronut/pp/tree/master/volrender/*. The *glutils.py* file can be downloaded from *https://github.com/electronut/pp/tree/master/common/*.

Generating a 3D Texture

The first step is to read the volumetric data from a folder containing images, as shown in the following code. To see the complete *volreader.py* code, skip ahead to "The Complete 3D Texture Code" on page 199.

```python
def loadVolume(dirName):
    """read volume from directory as a 3D texture"""
    # list images in directory
❶   files = sorted(os.listdir(dirName))
    print('loading images from: %s' % dirName)
    imgDataList = []
    count = 0
    width, height = 0, 0
    for file in files:
❷       file_path = os.path.abspath(os.path.join(dirName, file))
        try:
            # read image
❸           img = Image.open(file_path)
            imgData = np.array(img.getdata(), np.uint8)

            # check if all images are of the same size
❹           if count is 0:
                width, height = img.size[0], img.size[1]
```

```
                imgDataList.append(imgData)
            else:
❺              if (width, height) == (img.size[0], img.size[1]):
                    imgDataList.append(imgData)
            else:
                print('mismatch')
                raise RunTimeError("image size mismatch")
            count += 1
            #print img.size
        except:
            # skip
            print('Invalid image: %s' % file_path)

    # load image data into single array
    depth = count
❻  data = np.concatenate(imgDataList)
    print('volume data dims: %d %d %d' % (width, height, depth))

    # load data into 3D texture
❼  texture = glGenTextures(1)
    glPixelStorei(GL_UNPACK_ALIGNMENT, 1)
    glBindTexture(GL_TEXTURE_3D, texture)
    glTexParameterf(GL_TEXTURE_3D, GL_TEXTURE_WRAP_S, GL_CLAMP_TO_EDGE)
    glTexParameterf(GL_TEXTURE_3D, GL_TEXTURE_WRAP_T, GL_CLAMP_TO_EDGE)
    glTexParameterf(GL_TEXTURE_3D, GL_TEXTURE_WRAP_R, GL_CLAMP_TO_EDGE)
    glTexParameterf(GL_TEXTURE_3D, GL_TEXTURE_MAG_FILTER, GL_LINEAR)
    glTexParameterf(GL_TEXTURE_3D, GL_TEXTURE_MIN_FILTER, GL_LINEAR)
❽  glTexImage3D(GL_TEXTURE_3D, 0, GL_RED,
                width, height, depth, 0,
                GL_RED, GL_UNSIGNED_BYTE, data)
    # return texture
❾  return (texture, width, height, depth)
```

The loadVolume() method first lists the files in the given directory using the listdir() method from the os module ❶; then you load the image files themselves. At ❷, the filename is appended to the directory using os.path.abspath() and os.path.join(), eliminating the need to deal with relative file paths and operating system (OS)–specific path conventions. (You often see this useful idiom in Python code that traverses files and directories.)

At ❸, you use the Image class from Python Imaging Library (PIL) to load the image into an 8-bit numpy array. If the file specified is not an image or if the image fails to load, an exception is thrown, and you catch it to print an error.

Because you are loading these image slices into a 3D texture, you need to ensure they all have the same dimensions (width × height), which you confirm at ❹ and ❺. You store the image dimensions for the first image and compare them against new incoming images. Once all the images are loaded into individual arrays, create the final array containing the 3D data by joining these arrays using the concatenate() method from numpy ❻.

At ❼ and in the lines that follow, you create an OpenGL texture and set parameters for filtering and unpacking. Then, at ❽, load the 3D data array into the OpenGL texture. The format used here is GL_RED, and the data format is GL_UNSIGNED_BYTE because you have only one 8-bit value associated with each pixel in the data.

Finally, at ❾, you return the OpenGL texture ID and the dimensions of the 3D texture.

The Complete 3D Texture Code

Here is the full code listing. You can also find the *volreader.py* file at *https:// github.com/electronut/pp/tree/master/volrender/*.

```python
import os
import numpy as np
from PIL import Image

import OpenGL
from OpenGL.GL import *

from scipy import misc

def loadVolume(dirName):
    """read volume from directory as a 3D texture"""
    # list images in directory
    files = sorted(os.listdir(dirName))
    print('loading images from: %s' % dirName)
    imgDataList = []
    count = 0
    width, height = 0, 0
    for file in files:
        file_path = os.path.abspath(os.path.join(dirName, file))
        try:
            # read image
            img = Image.open(file_path)
            imgData = np.array(img.getdata(), np.uint8)

            # check if all are of the same size
            if count is 0:
                width, height = img.size[0], img.size[1]
                imgDataList.append(imgData)
            else:
                if (width, height) == (img.size[0], img.size[1]):
                    imgDataList.append(imgData)
                else:
                    print('mismatch')
                    raise RunTimeError("image size mismatch")
            count += 1
            #print img.size
        except:
            # skip
            print('Invalid image: %s' % file_path)

    # load image data into single array
    depth = count
```

```
    data = np.concatenate(imgDataList)
    print('volume data dims: %d %d %d' % (width, height, depth))

    # load data into 3D texture
    texture = glGenTextures(1)
    glPixelStorei(GL_UNPACK_ALIGNMENT, 1)
    glBindTexture(GL_TEXTURE_3D, texture)
    glTexParameterf(GL_TEXTURE_3D, GL_TEXTURE_WRAP_S, GL_CLAMP_TO_EDGE)
    glTexParameterf(GL_TEXTURE_3D, GL_TEXTURE_WRAP_T, GL_CLAMP_TO_EDGE)
    glTexParameterf(GL_TEXTURE_3D, GL_TEXTURE_WRAP_R, GL_CLAMP_TO_EDGE)
    glTexParameterf(GL_TEXTURE_3D, GL_TEXTURE_MAG_FILTER, GL_LINEAR)
    glTexParameterf(GL_TEXTURE_3D, GL_TEXTURE_MIN_FILTER, GL_LINEAR)
    glTexImage3D(GL_TEXTURE_3D, 0, GL_RED,
                 width, height, depth, 0,
                 GL_RED, GL_UNSIGNED_BYTE, data)
    #return texture
    return (texture, width, height, depth)


# load texture
def loadTexture(filename):
    img = Image.open(filename)
    img_data = np.array(list(img.getdata()), 'B')
    texture = glGenTextures(1)
    glPixelStorei(GL_UNPACK_ALIGNMENT,1)
    glBindTexture(GL_TEXTURE_2D, texture)
    glTexParameterf(GL_TEXTURE_2D, GL_TEXTURE_WRAP_S, GL_CLAMP_TO_EDGE)
    glTexParameterf(GL_TEXTURE_2D, GL_TEXTURE_WRAP_T, GL_CLAMP_TO_EDGE)
    glTexParameterf(GL_TEXTURE_2D, GL_TEXTURE_MAG_FILTER, GL_LINEAR)
    glTexParameterf(GL_TEXTURE_2D, GL_TEXTURE_MIN_FILTER, GL_LINEAR)
    glTexImage2D(GL_TEXTURE_2D, 0, GL_RGBA, img.size[0], img.size[1],
                 0, GL_RGBA, GL_UNSIGNED_BYTE, img_data)
    return texture
```

Generating Rays

The code for generating the rays is encapsulated in a class called RayCube.
This class is responsible for drawing the color cube and has methods to draw
the back-faces of the cube to an FBO or texture and to draw the front-faces
of the cube to the screen. To see the complete *raycube.py* code, skip ahead to
"The Complete Ray Generation Code" on page 206.

First, let's define the shaders used by this class:

❶ strVS = """
```
#version 330 core

layout(location = 1) in vec3 cubePos;
layout(location = 2) in vec3 cubeCol;

uniform mat4 uMVMatrix;
uniform mat4 uPMatrix;
out vec4 vColor;
```

```
void main()
{
    // set back-face color
    vColor = vec4(cubeCol.rgb, 1.0);

    // transformed position
    vec4 newPos = vec4(cubePos.xyz, 1.0);

    // set position
    gl_Position = uPMatrix * uMVMatrix * newPos;

}
"""
```
❷ strFS = """
```
#version 330 core

in vec4 vColor;
out vec4 fragColor;

void main()
{
    fragColor = vColor;
}
"""
```

At ❶, you define the vertex shader used by the RayCube class. This shader has two input attributes, cubePos and cubeCol, which are used to access the position and color values of the vertices, respectively. The modelview and projection matrices are passed in with the uniform variables uMVMatrix and pMatrix, respectively. The vColor variable is declared as output because it needs to be passed on to the fragment shader, where it will be interpolated. The fragment shader implemented at ❷ sets the fragment color to the (interpolated) value of the incoming vColor set in the vertex shader.

Defining the Color Cube Geometry

Now let's look at the geometry of the color cube, defined in the RayCube class:

```
    # cube vertices
❶  vertices = numpy.array([
        0.0, 0.0, 0.0,
        1.0, 0.0, 0.0,
        1.0, 1.0, 0.0,
        0.0, 1.0, 0.0,
        0.0, 0.0, 1.0,
        1.0, 0.0, 1.0,
        1.0, 1.0, 1.0,
        0.0, 1.0, 1.0
        ], numpy.float32)
```

```
# cube colors
❷      colors = numpy.array([
            0.0, 0.0, 0.0,
            1.0, 0.0, 0.0,
            1.0, 1.0, 0.0,
            0.0, 1.0, 0.0,
            0.0, 0.0, 1.0,
            1.0, 0.0, 1.0,
            1.0, 1.0, 1.0,
            0.0, 1.0, 1.0
            ], numpy.float32)

       # individual triangles
❸      indices = numpy.array([
            4, 5, 7,
            7, 5, 6,
            5, 1, 6,
            6, 1, 2,
            1, 0, 2,
            2, 0, 3,
            0, 4, 3,
            3, 4, 7,
            6, 2, 7,
            7, 2, 3,
            4, 0, 5,
            5, 0, 1
            ], numpy.int16)
```

The shaders are compiled, and the program object is created in the RayCube constructor. The cube geometry is defined at ❶, and the colors are defined at ❷.

The color cube has six faces, each of which can each be drawn as two triangles for a total of 6×6, or 36, vertices. But rather than specify all 36 vertices, you specify the cube's eight vertices and then define the triangles using an indices array, as shown at ❸ and illustrated in Figure 11-5.

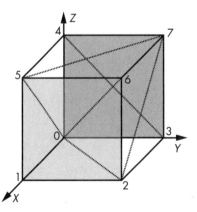

Figure 11-5: Using indexing, a cube can be represented as a collection of triangles, with each face composed of two triangles.

Next, you need to put the vertex information into buffers.

```
# set up vertex array object (VAO)
self.vao = glGenVertexArrays(1)
glBindVertexArray(self.vao)

# vertex buffer
self.vertexBuffer = glGenBuffers(1)
glBindBuffer(GL_ARRAY_BUFFER, self.vertexBuffer)
glBufferData(GL_ARRAY_BUFFER, 4*len(vertices), vertices, GL_STATIC_DRAW)

# vertex buffer - cube vertex colors
self.colorBuffer = glGenBuffers(1)
glBindBuffer(GL_ARRAY_BUFFER, self.colorBuffer)
glBufferData(GL_ARRAY_BUFFER, 4*len(colors), colors, GL_STATIC_DRAW)

# index buffer
self.indexBuffer = glGenBuffers(1)
glBindBuffer(GL_ELEMENT_ARRAY_BUFFER, self.indexBuffer);
glBufferData(GL_ELEMENT_ARRAY_BUFFER, 2*len(indices), indices,
            GL_STATIC_DRAW)
```

As with previous projects, you create and bind to a Vertex Array Object (VAO) and then define the buffers it manages. One difference here is that at ❶, the indices array is given the designation GL_ELEMENT_ARRAY_BUFFER, which means the elements in its buffer will be used to index and access the data in the color and vertex buffers.

Creating the Frame Buffer Object

Now let's jump to the method that creates the frame buffer object, where you'll direct your rendering.

```
def initFBO(self):
    # create frame buffer object
    self.fboHandle = glGenFramebuffers(1)
    # create texture
    self.texHandle = glGenTextures(1)
    # create depth buffer
    self.depthHandle = glGenRenderbuffers(1)

    # bind
    glBindFramebuffer(GL_FRAMEBUFFER, self.fboHandle)

    glActiveTexture(GL_TEXTURE0)
    glBindTexture(GL_TEXTURE_2D, self.texHandle)

    # set parameters to draw the image at different sizes
    glTexParameteri(GL_TEXTURE_2D, GL_TEXTURE_MIN_FILTER, GL_LINEAR)
    glTexParameteri(GL_TEXTURE_2D, GL_TEXTURE_MAG_FILTER, GL_LINEAR)
    glTexParameteri(GL_TEXTURE_2D, GL_TEXTURE_WRAP_S, GL_CLAMP_TO_EDGE)
    glTexParameteri(GL_TEXTURE_2D, GL_TEXTURE_WRAP_T, GL_CLAMP_TO_EDGE)
```

```
        # set up texture
        glTexImage2D(GL_TEXTURE_2D, 0, GL_RGBA, self.width, self.height,
                     0, GL_RGBA, GL_UNSIGNED_BYTE, None)

        # bind texture to FBO
❷      glFramebufferTexture2D(GL_FRAMEBUFFER, GL_COLOR_ATTACHMENT0,
                              GL_TEXTURE_2D, self.texHandle, 0)

        # bind
❸      glBindRenderbuffer(GL_RENDERBUFFER, self.depthHandle)
        glRenderbufferStorage(GL_RENDERBUFFER, GL_DEPTH_COMPONENT24,
                              self.width, self.height)

        # bind depth buffer to FBO
        glFramebufferRenderbuffer(GL_FRAMEBUFFER, GL_DEPTH_ATTACHMENT,
                                  GL_RENDERBUFFER, self.depthHandle)

        # check status
❹      status = glCheckFramebufferStatus(GL_FRAMEBUFFER)
        if status == GL_FRAMEBUFFER_COMPLETE:
            pass
            #print "fbo %d complete" % self.fboHandle
        elif status == GL_FRAMEBUFFER_UNSUPPORTED:
            print "fbo %d unsupported" % self.fboHandle
        else:
            print "fbo %d Error" % self.fboHandle
```

Here you create a frame buffer object, a 2D texture, and a render buffer object; then, at ❶, you set up the texture parameters. The texture is bound to the frame buffer at ❷; at ❸ and in the lines that follow, the render buffer sets up a 24-bit depth buffer and is attached to the frame buffer. At ❹, you check the status of the frame buffers and print a status message if something goes wrong. Now, as long as the frame buffer and render buffer are bound correctly, all of your rendering will go into the texture.

Rendering the Back-Faces of the Cube

Here is the code for rendering the back-faces of the color cube:

```
    def renderBackFace(self, pMatrix, mvMatrix):
        """renders back-face of ray-cube to a texture and returns it"""
        # render to FBO
❶      glBindFramebuffer(GL_FRAMEBUFFER, self.fboHandle)
        # set active texture
        glActiveTexture(GL_TEXTURE0)
        # bind to FBO texture
        glBindTexture(GL_TEXTURE_2D, self.texHandle)

        # render cube with face culling enabled
❷      self.renderCube(pMatrix, mvMatrix, self.program, True)

        # unbind texture
❸      glBindTexture(GL_TEXTURE_2D, 0)
```

```
glBindFramebuffer(GL_FRAMEBUFFER, 0)
glBindRenderbuffer(GL_RENDERBUFFER, 0)

# return texture ID
return self.texHandle
```
❹

At ❶, bind the FBO, set the active texture unit, and bind to the texture handle so that you can render to the FBO. At ❷, you call the renderCube() method in RayCube, with a face-culling flag as an argument to allow you to draw either the front-face or the back-face of the cube using the same code. Set the flag to True to make the back-faces appear in the FBO texture.

At ❸, you make the necessary calls to unbind from the FBO so that other rendering code is unaffected. The FBO texture ID is returned at ❹ for use in the next stage of your algorithm.

Rendering the Front-Faces of the Cube

The following code is used to draw the front-faces of the color cube during the second rendering pass of the ray casting algorithm. It simply calls the renderCube() method discussed in the previous section, with the face-culling flag set to False.

```
def renderFrontFace(self, pMatrix, mvMatrix, program):
    """render front-face of ray-cube"""
    # no face culling
    self.renderCube(pMatrix, mvMatrix, program, False)
```

Rendering the Whole Cube

Now let's look at the renderCube() method, which draws the color cube discussed previously:

```
def renderCube(self, pMatrix, mvMatrix, program, cullFace):
    """renderCube uses face culling if flag set"""

    glClear(GL_COLOR_BUFFER_BIT | GL_DEPTH_BUFFER_BIT)

    # set shader program
    glUseProgram(program)

    # set projection matrix
    glUniformMatrix4fv(glGetUniformLocation(program, b'uPMatrix'),
                       1, GL_FALSE, pMatrix)

    # set modelview matrix
    glUniformMatrix4fv(glGetUniformLocation(program, b'uMVMatrix'),
                       1, GL_FALSE, mvMatrix)

    # enable face culling
    glDisable(GL_CULL_FACE)
```

```
❶          if cullFace:
                glFrontFace(GL_CCW)
                glCullFace(GL_FRONT)
                glEnable(GL_CULL_FACE)

            # bind VAO
            glBindVertexArray(self.vao)

            # animated slice
❷           glDrawElements(GL_TRIANGLES, self.nIndices, GL_UNSIGNED_SHORT, None)

            # unbind VAO
            glBindVertexArray(0)

            # reset cull face
            if cullFace:
                # disable face culling
                glDisable(GL_CULL_FACE)
```

As you can see in this listing, you clear the color and depth buffers and then select the shader program and set the transformation matrices. At ❶, you set a flag to control face culling, which determines whether the cube's front-face or back-face is drawn. Also, you use glDrawElements() ❷ because you're using an index array to render the cube, rather than a vertex array.

The Resize Handler

Because the FBO is created for a particular window size, you need to re-create it when the window size changes. To do that, you create a resize handler for the RayCube class, as shown here:

```
❶      def reshape(self, width, height):
            self.width = width
            self.height = height
            self.aspect = width/float(height)
            # re-create FBO
            self.clearFBO()
            self.initFBO()
```

The reshape() function ❶ is called when the OpenGL window is resized.

The Complete Ray Generation Code

Here is the full code listing. You can also find the *raycube.py* file at *https://github.com/electronut/pp/tree/master/volrender/*.

```
import OpenGL
from OpenGL.GL import *
from OpenGL.GL.shaders import *

import numpy, math, sys
import volreader, glutils
```

```
strVS = """
#version 330 core

layout(location = 1) in vec3 cubePos;
layout(location = 2) in vec3 cubeCol;

uniform mat4 uMVMatrix;
uniform mat4 uPMatrix;
out vec4 vColor;

void main()
{
    // set back face color
    vColor = vec4(cubeCol.rgb, 1.0);

    // transformed position
    vec4 newPos = vec4(cubePos.xyz, 1.0);

    // set position
    gl_Position = uPMatrix * uMVMatrix * newPos;

}
"""
strFS = """
#version 330 core

in vec4 vColor;
out vec4 fragColor;

void main()
{
    fragColor = vColor;
}
"""

class RayCube:
    """class used to generate rays used in ray casting"""

    def __init__(self, width, height):
        """RayCube constructor"""

        # set dims
        self.width, self.height = width, height

        # create shader
        self.program = glutils.loadShaders(strVS, strFS)

        # cube vertices
        vertices = numpy.array([
                0.0, 0.0, 0.0,
                1.0, 0.0, 0.0,
                1.0, 1.0, 0.0,
                0.0, 1.0, 0.0,
                0.0, 0.0, 1.0,
```

```
            1.0, 0.0, 1.0,
            1.0, 1.0, 1.0,
            0.0, 1.0, 1.0
            ], numpy.float32)

# cube colors
colors = numpy.array([
        0.0, 0.0, 0.0,
        1.0, 0.0, 0.0,
        1.0, 1.0, 0.0,
        0.0, 1.0, 0.0,
        0.0, 0.0, 1.0,
        1.0, 0.0, 1.0,
        1.0, 1.0, 1.0,
        0.0, 1.0, 1.0
        ], numpy.float32)

# individual triangles
indices = numpy.array([
        4, 5, 7,
        7, 5, 6,
        5, 1, 6,
        6, 1, 2,
        1, 0, 2,
        2, 0, 3,
        0, 4, 3,
        3, 4, 7,
        6, 2, 7,
        7, 2, 3,
        4, 0, 5,
        5, 0, 1
        ], numpy.int16)

self.nIndices = indices.size

# set up vertex array object (VAO)
self.vao = glGenVertexArrays(1)
glBindVertexArray(self.vao)

#vertex buffer
self.vertexBuffer = glGenBuffers(1)
glBindBuffer(GL_ARRAY_BUFFER, self.vertexBuffer)
glBufferData(GL_ARRAY_BUFFER, 4*len(vertices), vertices, GL_STATIC_DRAW)

# vertex buffer - cube vertex colors
self.colorBuffer = glGenBuffers(1)
glBindBuffer(GL_ARRAY_BUFFER, self.colorBuffer)
glBufferData(GL_ARRAY_BUFFER, 4*len(colors), colors, GL_STATIC_DRAW);

# index buffer
self.indexBuffer = glGenBuffers(1)
glBindBuffer(GL_ELEMENT_ARRAY_BUFFER, self.indexBuffer);
glBufferData(GL_ELEMENT_ARRAY_BUFFER, 2*len(indices), indices,
            GL_STATIC_DRAW)
```

```
        # enable attrs using the layout indices in shader
        aPosLoc = 1
        aColorLoc = 2

        # bind buffers:
        glEnableVertexAttribArray(1)
        glEnableVertexAttribArray(2)

        # vertex
        glBindBuffer(GL_ARRAY_BUFFER, self.vertexBuffer)
        glVertexAttribPointer(aPosLoc, 3, GL_FLOAT, GL_FALSE, 0, None)

        # color
        glBindBuffer(GL_ARRAY_BUFFER, self.colorBuffer)
        glVertexAttribPointer(aColorLoc, 3, GL_FLOAT, GL_FALSE, 0, None)
        # index
        glBindBuffer(GL_ELEMENT_ARRAY_BUFFER, self.indexBuffer)

        # unbind VAO
        glBindVertexArray(0)

        # FBO
        self.initFBO()

    def renderBackFace(self, pMatrix, mvMatrix):
        """renders back-face of ray-cube to a texture and returns it"""
        # render to FBO
        glBindFramebuffer(GL_FRAMEBUFFER, self.fboHandle)
        # set active texture
        glActiveTexture(GL_TEXTURE0)
        # bind to FBO texture
        glBindTexture(GL_TEXTURE_2D, self.texHandle)

        # render cube with face culling enabled
        self.renderCube(pMatrix, mvMatrix, self.program, True)

        # unbind texture
        glBindTexture(GL_TEXTURE_2D, 0)
        glBindFramebuffer(GL_FRAMEBUFFER, 0)
        glBindRenderbuffer(GL_RENDERBUFFER, 0)

        # return texture ID
        return self.texHandle

    def renderFrontFace(self, pMatrix, mvMatrix, program):
        """render front face of ray-cube"""
        # no face culling
        self.renderCube(pMatrix, mvMatrix, program, False)

    def renderCube(self, pMatrix, mvMatrix, program, cullFace):
        """render cube use face culling if flag set"""

        glClear(GL_COLOR_BUFFER_BIT | GL_DEPTH_BUFFER_BIT)
```

```python
        # set shader program
        glUseProgram(program)

        # set projection matrix
        glUniformMatrix4fv(glGetUniformLocation(program, b'uPMatrix'),
                           1, GL_FALSE, pMatrix)

        # set modelview matrix
        glUniformMatrix4fv(glGetUniformLocation(program, b'uMVMatrix'),
                           1, GL_FALSE, mvMatrix)

        # enable face culling
        glDisable(GL_CULL_FACE)
        if cullFace:
            glFrontFace(GL_CCW)
            glCullFace(GL_FRONT)
            glEnable(GL_CULL_FACE)

        # bind VAO
        glBindVertexArray(self.vao)

        # animated slice
        glDrawElements(GL_TRIANGLES, self.nIndices, GL_UNSIGNED_SHORT, None)

        # unbind VAO
        glBindVertexArray(0)

        # reset cull face
        if cullFace:
            # disable face culling
            glDisable(GL_CULL_FACE)


    def reshape(self, width, height):
        self.width = width
        self.height = height
        self.aspect = width/float(height)
        # re-create FBO
        self.clearFBO()
        self.initFBO()

    def initFBO(self):
        # create frame buffer object
        self.fboHandle = glGenFramebuffers(1)
        # create texture
        self.texHandle = glGenTextures(1)
        # create depth buffer
        self.depthHandle = glGenRenderbuffers(1)

        # bind
        glBindFramebuffer(GL_FRAMEBUFFER, self.fboHandle)

        glActiveTexture(GL_TEXTURE0)
        glBindTexture(GL_TEXTURE_2D, self.texHandle)
```

```python
        # set parameters to draw the image at different sizes
        glTexParameteri(GL_TEXTURE_2D, GL_TEXTURE_MIN_FILTER, GL_LINEAR)
        glTexParameteri(GL_TEXTURE_2D, GL_TEXTURE_MAG_FILTER, GL_LINEAR)
        glTexParameteri(GL_TEXTURE_2D, GL_TEXTURE_WRAP_S, GL_CLAMP_TO_EDGE)
        glTexParameteri(GL_TEXTURE_2D, GL_TEXTURE_WRAP_T, GL_CLAMP_TO_EDGE)

        # set up texture
        glTexImage2D(GL_TEXTURE_2D, 0, GL_RGBA, self.width, self.height,
                     0, GL_RGBA, GL_UNSIGNED_BYTE, None)

        # bind texture to FBO
        glFramebufferTexture2D(GL_FRAMEBUFFER, GL_COLOR_ATTACHMENT0,
                               GL_TEXTURE_2D, self.texHandle, 0)

        # bind
        glBindRenderbuffer(GL_RENDERBUFFER, self.depthHandle)
        glRenderbufferStorage(GL_RENDERBUFFER, GL_DEPTH_COMPONENT24,
                              self.width, self.height)

        # bind depth buffer to FBO
        glFramebufferRenderbuffer(GL_FRAMEBUFFER, GL_DEPTH_ATTACHMENT,
                                  GL_RENDERBUFFER, self.depthHandle)

        # check status
        status = glCheckFramebufferStatus(GL_FRAMEBUFFER)
        if status == GL_FRAMEBUFFER_COMPLETE:
            pass
            #print "fbo %d complete" % self.fboHandle
        elif status == GL_FRAMEBUFFER_UNSUPPORTED:
            print("fbo %d unsupported" % self.fboHandle)
        else:
            print("fbo %d Error" % self.fboHandle)

        glBindTexture(GL_TEXTURE_2D, 0)
        glBindFramebuffer(GL_FRAMEBUFFER, 0)
        glBindRenderbuffer(GL_RENDERBUFFER, 0)
        return

    def clearFBO(self):
        """clears old FBO"""
        # delete FBO
        if glIsFramebuffer(self.fboHandle):
            glDeleteFramebuffers(int(self.fboHandle))

        # delete texture
        if glIsTexture(self.texHandle):
            glDeleteTextures(int(self.texHandle))


    def close(self):
        """call this to free up OpenGL resources"""
        glBindTexture(GL_TEXTURE_2D, 0)
        glBindFramebuffer(GL_FRAMEBUFFER, 0)
        glBindRenderbuffer(GL_RENDERBUFFER, 0)
```

```
        # delete FBO
        if glIsFramebuffer(self.fboHandle):
            glDeleteFramebuffers(int(self.fboHandle))

        # delete texture
        if glIsTexture(self.texHandle):
            glDeleteTextures(int(self.texHandle))

        # delete render buffer
        """
        if glIsRenderbuffer(self.depthHandle):
            glDeleteRenderbuffers(1, int(self.depthHandle))
            """
        # delete buffers
        """
        glDeleteBuffers(1, self._vertexBuffer)
        glDeleteBuffers(1, &_indexBuffer)
        glDeleteBuffers(1, &_colorBuffer)
        """
```

Volume Ray Casting

Next, implement the ray casting algorithm in the RayCastRender class. The core of the algorithm happens inside the fragment shader used by this class, which also uses the RayCube class to help generate the rays. To see the complete *raycast.py* code, skip ahead to "The Complete Volume Ray Casting Code" on page 216.

Begin by creating a RayCube object and loading the shaders in its constructor.

```
        def __init__(self, width, height, volume):
            """RayCastRender construction"""

            # create RayCube object
❶          self.raycube = raycube.RayCube(width, height)

            # set dimensions
            self.width = width
            self.height = height
            self.aspect = width/float(height)

            # create shader
❷          self.program = glutils.loadShaders(strVS, strFS)
            # texture
❸          self.texVolume, self.Nx, self.Ny, self.Nz = volume

            # initialize camera
❹          self.camera = Camera()
```

The constructor creates an object of type RayCube at ❶, which is used to generate rays. At ❷, load the shaders used by the ray casting; then at ❸, set the OpenGL 3D texture and dimensions, which are passed in as a tuple into the RayCastRender constructor. At ❹, you create a Camera class that you'll use to set up the OpenGL perspective transformation for the 3D rendering. (This class is basically the same as the one used in Chapter 10.)

Here is the rendering method for RayCastRender:

```
    def draw(self):

        # build projection matrix
❶       pMatrix = glutils.perspective(45.0, self.aspect, 0.1, 100.0)

        # modelview matrix
❷       mvMatrix = glutils.lookAt(self.camera.eye, self.camera.center,
                                  self.camera.up)

        # render

        # generate ray-cube back-face texture
❸       texture = self.raycube.renderBackFace(pMatrix, mvMatrix)

        # set shader program
❹       glUseProgram(self.program)

        # set window dimensions
        glUniform2f(glGetUniformLocation(self.program, b"uWinDims"),
                    float(self.width), float(self.height))

        # bind to texture unit 0, which represents back-faces of cube
❺       glActiveTexture(GL_TEXTURE0)
        glBindTexture(GL_TEXTURE_2D, texture)
        glUniform1i(glGetUniformLocation(self.program, b"texBackFaces"), 0)

        # texture unit 1: 3D volume texture
❻       glActiveTexture(GL_TEXTURE1)
        glBindTexture(GL_TEXTURE_3D, self.texVolume)
        glUniform1i(glGetUniformLocation(self.program, b"texVolume"), 1)

        # draw front-face of cubes
❼       self.raycube.renderFrontFace(pMatrix, mvMatrix, self.program)
```

At ❶, you set up a perspective projection matrix for the rendering, using the glutils.perspective() utility method. Then, you set the current camera parameters into the glutils.lookAt() method at ❷. At ❸, the first pass of the rendering is done, which uses the renderBackFace() method in RayCube to draw the back-faces of the color cube into a texture. (This method also returns the ID of the generated texture.)

At ❹, enable the shaders for the ray casting algorithm; then at ❺, set up the texture returned at ❸ to be used in the shader program as texture unit 0. At ❻, you set up the 3D texture created from the volumetric data you read in as texture unit 1 so that now both textures will be available from your shaders. Finally, at ❼, you render the front-faces of the cube using the renderFrontFace() method in RayCube. When this code is executed, the shaders for RayCastRender will act on the vertices and fragments.

The Vertex Shader

Now you come to the shaders used by RayCastRender. Let's look at the vertex shader first:

```
#version 330 core

❶ layout(location = 1) in vec3 cubePos;
   layout(location = 2) in vec3 cubeCol;

❷ uniform mat4 uMVMatrix;
   uniform mat4 uPMatrix;

❸ out vec4 vColor;

   void main()
   {
       // set position
❹     gl_Position = uPMatrix * uMVMatrix * vec4(cubePos.xyz, 1.0);

       // set color
❺     vColor = vec4(cubeCol.rgb, 1.0);
   }
```

Starting at ❶, you set the input variables of position and color. The layout uses the same indices as defined in the RayCube vertex shader because RayCastRender uses the VBO defined in that class to draw the geometry, and the locations in the shaders have to match. At ❷ and in the line that follows, define the input transformation matrices. Then, set a color value as the shader output at ❸. The usual transformation that computes the built-in gl_Position output is included at ❹, and at ❺, you set the output as the current color of the cube vertex, which will be interpolated across vertices to give you the correct color in the fragment shader.

The Fragment Shader

The fragment shader is the star of the show. It implements the core of the ray casting algorithm.

```
#version 330 core

in vec4 vColor;

uniform sampler2D texBackFaces;
uniform sampler3D texVolume;
uniform vec2 uWinDims;

out vec4 fragColor;
```

```
void main()
{
    // start of ray
❶   vec3 start = vColor.rgb;

    // calculate texture coordinates at fragment,
    // which is a fraction of window coordinates
❷   vec2 texc = gl_FragCoord.xy/uWinDims.xy;

    // get end of ray by looking up back-face color
❸   vec3 end = texture(texBackFaces, texc).rgb;

    // calculate ray direction
❹   vec3 dir = end - start;

    // normalized ray direction
    vec3 norm_dir = normalize(dir);

    // the length from front to back is calculated and
    // used to terminate the ray
    float len = length(dir.xyz);

    // ray step size
    float stepSize = 0.01;

    // x-ray projection
    vec4 dst = vec4(0.0);

    // step through the ray
❺   for(float t = 0.0; t < len; t += stepSize) {

        // set position to end point of ray
❻       vec3 samplePos = start + t*norm_dir;

        // get texture value at position
❼       float val = texture(texVolume, samplePos).r;
        vec4 src = vec4(val);

        // set opacity
❽       src.a *= 0.1;
        src.rgb *= src.a;

        // blend with previous value
❾       dst = (1.0 - dst.a)*src + dst;

        // exit loop when alpha exceeds threshold
❿       if(dst.a >= 0.95)
            break;
    }

    // set fragment color
    fragColor = dst;
}
```

The input to the fragment shader is the cube vertex color. The fragment shader also has access to the 2D texture generated by rendering the color cube, the 3D texture containing the data, and the dimensions of the OpenGL window.

While the fragment shader executes, you send in the front-faces of the cube, so by looking up the incoming color value at ❶, you get the starting point of the ray that goes into this cube. (Recall the discussion in "Generating Rays" on page 193 about the connection between the colors in the cube and ray directions.)

At ❷, you calculate the texture coordinate of the incoming fragment on the screen. Divide the location of the fragment in window coordinates by the window dimensions to map in the range [0, 1]. The ending point of the ray is obtained at ❸ by looking up the back-face color of the cube using this texture coordinate.

At ❹, you calculate the ray direction and then calculate the normalized direction and length of this ray, which will be useful in the ray casting computation. Then, at ❺, you loop through the volume using the ray's starting point and direction until it hits the ray's endpoint. Compute the ray's current position inside the data volume at ❻, and at ❼, look up the data value at this point.

The blending equation, which gives you the x-ray effect, is performed at ❽ and ❾. You combine the dst value with the current value of the intensity (which is attenuated using the alpha value), and the process continues along the ray. (The alpha value keeps increasing.)

At ❿, you check this alpha value until it equals the maximum threshold of 0.95 and then exit this loop. The end result is a sort of average opacity through the volume at each pixel, which produces a "see-through" or x-ray effect. (Try varying the threshold and alpha attenuation to produce different effects.)

The Complete Volume Ray Casting Code

Here is the full code listing. You can also find the *raycast.py* file at *https://github.com/electronut/pp/tree/master/volrender/*.

```
import OpenGL
from OpenGL.GL import *
from OpenGL.GL.shaders import *

import numpy as np
import math, sys

import raycube, glutils, volreader

strVS = """
#version 330 core

layout(location = 1) in vec3 cubePos;
layout(location = 2) in vec3 cubeCol;
```

```
uniform mat4 uMVMatrix;
uniform mat4 uPMatrix;

out vec4 vColor;

void main()
{
    // set position
    gl_Position = uPMatrix * uMVMatrix * vec4(cubePos.xyz, 1.0);

    // set color
    vColor = vec4(cubeCol.rgb, 1.0);
}
"""
strFS = """
#version 330 core

in vec4 vColor;

uniform sampler2D texBackFaces;
uniform sampler3D texVolume;
uniform vec2 uWinDims;

out vec4 fragColor;

void main()
{
    // start of ray
    vec3 start = vColor.rgb;

    // calculate texture coords at fragment,
    // which is a fraction of window coords
    vec2 texc = gl_FragCoord.xy/uWinDims.xy;

    // get end of ray by looking up back-face color
    vec3 end = texture(texBackFaces, texc).rgb;

    // calculate ray direction
    vec3 dir = end - start;

    // normalized ray direction
    vec3 norm_dir = normalize(dir);

    // the length from front to back is calculated and
    // used to terminate the ray
    float len = length(dir.xyz);

    // ray step size
    float stepSize = 0.01;

    // x-ray projection
    vec4 dst = vec4(0.0);
```

```
        // step through the ray
        for(float t = 0.0; t < len; t += stepSize) {

            // set position to end point of ray
            vec3 samplePos = start + t*norm_dir;

            // get texture value at position
            float val = texture(texVolume, samplePos).r;
            vec4 src = vec4(val);

            // set opacity
            src.a *= 0.1;
            src.rgb *= src.a;

            // blend with previous value
            dst = (1.0 - dst.a)*src + dst;

            // exit loop when alpha exceeds threshold
            if(dst.a >= 0.95)
                break;
        }

        // set fragment color
        fragColor =  dst;
}
"""

class Camera:
    """helper class for viewing"""
    def __init__(self):
        self.r = 1.5
        self.theta = 0
        self.center = [0.5, 0.5, 0.5]
        self.eye = [0.5 + self.r, 0.5, 0.5]
        self.up = [0.0, 0.0, 1.0]

    def rotate(self, clockWise):
        """rotate eye by one step"""
        if clockWise:
            self.theta = (self.theta + 5) % 360
        else:
            self.theta = (self.theta - 5) % 360
        # recalculate eye
        self.eye = [0.5 + self.r*math.cos(math.radians(self.theta)),
                    0.5 + self.r*math.sin(math.radians(self.theta)),
                    0.5]

class RayCastRender:
    """class that does Ray Casting"""

    def __init__(self, width, height, volume):
        """RayCastRender constr"""

        # create RayCube object
        self.raycube = raycube.RayCube(width, height)
```

```python
        # set dimensions
        self.width = width
        self.height = height
        self.aspect = width/float(height)

        # create shader
        self.program = glutils.loadShaders(strVS, strFS)
        # texture
        self.texVolume, self.Nx, self.Ny, self.Nz = volume

        # initialize camera
        self.camera = Camera()

    def draw(self):

        # build projection matrix
        pMatrix = glutils.perspective(45.0, self.aspect, 0.1, 100.0)

        # modelview matrix
        mvMatrix = glutils.lookAt(self.camera.eye, self.camera.center,
                                  self.camera.up)
        # render

        # generate ray-cube back-face texture
        texture = self.raycube.renderBackFace(pMatrix, mvMatrix)

        # set shader program
        glUseProgram(self.program)

        # set window dimensions
        glUniform2f(glGetUniformLocation(self.program, b"uWinDims"),
                    float(self.width), float(self.height))

        # texture unit 0, which represents back-faces of cube
        glActiveTexture(GL_TEXTURE0)
        glBindTexture(GL_TEXTURE_2D, texture)
        glUniform1i(glGetUniformLocation(self.program, b"texBackFaces"), 0)

        # texture unit 1: 3D volume texture
        glActiveTexture(GL_TEXTURE1)
        glBindTexture(GL_TEXTURE_3D, self.texVolume)
        glUniform1i(glGetUniformLocation(self.program, b"texVolume"), 1)

        # draw front face of cubes
        self.raycube.renderFrontFace(pMatrix, mvMatrix, self.program)

        #self.render(pMatrix, mvMatrix)

    def keyPressed(self, key):
        if key == 'l':
            self.camera.rotate(True)
        elif key == 'r':
            self.camera.rotate(False)
```

```
def reshape(self, width, height):
    self.width = width
    self.height = height
    self.aspect = width/float(height)
    self.raycube.reshape(width, height)

def close(self):
    self.raycube.close()
```

2D Slicing

In addition to showing the 3D view of the volumetric data, you also want to show 2D slices of the data in the *x*, *y*, and *z* directions onscreen. This code is encapsulated in a class called SliceRender, which creates 2D volumetric slices. To see the complete *slicerender.py* code, skip ahead to "The Complete 2D Slicing Code" on page 224.

Here is the initialization code that sets up the geometry for the slices:

```
                # set up vertex array object (VAO)
                self.vao = glGenVertexArrays(1)
                glBindVertexArray(self.vao)

                # define quad vertices
❶               vertexData = numpy.array([ 0.0, 1.0, 0.0,
                                           0.0, 0.0, 0.0,
                                           1.0, 1.0, 0.0,
                                           1.0, 0.0, 0.0], numpy.float32)

                # vertex buffer
                self.vertexBuffer = glGenBuffers(1)
                glBindBuffer(GL_ARRAY_BUFFER, self.vertexBuffer)
                glBufferData(GL_ARRAY_BUFFER, 4*len(vertexData), vertexData,
                            GL_STATIC_DRAW)
                # enable arrays
                glEnableVertexAttribArray(self.vertIndex)
                # set buffers
                glBindBuffer(GL_ARRAY_BUFFER, self.vertexBuffer)
                glVertexAttribPointer(self.vertIndex, 3, GL_FLOAT, GL_FALSE, 0, None)

                # unbind VAO
                glBindVertexArray(0)
```

This code sets up a VAO to manage the VBO, as in earlier examples. The geometry defined at ❶ is a square in the *xy* plane. (The vertex order is that of the GL_TRIANGLE_STRIP, introduced in Chapter 9.) So whether or not you are showing the slices perpendicular to *x*, *y*, or *z*, you use the same geometry. What changes between these cases is the data plane that you pick to display from within the 3D texture. I'll return to this when I discuss the vertex shader.

Next, render the 2D slices using `SliceRender`:

```python
def draw(self):
    # clear buffers
    glClear(GL_COLOR_BUFFER_BIT | GL_DEPTH_BUFFER_BIT)
    # build projection matrix
➊   pMatrix = glutils.ortho(-0.6, 0.6, -0.6, 0.6, 0.1, 100.0)
    # modelview matrix
➋   mvMatrix = numpy.array([1.0, 0.0, 0.0, 0.0,
                            0.0, 1.0, 0.0, 0.0,
                            0.0, 0.0, 1.0, 0.0,
                            -0.5, -0.5, -1.0, 1.0], numpy.float32)
    # use shader
    glUseProgram(self.program)

    # set projection matrix
    glUniformMatrix4fv(self.pMatrixUniform, 1, GL_FALSE, pMatrix)

    # set modelview matrix
    glUniformMatrix4fv(self.mvMatrixUniform, 1, GL_FALSE, mvMatrix)

    # set current slice fraction
➌   glUniform1f(glGetUniformLocation(self.program, b"uSliceFrac"),
                float(self.currSliceIndex)/float(self.currSliceMax))
    # set current slice mode
➍   glUniform1i(glGetUniformLocation(self.program, b"uSliceMode"),
                self.mode)

    # enable texture
    glActiveTexture(GL_TEXTURE0)
    glBindTexture(GL_TEXTURE_3D, self.texture)
    glUniform1i(glGetUniformLocation(self.program, b"tex"), 0)

    # bind VAO
    glBindVertexArray(self.vao)
    # draw
    glDrawArrays(GL_TRIANGLE_STRIP, 0, 4)
    # unbind VAO
    glBindVertexArray(0)
```

Each 2D slice is a square, which you build up using an OpenGL triangle strip primitive. This code goes through the render setup for the triangle strip. Note that you implement the orthographic projection using the glutils.ortho() method. At ➊, you set up a projection that adds 0.1 buffer around the unit square representing the slice. When you draw something with OpenGL, the default view (without any transformation applied) puts the eye at (0, 0, 0) and looking down the z-axis with the y-axis pointing up. At ➋, you apply the translation (−0.5, −0.5, −1.0) to your geometry to center it around the z-axis. You set the current slice fraction at ➌ (where, for example, the 10th slice out of 100 would be 0.1), set the slice mode at ➍ (to view the slices in the *x*, *y*, or *z* direction, as represented by the integers 0, 1, and 2, respectively), and set both values to the shaders.

The Vertex Shader

Now let's look at the vertex shader for SliceRender:

```
# version 330 core

in vec3 aVert;

uniform mat4 uMVMatrix;
uniform mat4 uPMatrix;

uniform float uSliceFrac;
uniform int uSliceMode;

out vec3 texcoord;

void main() {

    // x slice
    if (uSliceMode == 0) {
❶        texcoord = vec3(uSliceFrac, aVert.x, 1.0-aVert.y);
    }
    // y slice
    else if (uSliceMode == 1) {
❷        texcoord = vec3(aVert.x, uSliceFrac, 1.0-aVert.y);
    }
    // z slice
    else {
❸        texcoord = vec3(aVert.x, 1.0-aVert.y, uSliceFrac);
    }

    // calculate transformed vertex
    gl_Position = uPMatrix * uMVMatrix * vec4(aVert, 1.0);
}
```

The vertex shader takes the triangle strip vertex array as input and sets a texture coordinate as output. The current slice fraction and slice mode are passed in as uniform variables.

At ❶, you calculate the texture coordinates for the x slice. Because you are slicing perpendicular to the x direction, you want a slice parallel to the yz plane. The 3D vertices coming in to the vertex shader also double as the 3D texture coordinates because they are in the range [0, 1], so the texture coordinates are given as (f, Vx, Vy), where f is the fraction of the slice number in the direction of the x-axis and where Vx and Vy are the vertex coordinates. Unfortunately, the resulting image will appear upside down because the OpenGL coordinate system has its origin at the bottom left, with the y direction pointing up; this is the reverse of what you want. To resolve this problem, you change the texture coordinate t to $(1 - t)$ and use (f, Vx, $1 - Vy$), as shown at ❶. At ❷ and ❸, you use similar logic to compute the texture coordinates for the y and z direction slices.

The Fragment Shader

Here is the fragment shader:

```
# version 330 core

in vec3 texcoord;

uniform sampler3D texture;

out vec4 fragColor;

void main() {
    // look up color in texture
    vec4 col = texture(tex, texcoord);
    fragColor = col.rrra;
}
```

At ❶, the fragment shader declares texcoord as input, which was set as output in the vertex shader. The texture sampler is declared as a uniform at ❷. At ❸, you look up the texture color using texcoord, and at ❹, you set fragColor as the output. (Because you read in your texture only as the red channel, you use col.rrra.)

A User Interface for 2D Slicing

Now you need a way for the user to slice through the data. Do this using the keyboard handler for SliceRender.

```
    def keyPressed(self, key):
        """keypress handler"""
        if key == 'x':
            self.mode = SliceRender.XSLICE
            # reset slice index
            self.currSliceIndex = int(self.Nx/2)
            self.currSliceMax = self.Nx
        elif key == 'y':
            self.mode = SliceRender.YSLICE
            # reset slice index
            self.currSliceIndex = int(self.Ny/2)
            self.currSliceMax = self.Ny
        elif key == 'z':
            self.mode = SliceRender.ZSLICE
            # reset slice index
            self.currSliceIndex = int(self.Nz/2)
            self.currSliceMax = self.Nz
        elif key == 'l':
            self.currSliceIndex = (self.currSliceIndex + 1) % self.currSliceMax
        elif key == 'r':
            self.currSliceIndex = (self.currSliceIndex - 1) % self.currSliceMax
```

When the X, Y, or Z keys are pressed on the keyboard, SliceRender switches to the *x*, *y*, or *z* slice mode. You can see this in action at ❶ for the *x* slice where you set the current slice index to the middle of the data and update the maximum slice number. When the left or right arrow keys on the keyboard are pressed, you page through the slices. At ❷, the slice index is incremented when the right arrow is pressed. The modulo operator (%) ensures that the index "rolls over" to 0 when you exceed the maximum value.

The Complete 2D Slicing Code

Here is the full code listing. You can also find the *slicerender.py* file at *https://github.com/electronut/pp/tree/master/volrender/*.

```
import OpenGL
from OpenGL.GL import *
from OpenGL.GL.shaders import *
import numpy, math, sys

import volreader, glutils

strVS = """
# version 330 core

in vec3 aVert;

uniform mat4 uMVMatrix;
uniform mat4 uPMatrix;

uniform float uSliceFrac;
uniform int uSliceMode;

out vec3 texcoord;

void main() {

    // x slice
    if (uSliceMode == 0) {
        texcoord = vec3(uSliceFrac, aVert.x, 1.0-aVert.y);
    }
    // y slice
    else if (uSliceMode == 1) {
        texcoord = vec3(aVert.x, uSliceFrac, 1.0-aVert.y);
    }
    // z slice
    else {
        texcoord = vec3(aVert.x, 1.0-aVert.y, uSliceFrac);
    }

    // calculate transformed vertex
    gl_Position = uPMatrix * uMVMatrix * vec4(aVert, 1.0);
}
```

```
"""
strFS = """
# version 330 core

in vec3 texcoord;

uniform sampler3D tex;

out vec4 fragColor;

void main() {
    // look up color in texture
    vec4 col = texture(tex, texcoord);
    fragColor = col.rrra;
}

"""

class SliceRender:
    # slice modes
    XSLICE, YSLICE, ZSLICE = 0, 1, 2

    def __init__(self, width, height, volume):
        """SliceRender constructor"""
        self.width = width
        self.height = height
        self.aspect = width/float(height)

        # slice mode
        self.mode = SliceRender.ZSLICE

        # create shader
        self.program = glutils.loadShaders(strVS, strFS)

        glUseProgram(self.program)

        self.pMatrixUniform = glGetUniformLocation(self.program, b'uPMatrix')
        self.mvMatrixUniform = glGetUniformLocation(self.program,
                                                    b"uMVMatrix")

        # attributes
        self.vertIndex = glGetAttribLocation(self.program, b"aVert")

        # set up vertex array object (VAO)
        self.vao = glGenVertexArrays(1)
        glBindVertexArray(self.vao)

        # define quad vertices
        vertexData = numpy.array([ 0.0, 1.0, 0.0,
                                   0.0, 0.0, 0.0,
                                   1.0, 1.0, 0.0,
                                   1.0, 0.0, 0.0], numpy.float32)
        # vertex buffer
        self.vertexBuffer = glGenBuffers(1)
        glBindBuffer(GL_ARRAY_BUFFER, self.vertexBuffer)
```

```python
        glBufferData(GL_ARRAY_BUFFER, 4*len(vertexData), vertexData,
                    GL_STATIC_DRAW)
        # enable arrays
        glEnableVertexAttribArray(self.vertIndex)
        # set buffers
        glBindBuffer(GL_ARRAY_BUFFER, self.vertexBuffer)
        glVertexAttribPointer(self.vertIndex, 3, GL_FLOAT, GL_FALSE, 0, None)

        # unbind VAO
        glBindVertexArray(0)

        # load texture
        self.texture, self.Nx, self.Ny, self.Nz = volume

        # current slice index
        self.currSliceIndex = int(self.Nz/2);
        self.currSliceMax = self.Nz;


    def reshape(self, width, height):
        self.width = width
        self.height = height
        self.aspect = width/float(height)

    def draw(self):
        # clear buffers
        glClear(GL_COLOR_BUFFER_BIT | GL_DEPTH_BUFFER_BIT)
        # build projection matrix
        pMatrix = glutils.ortho(-0.6, 0.6, -0.6, 0.6, 0.1, 100.0)
        # modelview matrix
        mvMatrix = numpy.array([1.0, 0.0, 0.0, 0.0,
                                0.0, 1.0, 0.0, 0.0,
                                0.0, 0.0, 1.0, 0.0,
                                -0.5, -0.5, -1.0, 1.0], numpy.float32)
        # use shader
        glUseProgram(self.program)

        # set projection matrix
        glUniformMatrix4fv(self.pMatrixUniform, 1, GL_FALSE, pMatrix)

        # set modelview matrix
        glUniformMatrix4fv(self.mvMatrixUniform, 1, GL_FALSE, mvMatrix)

        # set current slice fraction
        glUniform1f(glGetUniformLocation(self.program, b"uSliceFrac"),
                    float(self.currSliceIndex)/float(self.currSliceMax))
        # set current slice mode
        glUniform1i(glGetUniformLocation(self.program, b"uSliceMode"),
                    self.mode)

        # enable texture
        glActiveTexture(GL_TEXTURE0)
        glBindTexture(GL_TEXTURE_3D, self.texture)
        glUniform1i(glGetUniformLocation(self.program, b"tex"), 0)
```

```
        # bind VAO
        glBindVertexArray(self.vao)
        # draw
        glDrawArrays(GL_TRIANGLE_STRIP, 0, 4)
        # unbind VAO
        glBindVertexArray(0)

    def keyPressed(self, key):
        """keypress handler"""
        if key == 'x':
            self.mode = SliceRender.XSLICE
            # reset slice index
            self.currSliceIndex = int(self.Nx/2)
            self.currSliceMax = self.Nx
        elif key == 'y':
            self.mode = SliceRender.YSLICE
            # reset slice index
            self.currSliceIndex = int(self.Ny/2)
            self.currSliceMax = self.Ny
        elif key == 'z':
            self.mode = SliceRender.ZSLICE
            # reset slice index
            self.currSliceIndex = int(self.Nz/2)
            self.currSliceMax = self.Nz
        elif key == 'l':
            self.currSliceIndex = (self.currSliceIndex + 1) % self.currSliceMax
        elif key == 'r':
            self.currSliceIndex = (self.currSliceIndex - 1) % self.currSliceMax

    def close(self):
        pass
```

Putting the Code Together

Let's take a quick look at the main file in the project *volrender.py*. This file
uses a class RenderWin, which creates and manages the GLFW OpenGL window. (I won't cover this class in detail because it's similar to the class used
in Chapters 9 and 10.) To see the complete *volrender.py* code, skip ahead to
"The Complete Main File Code" on page 228.

In the initialization code for this class, you create the renderer as follows:

```
        # load volume data
❶       self.volume = volreader.loadVolume(imageDir)
        # create renderer
❷       self.renderer = RayCastRender(self.width, self.height, self.volume)
```

At ❶, you read the 3D data into an OpenGL texture. At ❷, you create
an object of type RayCastRender to display the data.

Pressing V on the keyboard toggles the code between volume and slice rendering. Here is the keyboard handler for RenderWindow:

```python
def onKeyboard(self, win, key, scancode, action, mods):
    # print 'keyboard: ', win, key, scancode, action, mods
    # ESC to quit
    if key is glfw.GLFW_KEY_ESCAPE:
        self.renderer.close()
        self.exitNow = True
    else:
❶      if action is glfw.GLFW_PRESS or action is glfw.GLFW_REPEAT:
            if key == glfw.GLFW_KEY_V:
                # toggle render mode
❷              if isinstance(self.renderer, RayCastRender):
                    self.renderer = SliceRender(self.width, self.height,
                                                self.volume)
                else:
                    self.renderer = RayCastRender(self.width, self.height,
                                                  self.volume)
                # call reshape on renderer
                self.renderer.reshape(self.width, self.height)
            else:
                # send keypress to renderer
❸              keyDict = {glfw.GLFW_KEY_X: 'x', glfw.GLFW_KEY_Y: 'y',
                           glfw.GLFW_KEY_Z: 'z', glfw.GLFW_KEY_LEFT: 'l',
                           glfw.GLFW_KEY_RIGHT: 'r'}
                try:
                    self.renderer.keyPressed(keyDict[key])
                except:
                    pass
```

Pressing ESC quits the program. Other keypresses (V, X, Y, Z, and so on) are handled at ❶ (set so that it works whether you have just pressed the key down or if you are keeping it pressed). At ❷, if V is pressed, you toggle the renderer between volume and slice, using Python's isinstance() method to identify the current class type.

To handle keypress events other than ESC, you use a dictionary ❸ and pass the key pressed to the renderer's keyPressed() handler.

NOTE   *I'm choosing not to pass in the glfw.KEY values directly and using a dictionary to convert these to character values instead, because it's good practice to reduce dependencies in source files. Currently, the only file in this project that depends on GLFW is volrender.py. If you were to pass GLFW-specific types into other code, they would need to import and depend on the GLFW library, but if you were to switch to yet another OpenGL windowing toolkit, the code would become messy.*

The Complete Main File Code

Here is the full code listing. You can also find the *volrender.py* file at *https://github.com/electronut/pp/tree/master/volrender/*.

```python
import sys, argparse, os
from slicerender import *
from raycast import *
import glfw

class RenderWin:
    """GLFW Rendering window class"""
    def __init__(self, imageDir):

        # save current working directory
        cwd = os.getcwd()

        # initialize glfw; this changes cwd
        glfw.glfwInit()

        # restore cwd
        os.chdir(cwd)

        # version hints
        glfw.glfwWindowHint(glfw.GLFW_CONTEXT_VERSION_MAJOR, 3)
        glfw.glfwWindowHint(glfw.GLFW_CONTEXT_VERSION_MINOR, 3)
        glfw.glfwWindowHint(glfw.GLFW_OPENGL_FORWARD_COMPAT, GL_TRUE)
        glfw.glfwWindowHint(glfw.GLFW_OPENGL_PROFILE,
                            glfw.GLFW_OPENGL_CORE_PROFILE)

        # make a window
        self.width, self.height = 512, 512
        self.aspect = self.width/float(self.height)
        self.win = glfw.glfwCreateWindow(self.width, self.height, b"volrender")
        # make context current
        glfw.glfwMakeContextCurrent(self.win)

        # initialize GL
        glViewport(0, 0, self.width, self.height)
        glEnable(GL_DEPTH_TEST)
        glClearColor(0.0, 0.0, 0.0, 0.0)

        # set window callbacks
        glfw.glfwSetMouseButtonCallback(self.win, self.onMouseButton)
        glfw.glfwSetKeyCallback(self.win, self.onKeyboard)
        glfw.glfwSetWindowSizeCallback(self.win, self.onSize)

        # load volume data
        self.volume =  volreader.loadVolume(imageDir)
        # create renderer
        self.renderer = RayCastRender(self.width, self.height, self.volume)

        # exit flag
        self.exitNow = False

    def onMouseButton(self, win, button, action, mods):
        # print 'mouse button: ', win, button, action, mods
        pass
```

```python
    def onKeyboard(self, win, key, scancode, action, mods):
        # print 'keyboard: ', win, key, scancode, action, mods
        # ESC to quit
        if key is glfw.GLFW_KEY_ESCAPE:
            self.renderer.close()
            self.exitNow = True
        else:
            if action is glfw.GLFW_PRESS or action is glfw.GLFW_REPEAT:
                if key == glfw.GLFW_KEY_V:
                    # toggle render mode
                    if isinstance(self.renderer, RayCastRender):
                        self.renderer = SliceRender(self.width, self.height,
                                                    self.volume)
                    else:
                        self.renderer = RayCastRender(self.width, self.height,
                                                      self.volume)
                    # call reshape on renderer
                    self.renderer.reshape(self.width, self.height)
                else:
                    # send keypress to renderer
                    keyDict = {glfw.GLFW_KEY_X: 'x', glfw.GLFW_KEY_Y: 'y',
                               glfw.GLFW_KEY_Z: 'z', glfw.GLFW_KEY_LEFT: 'l',
                               glfw.GLFW_KEY_RIGHT: 'r'}
                    try:
                        self.renderer.keyPressed(keyDict[key])
                    except:
                        pass

    def onSize(self, win, width, height):
        #print 'onsize: ', win, width, height
        self.width = width
        self.height = height
        self.aspect = width/float(height)
        glViewport(0, 0, self.width, self.height)
        self.renderer.reshape(width, height)

    def run(self):
        # start loop
        while not glfw.glfwWindowShouldClose(self.win) and not self.exitNow:
            # render
            self.renderer.draw()
            # swap buffers
            glfw.glfwSwapBuffers(self.win)
            # wait for events
            glfw.glfwWaitEvents()
        # end
        glfw.glfwTerminate()

# main() function
def main():
  print('starting volrender...')
  # create parser
  parser = argparse.ArgumentParser(description="Volume Rendering...")
  # add expected arguments
  parser.add_argument('--dir', dest='imageDir', required=True)
```

```
# parse args
args = parser.parse_args()

# create render window
rwin = RenderWin(args.imageDir)
rwin.run()

# call main
if __name__ == '__main__':
    main()
```

Running the Program

Here is a sample run of the application using data from the Stanford
Volume Data Archive.[3]

```
$ python volrender.py --dir mrbrain-8bit/
```

You should see something like Figure 11-6.

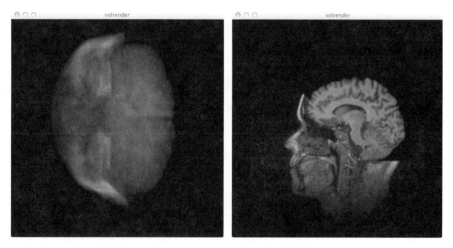

Figure 11-6: Sample run of volrender.py. The image on the left is the volumetric rendering,
and the image on the right is a 2D slice.

Summary

In this chapter, you implemented the volume ray casting algorithm using
Python and OpenGL. You learned how to use GLSL shaders to implement
this algorithm efficiently, as well as how to create 2D slices from the volumetric data.

---

3. http://graphics.stanford.edu/data/voldata/

Experiments!

Here are a few ways you could keep tinkering with the volume ray casting program:

1. Currently, it's hard to see the boundary of the volumetric data "cube" in the ray casting mode. Implement a class `WireFrame` that draws a box around this cube. Color the x-, y-, and z-axes red, green, and blue, respectively, and give each its own shaders. You will use `WireFrame` from within the `RayCastRender` class.

2. Implement data scaling. In the current implementation, you are drawing a cube for the volume and a square for 2D slices, which assumes you have a symmetric data set (that the number of slices are the same in each direction), but most real data has a varying number of slices. Medical data, in particular, often has fewer slices in the z direction, with dimensions such as 256×256×99, for example. To display this data correctly, you have to introduce a scale into your computations. One way to do so is to apply the scale to the cube vertices (3D volume) and square vertices (2D slice). The user can then input the scaling parameters as command line arguments.

3. Our volume ray casting implementation uses x-ray casting to calculate the final color or intensity of a pixel. Another popular way to do this is to use *maximum intensity projection (MIP)* to set the maximum intensity at each pixel. Implement this in your code. (Hint: in the fragment shader of `RayCastRender`, modify the code that steps through the ray to check and set the maximum value along the ray, instead of blending values.)

4. Currently, the only UI you have implemented is rotation around the x-, y-, and z-axes. Implement a zoom feature so pressing I and O simultaneously will zoom in and out of the volume-rendered image. You could do this by setting the appropriate camera parameters in the `glutils.lookAt()` method, with one caveat: if you move your view inside the data cube, the ray casting will fail because OpenGL will clip the front-faces of the cube; the ray computation needed for ray casting requires both the front- and back-faces of the color cube to be rendered correctly. Instead, zoom by adjusting the field of view in the `glutils.projecton()` method.

PART V

HARDWARE HACKING

"Those parts of the system that you can hit with a hammer (not advised) are called hardware; those program instructions that you can only curse at are called software."
—Anonymous

12

INTRODUCTION TO THE ARDUINO

The Arduino is a simple *microcontroller* board and open source development environment on a programmable chip. All versions of the Arduino contain the standard components of a computer, such as memory, a processor, and an input/output system.

In this chapter, you begin your journey into the world of microcontrollers with the help of the Arduino. You'll learn the basics of the Arduino platform and how to build Arduino programs in the Arduino programming language (a version of C++). You'll learn how to program an Arduino to gather data from a simple light sensor circuit that you'll build and then send this data to your computer via a serial port. Next you'll use pySerial to interface with the Arduino over a serial port, gather data, and graph it in real time using matplotlib. The graph will scroll to the right as new values come in, much like an EKG monitor. Figure 12-1 shows the circuit setup.

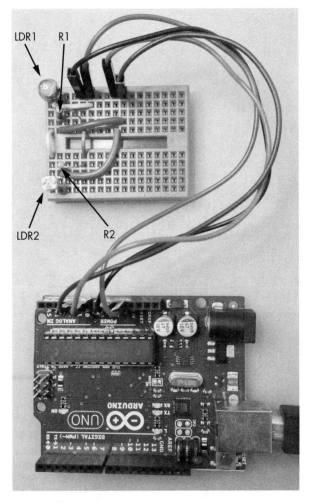

Figure 12-1: A simple light-dependent resistor (LDR) circuit assembled on a breadboard and connected to an Arduino Uno

The Arduino

The Arduino is a platform built around a class of microcontroller chips called the Atmel AVR. There are many Arduino boards on the market, of varying size and capabilities. Figure 12-2 highlights some of the major components in the Arduino Uno boards, one of the more common varieties available. The headers on the Arduino board (as shown in Figure 12-2) allow you to access the analog and digital pins of the microcontroller so you can talk to other electronics by sending and receiving data. (I recommend *Arduino Workshop* by John Boxall [No Starch Press, 2013] to get a better understanding of the electronics and programming aspects of the Arduino.)

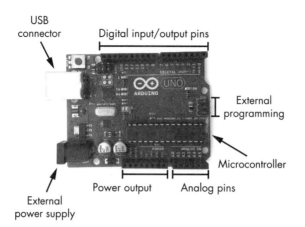

USB connector

Digital input/output pins

External programming

Microcontroller

Power output

Analog pins

External power supply

Figure 12-2: Components of the Arduino Uno board

NOTE   *Although I use the Arduino Uno board for the projects in this book, you should be able to use unofficial boards. If you do, see the Arduino website (http://arduino.cc/) to learn the differences between boards. For instance, some boards use different pin-numbering conventions from the Uno.*

The Arduino Uno board has a microcontroller chip, a universal serial bus (USB) connection, a jack for an external power supply, digital input/ output pins, analog pins, a power output that can be used by external circuits, and even pins for programming the chip directly.

The Arduino boards include a *bootloader*, which is a program that allows you to upload and run code on the microcontroller. If the bootloader weren't included, you would need to use an *in-circuit serial programming (ICSP)* programmer to interact with the microcontroller. (The Arduino makes ICSP possible with pins for external programming called the ICSP headers.) The Arduino is easy to program because you can connect it to a computer via the USB port and use the Arduino software to upload code to the board.

The most important component of an Arduino board is the AVR microcontroller, which is a computer on a chip. The AVR microcontroller on the Arduino Uno is an ATmega328 chip. It has a central processing unit (CPU), timers/counters, analog and digital pins, memory modules, and a clock module, among other things. The chip's CPU executes the programs you upload. The timer/counter modules can be used to create periodic events within the program (such as checking a digital pin value every second). The analog pins use an analog-to-digital converter (ADC) module to convert the incoming analog signals to digital values, and the digital pins can act as either input or output depending on how you set them.

The Arduino Ecosystem

The Arduino sits at the center of an ecosystem that combines a programming language with an integrated development environment (IDE), a supportive and inventive community, and a host of peripherals.

Language

The Arduino programming language is a simplified version of C++ with its origins in the Processing and Wiring prototyping languages. It is designed to be an easy language for people unfamiliar with programming. Programs written for the Arduino are called *sketches*. (For more on the Arduino programming language, visit *http://arduino.cc/.*)

IDE

The Arduino includes a simple IDE where you create sketches and upload them to the Arduino (see Figure 12-3). The IDE also includes a *serial monitor* that you can use to debug your applications by having the Arduino send information to the computer via the serial port. In addition, the IDE includes several example programs, as well as a bunch of standard libraries to perform common tasks and interface with external peripheral boards.

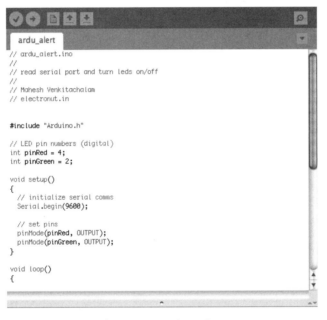

```
// ardu_alert.ino
//
// read serial port and turn leds on/off
//
// Mahesh Venkitachalam
// electronut.in


#include "Arduino.h"

// LED pin numbers (digital)
int pinRed = 4;
int pinGreen = 2;

void setup()
{
  // initialize serial comms
  Serial.begin(9600);

  // set pins
  pinMode(pinRed, OUTPUT);
  pinMode(pinGreen, OUTPUT);
}

void loop()
{
```

Figure 12-3: A sample program in the Arduino IDE

Community

The Arduino has a large user base, and if you have questions about a project, you can turn to the Arduino community for help. Too, the Arduino community has developed many open source libraries that you can use in your project, and if you're struggling with interfacing your Arduino to some sensor module, chances are someone has already solved the problem and a library is available to make your life easier.

Peripherals

As with any popular platform, an industry has been built around the Arduino platform. A huge number of *shields* (boards that fit conveniently over the Arduino and provide easy access to sensors and other electronics), *breakout boards* (which ease wiring up difficult-to-solder components/circuits), and other peripherals, many of which can simplify your projects, are available for Arduino. SparkFun Electronics (*https://www.sparkfun.com/*) and Adafruit Industries (*http://www.adafruit.com/*) are two companies that build a number of products that can be used with the Arduino.

Requirements

Now that you know some Arduino basics, let's see how we can program a board to read data from a light-sensing circuit. In addition to an Arduino, you'll also need two *resistors* and two *light-dependent resistors (LDRs)*. Resistors are used to reduce current flow through a circuit and to lower voltages. You'll use a light-dependent resistor (also called a *photoresistor*) whose electrical resistance decreases as the intensity of light hitting it increases. You'll also need a breadboard and wires to assemble the circuit, and a multimeter to check the connections.

Building the Light-Sensing Circuit

First you'll build your light-sensing circuit, which consists of two regular resistors and two LDRs. Figure 12-4 shows the circuit diagram for your light-sensing circuit. (Appendix B includes some basic information on how to start building electronic circuits.)

In Figure 12-4, VCC stands for a connection to the 5V output of the Arduino, which powers the circuit. The items labeled LDR1 and LDR2 are the two light-dependent resistors, and A0 and A1 are the Arduino's analog pins 0 and 1. (These analog pins allow the microcontroller to read voltage levels from external circuits.) You can also see the resistors R1 and R2 and a ground (GND) connection, which can be any of the GND pins on the Arduino. You can assemble your circuit on a *breadboard* (a plastic board with spring clips that are used to assemble circuits without soldering) using a few wires for the connections, as shown earlier in Figure 12-1.

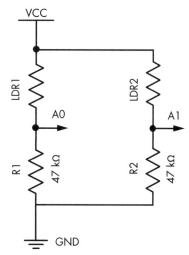

Figure 12-4: Schematic of a simple light-sensing circuit

How the Circuit Works

In this circuit, each LDR, and the resistor beneath it, act as a *resistor divider*, which is a simple circuit that uses two resistors to split an input voltage in two. This setup means the voltage at A0, for instance, is calculated as follows:

$$V_0 = V \frac{R_1}{R_{\mathrm{LDR}} + R_1}$$

R_1 is the resistance of the resistor, and R_{LDR} is the resistance of the LDR. V is the supply voltage, and V_0 is the voltage across R_1. As the intensity of light falling on the LDR changes, its resistance changes, and the voltage across it changes accordingly. The voltage (somewhere between 0 and 5 volts) is read at A0 and sent to your program as a 10-bit value, in the range [0, 1023]; that is, the voltage range is mapped to an integer range of [0, 1023].

The value of the R1 and R2 resistors that you'll use in the circuit will depend on your choice of LDR. When you shine light on the LDR, its electrical resistance decreases; as a result, R_{LDR} decreases, which means V_0 increases and a higher value is read in by the Arduino at the analog pin connected to this LDR. To determine the value of resistance that you need for R1 and R2, measure the resistance of the LDR using a multimeter under different light conditions and plug that value in to the voltage equation. You're looking for a good variation in voltage (from 0V to 5V) across the range of lighting conditions in which you will be using the LDR.

I ended up using 4.7k ohm resistors for R1 and R2 because my LDRs varied in resistance from about 10k ohms (in the dark) to 1k ohm (in bright light). Enter these values into the previous equation, and you'll see that you need a voltage range of 1.6V to 4V for the analog input. When you build the circuit, you can start with 4.7k ohm resistors and change them as needed.

The Arduino Sketch

Now let's write the Arduino sketch. Here's the code that runs on the Arduino to make it read signals from the circuit and send them to the computer over a serial port:

```
#include "Arduino.h"

void setup()
{
    // initialize serial communications
❶   Serial.begin(9600);
}

void loop()
{
    // read A0
❷   int val1 = analogRead(0);
    // read A1
❸   int val2 = analogRead(1);
```

```
       // print to serial
❹     Serial.print(val1);
       Serial.print(" ");
       Serial.print(val2);
       Serial.print("\n");
       // wait
❺     delay(50);
  }
```

At ❶, you enable serial communication inside the setup() method. Because setup() is called only when your program starts, this is a good place to put all of the initialization code. You initialize the *baud rate* (speed in bits per second) for the serial communications to 9600 here, which is the default for most devices and one that's fast enough for your purposes.

The main code is in the loop() method. At ❷, you read the current signal value from analog pin 0 (a 10-bit integer in the range [0, 1023]), and at ❸, you read the current signal value from pin 1. At ❹ and in the lines that follow, use Serial.print() to send the values to the computer, formatted as two integers separated by a space and followed by a newline character. At ❺, you use delay() to suspend operations for a set time period, 50 milliseconds in this case, before the loop repeats. The value you use here determines the rate at which the AVR microcontroller executes the loop() method.

To upload the sketch to your Arduino, connect the Arduino to your computer, bring up its IDE, and start a new project. Then enter the code into the sketch window and click **Verify** to compile the code. The IDE will print any syntax-related errors and warnings. If all is well, click **Upload** to send the sketch to the Arduino.

If you don't see any errors at this stage, bring up the Serial Monitor from the Tools menu of the Arduino software, and you should see something like this:

```
512  300
513  280
400  200
. . .
```

These are the analog values read from analog pins 0 and 1 and sent serially through the Arduino's USB port to your computer.

Creating the Real-Time Graph

To implement the scrolling real-time graph for your project, you'll use a deque, as discussed in Chapter 4. The deque consists of an array of *N* values; adding and removing values at either end is quickly done. As new values come in, they are appended to the deque, and the oldest value is popped off. By plotting the values at regular intervals, you'll produce a real-time graph with the newest data always added on the left.

The Python Code

Now let's look at the Python program that reads from the serial port. (For the complete project code, you can skip ahead to "The Complete Python Code" on page 244.) To help better organize your code, define a class AnalogPlot, which holds the data to be plotted. Here is the class constructor:

```
class AnalogPlot:
    # constructor
    def __init__(self, strPort, maxLen):
        # open serial port
❶       self.ser = serial.Serial(strPort, 9600)

❷       self.a0Vals = deque([0.0]*maxLen)
❸       self.a1Vals = deque([0.0]*maxLen)
❹       self.maxLen = maxLen
```

At ❶, the AnalogPlot constructor creates a Serial object from the pySerial library. You'll use this class for serial communications with the Arduino. The first argument to the Serial constructor is the port name string, which you can find in the IDE by selecting **Tools ▶ Serial Port** (on Windows, the string will be something like *COM3*; on Linux and OS X, it will be something like */dev/tty.usbmodem411*). The second argument to the Serial constructor is the baud rate, which you set to 9600 to match the rate you set in the Arduino sketch.

At ❷ and ❸, you create deque objects to hold the analog values. You initialize the deque objects with a list of zeros of size maxLen, the maximum number of values you'll plot at a given time. At ❹, this maxLen is stored in the AnalogPlot object.

To plot the analog values in real time, use the deque objects to buffer the most recent values, as shown in the AnalogPlot class.

```
    # add data
    def add(self, data):
        assert(len(data) == 2)
❶       self.addToDeq(self.a0Vals, data[0])
❷       self.addToDeq(self.a1Vals, data[1])

    # add to deque; pop oldest value
    def addToDeq(self, buf, val):
❸       buf.pop()
❹       buf.appendleft(val)
```

As you saw earlier, the Arduino sends only two analog integer values per line. In the add() method, the data values for each analog pin are added into two deque objects at ❶ and ❷, using the addToDeq() method. At ❸ and ❹, this method removes the oldest value from the tail of the deque using the pop() method and then appends the latest value to the head of the deque using the appendleft() method. When you plot values from this deque, the most recent value will always appear at left on the graph.

You use the `matplotlib animation` class to update the plot at set intervals. (You may recall seeing this in action in the Boids project in Chapter 5.) Here is the `update()` method in `AnalogPlot`, which will be called at each step in the plot animation:

```
# update plot
def update(self, frameNum, a0, a1):
    try:
❶      line = self.ser.readline()
❷      data = [float(val) for val in line.split()]
        # print data
        if(len(data) == 2):
❸          self.add(data)
❹          a0.set_data(range(self.maxLen), self.a0Vals)
❺          a1.set_data(range(self.maxLen), self.a1Vals)
    except:
❻      pass

    return a0, a1
```

The `update()` method reads in a line of serial data as a string at ❶, and at ❷, you use a Python list comprehension to convert the values to floating-point numbers and store them in a list. You use the `split()` method to split a string based on whitespace so that a string read from the serial port as `512 600\n` will be converted to `[512, 600]`.

After checking that the data has two values, you use `AnalogPlot add()` at ❸ to add the values to the deque. At ❹ and ❺, you use the `matplotlib set_data()` method to update the graph with the new values. The *x* values for each plot are the numbers [0, ... maxLen], which you set using the `range()` method. The *y* values are populated from the updated deque object.

All of this code is enclosed in a try block, and if an exception occurs, the code jumps to pass at ❻, where you ignore the reading (pass doesn't do anything). (You use the try block because serial data can sometimes be corrupted by a loose contact in your circuit, for example, and you don't want your program to crash just because some bad values are sent via the serial port.)

When you're ready to exit, you close the serial port to release any system resources, as shown here:

```
# clean up
def close(self):
    # close serial
    self.ser.flush()
    self.ser.close()
```

In your `main()` method, you need to set up the `matplotlib` animation:

```
# set up animation
❶  fig = plt.figure()
❷  ax = plt.axes(xlim=(0, maxLen), ylim=(0, 1023))
❸  a0, = ax.plot([], [])
```

```
❹    a1, = ax.plot([], [])
❺    anim = animation.FuncAnimation(fig, analogPlot.update,
                                        fargs=(a0, a1), interval=20)

     # show plot
❻    plt.show()
```

At ❶, you get the `matplotlib` `Figure` module, which contains all the plot elements. You access the `Axes` module and set the *x* and *y* limits for the graph at ❷. The *x* limit is the number of samples, and the *y* limit is 1023 since that's the top of the range of the analog values.

At ❸ and ❹, you create two blank line objects (a0 and a1), which you pass to the animation class to set up the callback that supplies the coordinates for each line. Then, at ❺, set up the animation by passing in the `analogPlot` `update()` method to be called with each animation step. You also specify the arguments to call that method and the time interval in milliseconds to 20. At ❻, you call `plt.show()` to start the animation.

The `main()` method of your program is also where you use the `argparse` Python module to support command line options.

```
# create parser
parser = argparse.ArgumentParser(description="LDR serial")
# add expected arguments
parser.add_argument('--port', dest='port', required=True)
parser.add_argument('--N', dest='maxLen', required=False)

# parse args
args = parser.parse_args()

strPort = args.port

# plot parameters
maxLen = 100
if args.maxLen:
    maxLen = int(args.maxLen)
```

The `--port` argument is required. It tells the program the name of the serial port where the data is received (find this in the Arduino IDE under **Tools ▶ Serial Port**). The `maxLen` argument is optional and can be used to set the number of points to plot at a time. (The default is 100 samples.)

The Complete Python Code

Here is the complete Python code for this project. You can also download the complete code listing from *https://github.com/electronut/pp/tree/master/arduino-ldr/ldr.py*.

```
import serial, argparse
from collections import deque
```

```python
import matplotlib.pyplot as plt
import matplotlib.animation as animation


# plot class
class AnalogPlot:
    # constructor
    def __init__(self, strPort, maxLen):
        # open serial port
        self.ser = serial.Serial(strPort, 9600)

        self.a0Vals = deque([0.0]*maxLen)
        self.a1Vals = deque([0.0]*maxLen)
        self.maxLen = maxLen

    # add data
    def add(self, data):
        assert(len(data) == 2)
        self.addToDeq(self.a0Vals, data[0])
        self.addToDeq(self.a1Vals, data[1])

    # add to deque; pop oldest value
    def addToDeq(self, buf, val):
        buf.pop()
        buf.appendleft(val)

    # update plot
    def update(self, frameNum, a0, a1):
        try:
            line = self.ser.readline()
            data = [float(val) for val in line.split()]
            # print data
            if(len(data) == 2):
                self.add(data)
                a0.set_data(range(self.maxLen), self.a0Vals)
                a1.set_data(range(self.maxLen), self.a1Vals)
        except:
            pass

        return a0, a1

    # clean up
    def close(self):
        # close serial
        self.ser.flush()
        self.ser.close()

# main() function
def main():
    # create parser
    parser = argparse.ArgumentParser(description="LDR serial")
    # add expected arguments
    parser.add_argument('--port', dest='port', required=True)
    parser.add_argument('--N', dest='maxLen', required=False)
```

```
# parse args
args = parser.parse_args()

#strPort = '/dev/tty.usbserial-A7006Yqh'
strPort = args.port

print('reading from serial port %s...' % strPort)

# plot parameters
maxLen = 100
if args.maxLen:
    maxLen = int(args.maxLen)

# create plot object
analogPlot = AnalogPlot(strPort, maxLen)

print('plotting data...')

# set up animation
fig = plt.figure()
ax = plt.axes(xlim=(0, maxLen), ylim=(0, 1023))
a0, = ax.plot([], [])
a1, = ax.plot([], [])
anim = animation.FuncAnimation(fig, analogPlot.update,
                               fargs=(a0, a1), interval=20)

# show plot
plt.show()

# clean up
analogPlot.close()

print('exiting.')


# call main
if __name__ == '__main__':
    main()
```

Running the Program

To test the program, assemble the LDR circuit, connect the Arduino to your computer, upload the sketch, and then run the Python code.

```
$ python3 --port /dev/tty.usbmodem411 ldr.py
```

Figure 12-5 shows sample output of the program, specifically, a graph generated when the LDRs are exposed to light and then covered. As you can see in the graph, when the resistance of the LDRs changes, the analog voltage read in by the Arduino also changes. The peak in the center occurred when I quickly passed my hand over the LDRs, and the flat part at the right occurred when I passed my hand over more slowly.

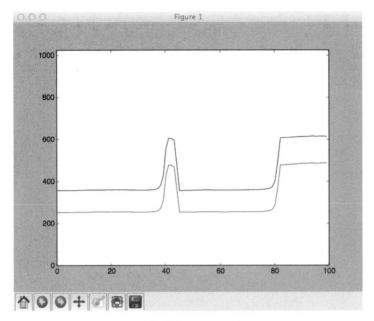

Figure 12-4: Sample run of the light-sensitive plotting program

The two LDRs have different resistance characteristics, which is why the lines don't coincide perfectly, but as you can see, they react to changes in light levels in the same way.

Summary

In this project, you were introduced to the world of microcontrollers and the Arduino platform. You learned Arduino programming syntax and how to upload a program to the Arduino. You also learned how to read analog values from an Arduino pin and create a simple LDR circuit. In addition, you learned how to send data from Arduino via the serial port and read it from the computer using Python. You also learned to visualize the data using a real-time scrolling graph and `matplotlib`.

Experiments!

Try these modifications to your Arduino project.

1. In your program, the graph scrolls from left to right; in other words, older values move to the right as new values come in from the left. Invert the scrolling direction so the graph moves from right to left.

2. The Arduino code reads analog values at regular intervals and sends them to the serial port. The incoming data could fluctuate in certain types of sensors, and applying some type of filtering to smooth out the data is common. Implement an averaging scheme for the LDR

data. (Hint: maintain a running average of *N* analog values read in for each LDR. The average value should be sent to the serial port at regular intervals. Decrease the delay() in the loop so it reads in values more quickly. Is the new graph of averages smoother than the original graph? Try different values for *N* and see what happens.)

3. You have two LDRs in your sensor circuit. Keeping these LDRs under a good source of light, sweep your hand over them. You should see a sharp change in the graphs—with one LDR plot line changing a little before the other one since it was obscured first. Can you use this information to detect the direction of movement of your hand? This is a basic gesture detection project. (Hint: the sharp change in the graph in the LDRs will happen at different times, telling you which LDR was obscured first and thus giving you the direction of hand movement.)

13

LASER AUDIO DISPLAY

In Chapter 12, you learned the basics of the Arduino, which is perfect for interfacing with low-level electronic devices. In this project, you'll leverage the Arduino to build hardware to produce interesting laser patterns from audio signals. This time, Python will do more of the heavy lifting. In addition to handling serial communications, it will perform computations based on real-time audio data and use that data to adjust the motors in a laser display rig.

For these purposes, think of a laser as an intense beam of light that remains focused in a tiny point, even when projected over a large distance. This focus is possible because the beam is organized so that its waves travel in one direction only and are in phase with each other. For this project, you'll use an inexpensive, easily obtainable laser pointer to create a laser pattern that changes in sync to music (or any audio input). You'll build hardware that creates interesting patterns using the laser pointer and two rotating mirrors attached to motors. You'll use the Arduino to set the direction and rotational speed of the motors, which you'll control with Python via the serial port. The Python program will read audio input, analyze it, and convert it to motor speed and direction data to control the motors. You'll also learn how to set the speed and direction of the motors to sync the patterns with music.

In this project, you will push your Arduino and Python knowledge further. Here are some of the topics we'll cover:

- Generating interesting patterns with a laser and two rotating mirrors
- Getting frequency information from a signal using fast Fourier transform
- Computing fast Fourier transform using numpy
- Reading audio data using pyaudio
- Setting up serial communications between a computer and an Arduino
- Driving motors with an Arduino

Generating Patterns with a Laser

To generate the laser patterns in this project, you'll use a laser pointer and two mirrors attached to the shafts of two small DC motors as shown in Figure 13-1. If you shine a laser at the surface of the flat mirror (mirror A), the reflection projected will remain a point, even if the motor is spinning. Because the plane of reflection of the laser is perpendicular to the spinning axis of the motor, it's as if the mirror is not rotating at all.

Now, say the mirror is attached at an angle to the shaft, as shown on the right in Figure 13-1 (mirror B). As the shaft rotates, the projected point will trace an ellipse, and if the motor is spinning fast enough, the viewer will perceive the moving dot as a continuous shape.

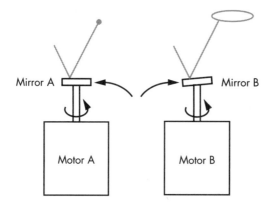

Figure 13-1: The flat mirror (mirror A) reflects a single dot. The reflection off the slanted mirror (mirror B) creates a circle as the motor spins.

What if you arrange the mirrors so that the point reflected off mirror A is projected onto mirror B? Now when motors A and B spin, the pattern created by the reflected point will be a combination of the two rotational movements of motors A and B, producing interesting patterns, as shown in Figure 13-2.

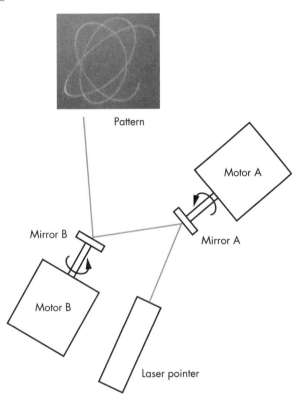

Figure 13-2: Reflecting laser light off two rotating, slanted mirrors produces interesting, complex patterns.

The exact patterns produced will depend on the speed and direction of rotation of the two motors, but they will be similar to the hypotrochoids produced by the Spirograph you explored in Chapter 2.

Motor Control

You'll use the Arduino to control the speed and direction of your motors. This setup requires some care to make sure it can take the relatively high voltage of the motors, because the Arduino can handle only so much current before it is damaged. You can protect the Arduino, simplify the design, and reduce development time by using the SparkFun TB6612FNG peripheral *breakout* board shown in Figure 13-3(a). Use the breakout board to control two motors simultaneously from an Arduino.

Figure 13-3: SparkFun Motor Driver 1A Dual TB6612FNG

Figure 13-3(b) shows the soldered backside of the breakout board. The
A and *B* in the pin names denote the two motors. The IN pins control the
direction of the motors, the 01 and 02 pins supply power to the motors, and
the PWM pins control the motor speeds. By writing to these pins, you can
control both the direction and speed of rotation for each motor, which is
exactly what you need for this project.

NOTE *You could replace this breakout part with any motor control circuit you're familiar
with, as long as you modify the Arduino sketch appropriately.*

The Fast Fourier Transform

Because the ultimate goal in this project is to control motor speeds based
on audio input, you need to be able to analyze the frequency of the audio.

Recall from Chapter 4 that tones from an acoustic instrument are a
mix of several frequencies or overtones. In fact, any sound can be decom-
posed into its constituent frequencies using Fourier transforms. When the
Fourier transform is applied to digital signals, the result is called the *discrete
Fourier transform (DFT)* because digital signals are comprised of many discrete
samples. In this project, you'll use Python to implement a *fast Fourier transform (FFT)* algorithm to compute the DFT. (Throughout this chapter I'll use
FFT to refer to both the algorithm and the result.)

Here is a simple example of an FFT. Figure 13-4 shows a signal that
combines just two sine waves, with the corresponding FFT below it. The
wave at the top can be expressed by the following equation, which sums
the two waves:

$$y(t) = 4\sin(2\pi 10 t) + 2.5\sin(2\pi 30 t)$$

Notice the 4 and 10 in the expression for the first wave—4 is the amplitude of the wave, and 10 is the frequency (in Hertz) of the wave. Meanwhile,
the second wave has an amplitude of 2.5 and a frequency of 30.

The FFT reveals the wave's component frequencies and their relative amplitude, showing peaks at 10 Hz and 30 Hz. The intensity of the first peak is about twice that of the second peak.

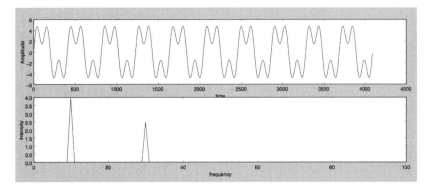

Figure 13-4: An audio signal captured from music (top) and its corresponding FFT (bottom)

Now let's look at a more complex example. Figure 13-5 shows an audio signal in the top frame and the corresponding FFT in the bottom frame.

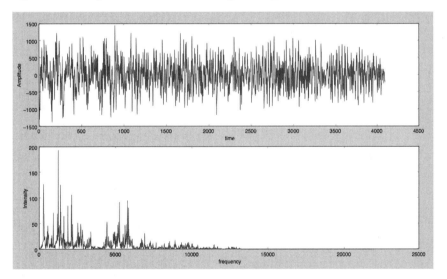

Figure 13-5: The FFT algorithm takes an amplitude signal (top) and computes its component frequencies (bottom).

The audio input, or *signal*, is in the *time domain* because the amplitude data varies with time. The FFT is in the *frequency domain*. Notice in the figure that the FFT displays a series of peaks showing the intensities of various frequencies in the signal.

To compute an FFT, you need a set of samples. The choice of the number of samples is a bit arbitrary, but a small sample size would not give you a good picture of the signal's frequency content and might also mean a higher computational load because you would need to compute more FFTs per second. On the other hand, a sample size that's too large would average out the changes in the signal, so you wouldn't be getting a "real-time" frequency response for the signal. For the sampling rate of 44100 Hz used for this project, a sample size of 2048 represents data for about 0.046 seconds.

For this project, you need to split the audio data into its constituent frequencies and use that information to control the motors. First, you'll split the range of frequencies (in Hz) into three bands: [0, 100], [100, 1000], and [1000, 2500]. You'll compute an average amplitude for each band, and each value will affect the motors and resulting laser pattern differently, as follows:

- Changes in the average amplitude of low frequencies will affect the speed of the first motor.
- Changes in the average amplitude of middle frequencies will affect the speed of the second motor.
- When high frequencies peak above a certain threshold, the first motor will change direction.

Requirements

Here's a list of the items you'll need to build this project:

- A small laser pointer
- Two DC motors like the ones used in a small toy (rated for 9V)
- Two small mirrors approximately 1 inch or less in diameter
- A SparkFun Motor Driver 1A Dual TB6612FNG
- An Arduino Uno or similar board
- Wire to make connections (single-core hookup wires with male pins on both sides work nicely)
- A four AA battery pack
- Some LEGO bricks to raise the motors and laser pointer off the mounting board so the mirrors can spin freely
- A rectangular sheet of cardboard or acrylic about 8 inches × 6 inches to mount the hardware
- A hot glue gun
- Soldering iron

Constructing the Laser Display

The first order of business is to attach the mirrors to the motors. The mirror has to be at a slight angle to the motor shaft. To attach the mirror, place it facedown on a flat surface and put a drop of hot glue in the center. Carefully dip the motor shaft in the glue, keeping it perpendicular to the mirror until the glue hardens (see Figure 13-6). To test it, spin the mirror with your hand while shining the laser pointer at it. You should find the reflection of the laser dot moves in an ellipse when projected on a flat surface. Do the same for the second mirror.

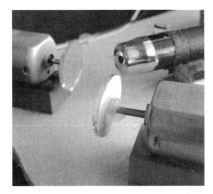

Figure 13-6: Attach the mirrors to each motor shaft at a slight angle.

Aligning the Mirrors

Next, align the laser pointer with the mirrors so that the laser reflects from mirror A to B, as shown in Figure 13-7. Be sure that the reflected laser light from mirror A stays within the circumference of mirror B for mirror A's entire range of rotation. (This will take some trial and error.) To test the arrangement, manually rotate mirror A. Also, be sure to position mirror B so that the light reflected from its surface will fall on a flat surface (like a wall) for the full range of rotation of both the mirrors.

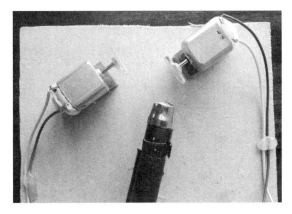

Figure 13-7: The alignment of the laser and the mirrors

NOTE *As you tweak things, you will need to keep the laser pointer on. If your laser pointer has an on button, tape it down to keep the laser pointer on. (Or see "Experiments!" on page 271 for a more elegant way to control the power of the laser pointer.)*

Once you're happy with the placement of the mirrors, hot glue the laser pointer and the two motors with attached mirrors onto three identical blocks to raise them up so that they'll be able to rotate freely. Next, place the blocks on the mounting board, and when you're happy with their arrangement, mark the location of each by tracing their edge with a pencil. Then glue the blocks onto the board.

Powering the Motors

If your motors did not come with wires attached to their terminals (most don't), solder wires to both terminals, being sure to leave sufficient wire (say 6 inches) so that you can attach the motors to the motor driver board. The motors are powered by four AA batteries in a battery pack, which you can hot glue to the back of the mounting board, as shown in Figure 13-8.

Figure 13-8: Glue the battery pack to the back of the mounting board.

Now test the hardware by spinning both mirrors with your hands as the laser shines on them. If you spin them fast enough, you should see some interesting patterns emerging in a glimpse of what's to come!

Wiring the Motor Driver

In this project, you'll use the Sparkfun Motor Driver (TB6612FNG) to control the motors with the Arduino. I won't go into the details of how this board works, but if you're curious, you can start by reading up on an *H bridge*, a common circuit design that uses *metal-oxide-semiconductor field-effect transistors (MOSFETs)* to control motors.

Now you'll connect the motors to the SparkFun motor driver and the Arduino. There are quite a few wires to connect, as listed in Table 13-1. Label one motor *A* and the other *B*, and keep to this convention when wiring them.

Table 13-1: SparkFun Motor Driver to Arduino Wiring

From	To
Arduino Digital Pin 12	TB6612FNG Pin BIN2
Arduino Digital Pin 11	TB6612FNG Pin BIN1
Arduino Digital Pin 10	TB6612FNG Pin STBY
Arduino Digital Pin 9	TB6612FNG Pin AIN1
Arduino Digital Pin 8	TB6612FNG Pin AIN2
Arduino Digital Pin 5	TB6612FNG Pin PWMB
Arduino Digital Pin 3	TB6612FNG Pin PWMA
Arduino 5V Pin	TB6612FNG Pin VCC
Arduino GND	TB6612FNG Pin GND
Arduino GND	Battery Pack GND (–)
Battery Pack VCC (+)	TB6612FNG Pin VM
Motor #1 Connector #1 (polarity doesn't matter)	TB6612FNG Pin A01
Motor #1 Connector #2 (polarity doesn't matter)	TB6612FNG Pin A02
Motor #2 Connector #1 (polarity doesn't matter)	TB6612FNG Pin B01
Motor #2 Connector #2 (polarity doesn't matter)	TB6612FNG Pin B02
Arduino USB connector	Computer's USB port

Figure 13-9 shows everything wired up.

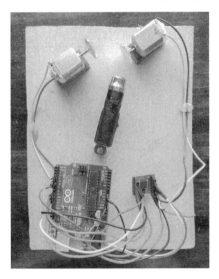

Figure 13-9: The completely wired laser display

Now let's work on the Arduino sketch.

The Arduino Sketch

You'll start the sketch by setting up the digital output pins of the Arduino. Then, in the main loop, you will read data coming in via the serial port and convert the data into parameters that need to be sent to the motor driver board. You'll also look at how to implement speed and direction control for the motors.

Configuring the Arduino's Digital Output Pins

First, map the Arduino's digital pins to the pins on the motor driver according to Table 13-1 and set the pins as outputs.

```
// motor A connected to A01 and A02
// motor B connected to B01 and B02

❶ int STBY = 10; //standby

// Motor A
int PWMA = 3;  //speed control
int AIN1 = 9;  //direction
int AIN2 = 8;  //direction

// Motor B
int PWMB = 5;  //speed control
int BIN1 = 11; //direction
❷ int BIN2 = 12; //direction

void setup(){

❸     pinMode(STBY, OUTPUT);

       pinMode(PWMA, OUTPUT);
       pinMode(AIN1, OUTPUT);
       pinMode(AIN2, OUTPUT);

       pinMode(PWMB, OUTPUT);
       pinMode(BIN1, OUTPUT);
       pinMode(BIN2, OUTPUT);

       // initialize serial communication
❹     Serial.begin(9600);
}
```

From ❶ to ❷, you map the names of the Arduino pins to the motor driver pins. For example, PWMA (Pulse With Modulation A) controls the speed of motor A and is assigned to Arduino pin 3. PWM is a way to power a device by sending digital pulses that switch on and off quickly such that the device "sees" a continuous voltage. The fraction of time that the digital pulse is on is called the *duty cycle* and is expressed as a percentage. By changing this percentage, you can provide varying power levels to a device. PWM is often used to control dimmable LEDs and motor speeds.

Then, you call the setup() method at ❸, and in the lines that follow, you set all seven digital pins as output. At ❹, you start serial communication, reading in serial data sent by the computer on the Arduino.

The Main Loop

The main loop in the sketch waits for serial data to arrive, parses it to extract the motor speed and direction, and uses that information to set the digital outputs for the driver board that controls the motors.

```
// main loop that reads the motor data sent by laser.py
void loop()
{
    // data sent is of the form 'H' (header), speed1, dir1, speed2, dir2
❶  if (Serial.available() >= 5) {
❷      if(Serial.read() == 'H') {
            // read the next 4 bytes
❸          byte s1 = Serial.read();
            byte d1 = Serial.read();
            byte s2 = Serial.read();
            byte d2 = Serial.read();

            // stop the motor if both speeds are 0
❹          if(s1 == 0 && s2 == 0) {
                stop();
            }
            else {
                // set the motors' speed and direction
❺              move(0, s1, d1);
                move(1, s2, d2);
            }
            // slight pause for 20 ms
❻          delay(20);
        }
        else {
            // if there is invalid data, stop the motors
❼          stop();
        }
    }
    else {
        // if there is no data, pause for 250 ms
❽      delay(250);
    }
}
```

The motor control data is sent as a set of 5 bytes: H followed by 4 single-byte numbers, s1, d1, s2, and d2, which represent the speed and direction of the motors. Since serial data comes in continuously, at ❶, you check to ensure that you have received at least 5 bytes. If not, you delay for 250 milliseconds ❽ and try to read the data again in the next cycle.

At ❷, you check that the first byte you read in is an H to ensure that you're at the beginning of a proper set of control data and that the next

4 bytes are what you expect them to be. If not, you stop the motors at ❼ because the data may have been corrupted by transmission or connection errors.

Beginning at ❸, the sketch reads the speed and direction data for the two motors. If both motor speeds are set to zero, stop the motors ❹. If not, the speed and direction values are assigned to the motors at ❺, using the move() method. At ❻, you add a small delay in data reading to allow the motors to keep up and to make sure you're not reading in data too fast.

Here is the move() method used to set the speed and direction of the motors:

```
    // set motor speed and direction
    // motor: A -> 1, B -> 0
    // direction: 1/0
    void move(int motor, int speed, int direction)
    {
        // disable standby
❶      digitalWrite(STBY, HIGH);

❷      boolean inPin1 = LOW;
        boolean inPin2 = HIGH;

❸      if(direction == 1){
            inPin1 = HIGH;
            inPin2 = LOW;
        }

        if(motor == 1){
❹          digitalWrite(AIN1, inPin1);
            digitalWrite(AIN2, inPin2);
            analogWrite(PWMA, speed);
        }
        else{
❺          digitalWrite(BIN1, inPin1);
            digitalWrite(BIN2, inPin2);
            analogWrite(PWMB, speed);
        }
    }
```

The motor driver has a standby mode to save power when the motors are off. You leave standby by writing HIGH to the standby pin at ❶. At ❷, you define two Boolean variables, which determine the direction of rotation of the motors. At ❸, if the direction argument is set to 1, you flip the values of these variables, which allows you to switch the motor's direction in the code that follows.

You set the pins AIN1, AIN2, and PWMA for motor A at ❹. Pins AIN1 and AIN1 control the motor's direction, and you use the Arduino digitalWrite() method to set one pin to HIGH (1) and one to LOW (0) as needed. In the case of pin PWMA, you send the PWM signal, which allows you to control the motor's speed, as described earlier. To control the value of the PWM, you use the analogWrite() method to write a value in the range [0, 255] to an Arduino output pin. (In contrast, the digitalWrite() method only lets you write either a 1 or 0 to the output pin.)

At ❺, you set the pins for motor B.

Stopping the Motors

To stop the motors, you write a LOW to the standby pin of the motor driver.

```
void stop(){
    //enable standby
    digitalWrite(STBY, LOW);
}
```

The Python Code

Now let's look at the Python code running on the computer. This code does the heavy lifting: it reads in audio, computes the FFT, and sends serial data to the Arduino. You can find the complete project code in "The Complete Python Code" on page 267.

Selecting the Audio Device

First, you need to read in the audio data with the help of the pyaudio module. Initialize the pyaudio module like this:

```
p = pyaudio.PyAudio()
```

Next, you access the computer's audio input device using the helper functions in pyaudio, as shown in the code for the getInputDevice() method:

```
    # get pyaudio input device
    def getInputDevice(p):
❶       index = None
❷       nDevices = p.get_device_count()
        print('Found %d devices. Select input device:' % nDevices)
        # print all devices found
        for i in range(nDevices):
❸           deviceInfo = p.get_device_info_by_index(i)
❹           devName = deviceInfo['name']
❺           print("%d: %s" % (i, devName))
        # get user selection
        try:
            # convert to integer
❻           index = int(input())
        except:
            pass

        # print the name of the chosen device
        if index is not None:
            devName = p.get_device_info_by_index(index)["name"]
```

```
                print("Input device chosen: %s" % devName)
❼        return index
```

At ❶, you set an index variable to None. (This index is the return value
for the function at ❼, and if it is returned as None, you know that no suitable input device was found.) At ❷, you use the get_device_count() method
to get the number of audio devices on the computer, including any audio
hardware such as microphones, line inputs, or line outputs. You then iterate
through all found devices, getting information about each.

The get_device_info_by_index() function at ❸ returns a dictionary
containing information about various features of each audio device, but
you're interested only in the name of the device because you're looking for
an input device. You store the device name at ❹, and at ❺, you print out the
index and name of the device. At ❻, you use the input() method to read the
selection from the user, converting the string read in to an integer index.
At ❼, this selected index is returned from the function.

Reading Data from the Input Device

Once you have selected the input device, you need to read data from it. To
do so, you first open the audio stream, as shown here. (Note that all the
code runs continuously in a while loop.)

```
        # set FFT sample length
❶    fftLen = 2**11
        # set sample rate
❷    sampleRate = 44100

        print('opening stream...')
❸    stream = p.open(format = pyaudio.paInt16,
                        channels = 1,
                        rate = sampleRate,
                        input = True,
                        frames_per_buffer = fftLen,
                        input_device_index = inputIndex)
```

At ❶, you set the length of the FFT buffer—the number of audio samples
you will use to compute the FFT—to 2048 (which is 2^{11}; FFT algorithms are
optimized for powers of 2). Then, you set the sampling rate for pyaudio to
44100 or 44.1 kHz ❷, which is standard for CD-quality recordings.

Next, you open the pyaudio stream ❸ and specify several options:

- pyaudio.paInt16 indicates that you're reading in the data as 16-bit
  integers.
- channels is set to 1 because you're reading the audio as a single channel.
- rate is set to the chosen sample rate of 44100 Hz.
- input is set to True.

- `frames_per_buffer` is set to the FFT buffer length.

- `input_device_index` is set to the device you chose in the `getInputDevice()` method.

Computing the FFT of the Data Stream

Here is the code you use to read data from the stream:

```
                # read a chunk of data
❶               data    = stream.read(fftLen)
                # convert the data to a numpy array
❷               dataArray = numpy.frombuffer(data, dtype=numpy.int16)
```

At ❶, you read the most recent `fftLen` samples from the audio input stream. Then you convert this data into a 16-bit integer numpy array at ❷. Now you compute the FFT of this data.

```
                # get FFT of data
❶               fftVals = numpy.fft.rfft(dataArray)*2.0/fftLen
                # get absolute values of complex numbers
❷               fftVals = numpy.abs(fftVals)
```

At ❶, you compute the FFT of the values in the numpy array, using the `rfft()` method from the numpy `fft` module. This method takes a signal composed of *real* numbers (like the audio data) and computes the FFT, which generally results in a set of *complex numbers*. The `2.0/fftLen` is a normalization factor you use to map the FFT values to the expected range. Then, because the `rfft()` method returns complex numbers, you use the numpy `abs()` method ❷ to get the magnitudes of these complex numbers, which are real.

Extracting Frequency Information from the FFT Values

Next, you extract the relevant frequency information from the FFT values.

```
                # average 3 frequency bands: 0-100 Hz, 100-1000 Hz, and 1000-2500 Hz
                levels = [numpy.sum(fftVals[0:100])/100,
                          numpy.sum(fftVals[100:1000])/900,
                          numpy.sum(fftVals[1000:2500])/1500]
```

To analyze the audio signal, you split the frequency range into three bands: 0 to 100 Hz, 100 to 1000 Hz, and 1000 to 2500 Hz. You are most interested in the lower, bass band (0–100 Hz) and the midrange (100–1000 Hz) frequencies, which roughly correspond to the beat and the vocals in a song, respectively. For each range, you compute the average FFT value using the `numpy.sum()` method in the code.

Converting Frequency to Motor Speed and Direction

Now convert this frequency information to motor speeds and directions.

```
                # 'H' (header), speed1, dir1, speed2, dir2
❶               vals = [ord('H'), 100, 1, 100, 1]
                # speed1
❷               vals[1] = int(5*levels[0]) % 255
                # speed2
❸               vals[3] = int(100 + levels[1]) % 255

                # dir
                d1 = 0
❹               if levels[2] > 0.1:
                    d1 = 1
                vals[2] = d1
❺               vals[4] = 0
```

At ❶, you initialize a list of motor speeds and direction values to be sent to the Arduino (the 5 bytes, starting with H discussed earlier). Use the built-in ord() function to convert the string to an integer and then fill in this list by converting the average values for the three frequency bands into motor speeds and directions.

NOTE   *This part is a hack, really—there's no particularly elegant rule governing these conversions. These values change constantly with the audio signal, and any method you come up with will change the motor speeds and affect the laser pattern along with the music. Just make sure your conversion puts the motor speeds in the [0, 255] range and that the directions are always set to 1 or 0. The method I chose was simply based on trial and error; I looked at FFT values while playing various types of music.*

At ❷, you take the value from the lowest frequency range, scale it by a factor of five, convert it to an integer, and use the modulus operator (%) to ensure that the value lies within the [0, 255] range. This value controls the speed of the first motor. At ❸, you add 100 to the middle frequency value and place it in the [0, 255] range. This value controls the speed of the second motor.

Then, at ❹, you switch the motor A direction whenever the value from the highest frequency range crosses the threshold of 0.1. The motor B direction is kept at a constant 0 ❺. (I found through trial and error that these methods produce a nice variation of patterns, but I encourage you to play with these values and create your own conversions. There are no wrong answers here.)

Testing the Motor Setup

Before testing the hardware with a live audio stream, let's check the motor setup. The function autoTest(), shown here, does just that:

```
# automatic test for sending motor speeds
def autoTest(ser):
    print('starting automatic test...')
    try:
        while True:
```

```
                  # for each direction combination
❶             for dr in [(0, 0), (1, 0), (0, 1), (1, 1)]:
                      # for a range of speeds
❷                 for j in range(25, 180, 10):
❸                     for i in range(25, 180, 10):
❹                         vals = [ord('H'), i, dr[0], j, dr[1]]
❺                         print(vals[1:])
❻                         data = struct.pack('BBBBB', *vals)
❼                         ser.write(data)
                          sleep(0.1)
          except KeyboardInterrupt:
              print('exiting...')
              # shut off motors
❽         vals = [ord('H'), 0, 1, 0, 1]
          data = struct.pack('BBBBB', *vals)
          ser.write(data)
          ser.close()
```

This method takes the two motors through a range of motions by varying the speed and direction of each. Because the direction can be clockwise
or counterclockwise for each motor, four such combinations are represented
in the outer loop at ❶. For each combination, the loops at ❷ and ❸ run the
motors at various speeds.

NOTE   *I'm using range(25, 180, 10), which means the speed varies from 25 to 180 in steps
of 10. I am not using the full range of motion of the motor [0, 255] here because the
motors barely turn below a speed of 25 and they spin really fast above 200.*

At ❹, you generate the 5-byte motor data values, and at ❺, you print
their direction and speed values. (The use of Python string splicing vals[1:]
will get all but the first element in the list.)

Pack the motor data into a byte array at ❻, and write it to the serial
port at ❼. Pressing CTRL-C interrupts this test, and at ❽, you handle this
exception by cleaning up, stopping the motors, and closing the serial port
like the responsible programmer you are.

Command Line Options

As with previous projects, you use the argparse module to parse command
line arguments for the program.

```
# main method
def main():
    # parse arguments
    parser = argparse.ArgumentParser(description='Analyzes audio input and
sends motor control information via serial port')
    # add arguments
    parser.add_argument('--port', dest='serial_port_name', required=True)
    parser.add_argument('--mtest', action='store_true', default=False)
    parser.add_argument('--atest', action='store_true', default=False)
    args = parser.parse_args()
```

In this code, the serial port is a required command line option. There are also two optional command line options: one for an automatic test (covered earlier) and another for a manual test (which I'll discuss shortly).

Here is what happens once the command line options are parsed in the main() method:

```
        # open serial port
        strPort = args.serial_port_name
        print('opening ', strPort)
❶       ser = serial.Serial(strPort, 9600)
        if args.mtest:
            manualTest(ser)
        elif args.atest:
            autoTest(ser)
        else:
❷            fftLive(ser)
```

At ❶, you use pySerial to open a serial port with the string passed in to the program. The speed of serial communications, or the baud rate, is set at 9,600 bits per second. If no other command arguments (--atest or --mtest) are used, you proceed at ❷ to the audio processing and FFT computation, encapsulated in the fftLive() method.

Manual Testing

This manual test lets you enter specific motor directions and speeds so that you can see their effects on the laser pattern.

```
    # manual test of motor direction and speeds
    def manualTest(ser):
        print('starting manual test...')
        try:
            while True:
                print('enter motor control info such as < 100 1 120 0 >')
❶                strIn = raw_input()
❷                vals = [int(val) for val in strIn.split()[:4]]
❸                vals.insert(0, ord('H'))
❹                data = struct.pack('BBBBB', *vals)
❺                ser.write(data)
        except:
            print('exiting...')
            # shut off the motors
❻            vals = [ord('H'), 0, 1, 0, 1]
            data = struct.pack('BBBBB', *vals)
            ser.write(data)
            ser.close()
```

At ❶, you use the raw_input() method to wait until the user enters a value at the command prompt. The expected entry is in the form 100 1 120 0, representing the speed and direction of motor A followed by that of motor B. Parse the string into a list of integers at ❷. At ❸, you insert an 'H' to complete the motor data, and at ❹ and ❺, you pack this data and send it through the serial port in the expected format. When the user interrupts the test using CTRL-C (or if any exception occurs), you clean up at ❻ by shutting down the motors and the serial port gracefully.

The Complete Python Code

Here is the complete Python code for this project. You'll can also find this at *https://github.com/electronut/pp/tree/master/arduino-laser/laser.py*.

```python
import sys, serial, struct
import pyaudio
import numpy
import math
from time import sleep
import argparse

# manual test of motor direction speeds
def manualTest(ser):
    print('staring manual test...')
    try:
        while True:
            print('enter motor control info: eg. < 100 1 120 0 >')
            strIn = raw_input()
            vals = [int(val) for val in strIn.split()[:4]]
            vals.insert(0, ord('H'))
            data = struct.pack('BBBBB', *vals)
            ser.write(data)
    except:
        print('exiting...')
        # shut off motors
        vals = [ord('H'), 0, 1, 0, 1]
        data = struct.pack('BBBBB', *vals)
        ser.write(data)
        ser.close()

# automatic test for sending motor speeds
def autoTest(ser):
    print('staring automatic test...')
    try:
        while True:
            # for each direction combination
            for dr in [(0, 0), (1, 0), (0, 1), (1, 1)]:
                # for a range of speeds
                for j in range(25, 180, 10):
                    for i in range(25, 180, 10):
                        vals = [ord('H'), i, dr[0], j, dr[1]]
                        print(vals[1:])
                        data = struct.pack('BBBBB', *vals)
                        ser.write(data)
                        sleep(0.1)
    except KeyboardInterrupt:
        print('exiting...')
```

```
        # shut off motors
        vals = [ord('H'), 0, 1, 0, 1]
        data = struct.pack('BBBBB', *vals)
        ser.write(data)
        ser.close()

# get pyaudio input device
def getInputDevice(p):
    index = None
    nDevices = p.get_device_count()
    print('Found %d devices. Select input device:' % nDevices)
    # print all devices found
    for i in range(nDevices):
        deviceInfo = p.get_device_info_by_index(i)
        devName = deviceInfo['name']
        print("%d: %s" % (i, devName))
    # get user selection
    try:
        # convert to integer
        index = int(input())
    except:
        pass

    # print the name of the chosen device
    if index is not None:
        devName = p.get_device_info_by_index(index)["name"]
        print("Input device chosen: %s" % devName)
    return index

# FFT of live audio
def fftLive(ser):
    # initialize pyaudio
    p = pyaudio.PyAudio()

    # get pyAudio input device index
    inputIndex = getInputDevice(p)

    # set FFT sample length
    fftLen = 2**11
    # set sample rate
    sampleRate = 44100

    print('opening stream...')
    stream = p.open(format = pyaudio.paInt16,
                    channels = 1,
                    rate = sampleRate,
                    input = True,
                    frames_per_buffer = fftLen,
                    input_device_index = inputIndex)
    try:
        while True:
            # read a chunk of data
            data  = stream.read(fftLen)
            # convert to numpy array
            dataArray = numpy.frombuffer(data, dtype=numpy.int16)
```

```python
            # get FFT of data
            fftVals = numpy.fft.rfft(dataArray)*2.0/fftLen
            # get absolute values of complex numbers
            fftVals = numpy.abs(fftVals)
            # average 3 frequency bands: 0-100 Hz, 100-1000 Hz and 1000-2500 Hz
            levels = [numpy.sum(fftVals[0:100])/100,
                        numpy.sum(fftVals[100:1000])/900,
                        numpy.sum(fftVals[1000:2500])/1500]

            # the data sent is of the form:
            # 'H' (header), speed1, dir1, speed2, dir2
            vals = [ord('H'), 100, 1, 100, 1]

            # speed1
            vals[1] = int(5*levels[0]) % 255
            # speed2
            vals[3] = int(100 + levels[1]) % 255

            # dir
            d1 = 0
            if levels[2] > 0.1:
                d1 = 1
            vals[2] = d1
            vals[4] = 0

            # pack data
            data = struct.pack('BBBBB', *vals)
            # write data to serial port
            ser.write(data)
            # a slight pause
            sleep(0.001)
    except KeyboardInterrupt:
        print('stopping...')
    finally:
        print('cleaning up')
        stream.close()
        p.terminate()
        # shut off motors
        vals = [ord('H'), 0, 1, 0, 1]
        data = struct.pack('BBBBB', *vals)
        ser.write(data)
        # close serial
        ser.flush()
        ser.close()

# main method
def main():
    # parse arguments
    parser = argparse.ArgumentParser(description='Analyzes audio input and
sends motor control information via serial port')
    # add arguments
    parser.add_argument('--port', dest='serial_port_name', required=True)
    parser.add_argument('--mtest', action='store_true', default=False)
    parser.add_argument('--atest', action='store_true', default=False)
```

```
args = parser.parse_args()

# open serial port
strPort = args.serial_port_name
print('opening ', strPort)
ser = serial.Serial(strPort, 9600)
if args.mtest:
    manualTest(ser)
elif args.atest:
    autoTest(ser)
else:
    fftLive(ser)

# call main function
if __name__ == '__main__':
    main()
```

Running the Program

To test the project, assemble the hardware, connect the Arduino to the computer, and upload the motor driver code into the Arduino. Make sure the battery pack is connected and that your laser pointer is on and projecting on a flat surface like a wall. I recommend testing the laser display part first by running the following program. (Don't forget to change the serial port string to match your computer!)

```
$ python3 laser.py --port /dev/tty.usbmodem411 --atest
('opening ', '/dev/tty.usbmodem1411')
staring automatic test...
[25, 0, 25, 0]
[35, 0, 25, 0]
[45, 0, 25, 0]
...
```

This test runs both motors through various combinations of speeds and direction. You should see different laser patterns projected onto your wall. To stop the program and the motors, press CTRL-C.

If the test succeeds, you're ready to move on to the real show. Start playing your favorite music on your computer and run the program as follows. (Again, watch that serial port string!)

```
$ python3 laser.py --port /dev/tty.usbmodem411
('opening ', '/dev/tty.usbmodem1411') Found 4 devices. Select input device: 0:
Built-in Microph
1: Built-in Output
2: BoomDevice
3: AirParrot
0
Input device chosen: Built-in Microph
opening stream...
```

You should see the laser display produce lots of interesting patterns that change in time with the music, as shown in Figure 13-10.

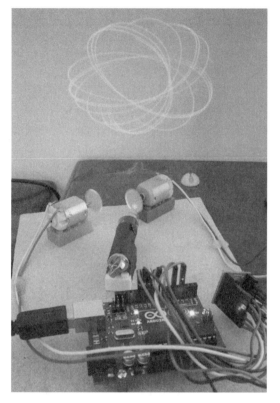

Figure 13-10: The complete wiring of the laser display and a pattern projected on the wall

Summary

In this chapter, you upped your Python and Arduino skills by building a more complex project. You learned how to control motors with Python and Arduino, and used numpy to get the FFT of audio data, serial communications, and even lasers!

Experiments!

Here are some ways you can modify this project:

1. The program used an arbitrary scheme to convert the FFT values into motor speed and direction data. Try changing this scheme. For example, experiment with different frequency bands and criteria for changing motor directions.

2. In this project, you converted frequency information gathered from the audio signal to motor speed and direction. Try making the motors move according to the overall "pulse" or volume of the music. For this, you can compute the *root mean square (RMS)* value of the amplitude of the signal. This computation is similar to the FFT calculation. Once you read in a chunk of audio data and put it into a numpy array x, you can compute the RMS value as follows:

```
rms = numpy.sqrt(numpy.mean(x**2))
```

Also, remember that the amplitude in your project was expressed as a 16-bit signed integer, which can have a maximum value of 32,768 (a useful number to keep in mind for normalization). Use this RMS amplitude in conjunction with the FFT to generate a greater variation of laser patterns.

3. In the project, you rather crudely used some tape to keep the laser pointer on to test and run your hardware setup. Can you find a better way to control the laser? Read up about optoisolators and relays,[1] which are devices you can use to switch external circuits on and off. To use these, you first need to hack your laser pointer so it can be toggled by an external switch. One way to do so is to glue the button of the laser pointer to the ON position permanently, remove the batteries, and solder two leads onto the battery contacts. Now you can switch the laser pointer on and off manually using these wires and the laser pointer's batteries. Next, replace this scheme with a digital switch by wiring the laser pointer through a relay or optoisolator and switching it on using a digital pin on your Arduino. If you use an optoisolator, you can toggle the laser on and off directly with the Arduino. If you're using a relay, you will also need a driver, usually in the form of a simple transistor-based circuit.

Once you have this set up, add some code so that when the Python program runs, a serial command is sent to the Arduino to switch on the laser pointer before the show starts.

---

1. "Relays and Optoisolators," What-When-How, *http://what-when-how.com/8051-microcontroller/ relays-and-optoisolators/*.

14

A RASPBERRY PI–BASED WEATHER MONITOR

When you find that you need more computational power or support for peripherals such as USB or *high-definition multimedia interface (HDMI)* video, you leave the realm of microcontrollers like the Arduino and enter the computer realm. The Raspberry Pi is a tiny computer that can perform high-level tasks such as these quite well, especially when compared to the Arduino.

Like the Arduino, the Raspberry Pi is used in numerous interesting projects. Although it can fit in the palm of your hand, it's a full computer (you can connect a monitor and keyboard to it), which has made it popular among educators and makers.

In this chapter, you'll use the Raspberry Pi together with a temperature and humidity sensor (DHT11) to build a web-based temperature- and humidity-monitoring system. The code you run on the Pi will start the Bottle web server, which will listen for incoming connections. When you access the Pi's Internet Protocol (IP) address on the local network, the

Bottle server should serve a web page containing a chart of the weather data. The handler on the Pi will communicate with the DHT11 sensor, retrieve data, and return it to the client, which will use the flot library to plot the sensor data in the browser. You'll also provide web-based control for a light-emitting diode (LED) attached to the Raspberry Pi. (This is just to demonstrate how you can control external devices via the Web using the Pi.)

NOTE *We'll use Python 2.7 in this project. The Raspbian OS on the Raspberry Pi comes with Python 2.7 (run as python on shell) and Python 3 (run as python3 on shell) installed. The code, as written, is compatible with both.*

The Hardware

Like any laptop or desktop computer sold today, a Pi has a central processing unit (CPU), random access memory (RAM), USB ports, video output, audio output, and network connectivity. But unlike most computers, the Pi is cheap: about $35. In addition, the Pi can easily interface with external hardware, thanks to its onboard general-purpose input/output (GPIO) pins, making it ideal for all kinds of embedded hardware projects. You'll connect it up with a DHT11 temperature and humidity sensor to monitor your environment.

The DHT11 Temperature and Humidity Sensor

The DHT11 (see Figure 14-1) is a popular sensor that measures temperature and humidity. It has four pins—VDD (+), GND (−), DATA, and a fourth that is not used. The DATA pin connects to a microcontroller (in this case, a Raspberry Pi), and both input and output run through this pin. You'll use the Adafruit Python library Adafruit_Python_DHT to communicate with a DHT11 to retrieve temperature and humidity data.

Figure 14-1: The DHT11 temperature and humidity sensor

The Raspberry Pi

As I write this, three models of Raspberry Pi are available: the Raspberry Pi 1 Model A+, the Raspberry Pi 1 Model B+, and the Raspberry Pi 2 Model B. For this project, I used an older Raspberry Pi Model B Rev 2, but the pin numbers used in this project are compatible across all models, and the code will work on any of the models without changes.

Figure 14-2 shows a Raspberry Pi Model B computer that has two USB ports, an HDMI connector, a composite video output jack, an audio output jack, a micro USB port for power supply, an Ethernet port, and 26 GPIO pins arranged as two columns of 13 pins each. It also has an SD card slot on the bottom side of the board (not shown). The Raspberry Pi uses a Broadcom BCM2835 chip, which has an ARM CPU that runs at 700 MHz and consumes very little power. (This explains why the Pi doesn't need any giant heat sinks to cool it down, like a desktop computer does). Model B also has 512MB of SDRAM. Most of these details are not important for this project, but they might come in handy if you want to impress folks with all the specs of your latest pocket computer.

Figure 14-2: The Raspberry Pi Model B

Setting Up Your Pi

Unlike the Arduino, you can't just plug the Raspberry Pi in to your computer and start coding. As a full-fledged computer, the Pi needs an operating system and a few peripherals. At a minimum, I suggest the peripherals shown in Figure 14-3.

- An 8GB or higher-capacity SD card with a suitable operating system
- A Pi-compatible USB Wi-Fi adapter
- A Pi-compatible power supply (The official recommendation is to use a 5V 1200 mA supply, or a 5V 2500 mA supply if you need to use all the USB ports.)
- A case to protect your precious Pi
- A keyboard and mouse (Consider a wireless combination that takes up only a single USB port for convenience.)
- A composite video cable or an HDMI cable (See Appendix C for more on using an HDMI cable with the Pi.)

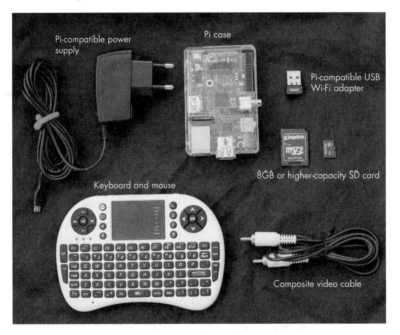

Figure 14-3: Recommended set of Raspberry Pi peripherals

NOTE *Be sure to check the list of peripherals known to work with the Pi at* http://elinux .org/RPI_VerifiedPeripherals *before purchasing.*

Installing and Configuring Software

Now it's time to set up your Raspberry Pi and get it ready for Python. I'll cover the required steps briefly in the following section, but you should watch the setup videos available at the Raspberry Pi Foundation's "Getting Started with NOOBS" page (*http://www.raspberrypi.org/help/noobs-setup/*) before installing.

The Operating System

Your Pi's operating system and files will reside on an external SD card. Although you have your choice of several operating systems, I suggest installing Raspbian. The operating system needs to be installed in a particular way, and rather than bore you here with the details (which may well change), I'll ask you to take a look at "RPi Easy SD Card Setup" on the Linux wiki at *http://elinux.org/RPi_Easy_SD_Card_Setup* or the "Using NOOBS" instructions at the same link, which is a bit more beginner-friendly.

Initial Configuration

Once you've installed your operating system, it's time for the first boot. Plug in your formatted SD card, hook up a composite video cable to a TV or monitor, attach the keyboard and mouse, and connect the Pi to the power supply. When the Pi boots, a program called `raspi-config` should start, and you should see various configuration options. (You'll find documentation for `raspi-config` at the Raspberry Pi Foundation's website: *https://www.raspberrypi.org/documentation/configuration/raspi-config.md*). Modify the configuration as follows:

1. Select **Expand Filesystem** to make use of the full SD card.
2. Select **Enable Boot to Desktop/Scratch** and then select **Desktop**.
3. Select **Change Time Zone** and set your time zone under Internationalization Options.
4. Go to Advanced Options and enable **Overscan**.
5. Go to SSH and enable remote command line access in the Advanced Options menu by choosing the **Enable or Disable SSH Server** option.

    Now select **Finish**; the Pi should reboot and display a desktop.

Wi-Fi Setup

You'll connect your Pi wirelessly in this project. Assuming that you installed a compatible Wi-Fi adapter (after consulting the *http://elinux.org/* site), Raspbian should automatically recognize the adapter when you plug it in. Assuming that all goes well, you'll set up a static IP address by editing the network configuration file using the built-in Nano editor. (Nano has a bare-bones UI, which can take some getting used to. The most important thing to remember is to press CTRL-X and enter **Yes** to save your file and exit.)

You'll run the commands in a terminal. Open LXTerminal (it should be installed with Raspbian) and enter the following:

```
$ sudo nano /etc/network/interfaces
```

This command opens the *interfaces* file, which you'll use to configure the network settings, as shown here:

```
auto lo

iface lo inet loopback
iface eth0 inet dhcp

allow-hotplug wlan0
iface wlan0 inet manual
wpa-roam /etc/wpa_supplicant/wpa_supplicant.conf
iface default inet static
address 192.x.x.x
netmask 255.255.255.0
gateway 192.x.x.x
```

Add or modify the address, netmask, and gateway lines at the end of the file to suit your local network. Enter the netmask for your network (likely 255.255.255.0), enter your network's gateway (run **ipconfig** on Linux from a Linux terminal; press WINDOWS and R keys and then run **ipconfig /all** on Windows; or choose **System Preferences ▸ Network** on OS X, and give your Pi a static network IP address that's different from that of any other devices on your network.

Now connect the Pi to your Wi-Fi network using the WiFi Config utility; you should see a shortcut for it on the desktop. (If you get stuck, try the Adafruit tutorials at *https://learn.adafruit.com/*. If all goes well, your Pi should connect to the Internet with the built-in browser Midori.)

Setting Up the Programming Environment

Next you'll install your development environment, including the RPi.GPIO package needed to talk to external hardware, the Bottle web framework, and the tools needed to install other Python packages on your Raspberry Pi. Make sure you're connected to the Internet and run these commands in a terminal, one at a time:

```
$ sudo apt-get update
$ sudo apt-get install python-setuptools
$ sudo apt-get install python-dev
$ sudo apt-get install python-rpi.gpio
$ sudo easy_install bottle
```

Now, download the latest version of the `flot` JavaScript plotting library from *http://www.flotcharts.org/*, expand it to create the *flot* directory, and copy this directory into the same folder as your program.

```
$ wget http://www.flotcharts.org/downloads/flot-x.zip
$ unzip flot-x.zip
$ mv flot myProjectDir/
```

Next, install the `Adafruit_Python_DHT` library (*https://github.com/adafruit/ Adafruit_Python_DHT/*), which you'll use to retrieve data from the DHT11 sensor attached to your Pi, by running these commands in a terminal:

```
$ git clone https://github.com/adafruit/Adafruit_Python_DHT.git
$ cd Adafruit_Python_DHT
$ sudo python setup.py install
```

The Raspberry Pi should now be set up with all the software you need to build your weather monitor.

Connecting via SSH

Rather than connect your Pi to a monitor and control it using a connected mouse and keyboard, it's much easier to work with the Pi by logging in to it from a desktop or laptop. Linux and OS X have built-in support for this sort of thing, in the form of Secure Shell (SSH). If you're using Windows, install PuTTY to connect to the Pi.

The following listing shows a typical SSH session:

```
❶ moksha:~ mahesh$ ssh pi@192.168.4.32
❷ pi@192.168.4.32's password:
❸ pi@raspberrypi ~ $ whoami
  pi
  pi@raspberrypi ~ $
```

In this session, at ❶, I've logged in to the Pi from my computer by entering the `ssh` command, the Pi's default username (*pi*), and its IP address as ssh *username@ip_address*. When you enter ssh ❷, you should be prompted for a password. The default is *raspberry*.

Once you think you've logged in to the Pi, make sure by entering the `whoami` command ❸. If the response is `pi` as shown earlier, you have logged in properly.

NOTE *It's a good idea to change your Pi's username and password to make it more secure. For more hints on working remotely with the Raspberry Pi, see Appendix C.*

The Bottle Web Framework

To monitor and control the Pi via a web interface, you'll need to have it run a web server. You'll use Bottle, a Python web framework with a simple interface. (In fact, the entire library consists of a single source file named *bottle.py*.) Here's the code needed to serve a simple web page using Bottle:

```python
from bottle import route, run

@route('/hello')
def hello():
    return "Hello Bottle World!"

run(host='192.168.x.x', port=xxxx, debug=True)
```

This code uses the Python decorator @route to define a route to a URL or path for the client to use to send a data request. The defined route calls the *routing function*, which returns a string. The run() method starts the Bottle server, which can now accept connections from clients. (Be sure to supply your own IP address and port number.) Note that I've set the debug flag to True to make it easier to diagnose problems.)

Now open a browser on any computer connected to the local network and enter **http://192.168.4.4:8080/hello**. Connect to your Pi and Bottle should serve you a web page with the line "Hello Bottle World!". With just a few lines of code, you've created a web server.

The client will make requests to the server (Bottle, running on the Pi) using the Asynchronous JavaScript and XML (AJAX) framework. To make your AJAX calls easy to write, you'll use the popular jQuery library.

PYTHON DECORATORS

A *decorator* in Python is @ syntax that takes a function as an argument and returns another function. A decorator provides a convenient way to "wrap" one function using another function. For example, this code

```python
@wrapper
def myFunc():
    return 'hi'
```

is equivalent to doing the following:

```python
myFunc = wrapper(myFunc)
```

Functions are first-class objects in Python that can be passed like variables.

Plotting with flot

Now let's look at how you'll plot your data. The flot library has an easy-to-use and powerful API that lets you create nice-looking graphs with minimal code. Basically, you set up some Hypertext Markup Language (HTML) to hold a chart and provide an array of values to plot, and Flot handles the rest, as shown in this example. (You'll find this code in the file *simple-flot.html* in the book's code repository.)

```
<html>
<head>
  <meta http-equiv="Content-Type" content="text/html; charset=utf-8">
  <title>SimpleFlot</title>
❶ <style>
    .demo-placeholder {
        width: 80%;
        height: 80%;
    }
  </style>
❷ <script language="javascript" type="text/javascript"
        src="flot/jquery.js"></script>
  <script language="javascript" type="text/javascript"
        src="flot/jquery.flot.js"></script>
  <script language="javascript" type="text/javascript">
❸ $(document).ready(function() {
        // create plot
❹   var data = [];
        for(var i = 0; i < 500; i ++) {
❺       data.push([i, Math.exp(-i/100)*Math.sin(Math.PI*i/10)]);
        }
❻   var plot = $.plot("#placeholder", [data]);
    });
  </script>
</head>

<body>
  <h3>A Simple Flot Plot</h3>
  <div class="demo-container">
❼ <div id="placeholder" class="demo-placeholder"></div>
  </div>
</body>
</html>
```

At ❶, you define a CSS class (demo-placeholder) to set the width and height of the placeholder element to hold your plot (which you'll define in the body of the document). At ❷, you declare the JavaScript files for the libraries you'll use in this HTML file: *jquery.js* and *flot.js*. (Note that jQuery comes bundled with flot, so you don't need to download it separately. Also, ensure that you put the top-level *flot* directory into the same directory that contains all the source code for this project.)

Next, you use JavaScript to generate values to plot. At ❸, you use the jQuery method $(document).ready() to define a function to be executed by the browser as soon as the HTML file is loaded. Inside that function, at ❹, you declare an empty JavaScript array and then loop 500 times, adding a value of the form [i, y] to this array ❺. Each value represents the x- and y-coordinates of this interesting function (chosen somewhat arbitrarily).

$$y(x) = e^{\frac{-x}{100}} \sin\left(\frac{2\pi}{10}x\right), \text{ for } x \text{ in the range } [0, 500]$$

At ❻, you call plot() from the flot library to do the plotting. At ❼, the plot() function takes as input the id of the HTML element that contains the plot (the placeholder element). When you load the resulting HTML file in a browser, you should see the plot shown in Figure 14-4.

A Simple Flot

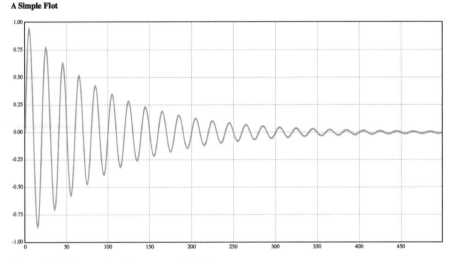

Figure 14-4: A sample plot created with flot

I used flot's default settings here, but you can customize your flot plots extensively by adjusting colors, using data points instead of lines, adding legends and titles, making the plot interactive, and more. (You'll see how when you design the chart for the weather data in "Plotting the Data" on page 285.)

Shutting Down the Pi

Never abruptly disconnect the power supply to a running Raspberry Pi or you'll likely corrupt your filesystem, making the Pi unbootable. To shut down the Pi's user interface if you're connected to it directly or from your computer, enter the following via SSH:

```
$ sudo shutdown -h now
```

NOTE *Before you run the previous command, you need to be sure that you are logged in to your Pi. Otherwise, you may end up shutting down your host computer—if you're running Linux, for instance.*

A few seconds after you enter the shutdown command, the Pi's yellow indicator LED should blink exactly 10 times. Now you can pull the plug safely.

Building the Hardware

In addition to the Pi and the peripherals mentioned earlier, you'll need one of each of the following, as well as hookup wires:

- DHT11 sensor
- 4.7k ohm resistor
- 100 ohm resistor
- Red LED
- Breadboard

Figure 14-5 shows how to wire everything up. The VDD pin of the DHT11 is connected to the +5V (pin #2 on the Pi), the DHT11 DATA pin is connected to pin #16 on the Pi, and the DHT11 GND pin is connected to GND on the Pi (pin #6). A 4.7k ohm resistor is connected between DATA and VDD. The *cathode* (negative) of the LED is connected to GND via a 100 ohm resistor, and the *anode* (positive) is connected to pin #18 of the Pi.

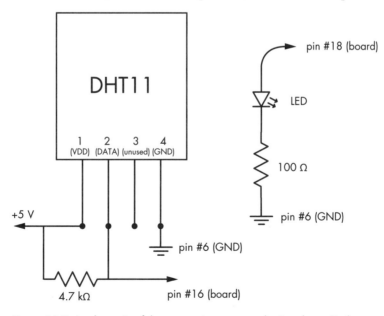

Figure 14-5: A schematic of the connections among the Raspberry Pi, the DHT11 circuit, and the LED

You can use a solderless breadboard to connect the DHT11 and LED circuits and test the setup, as shown in Figure 14-6. Then move the setup to a custom enclosure once you have it working to your satisfaction.

Figure 14-6: The Raspberry Pi, DHT11, and LED connected with a breadboard

The Code

Now, you'll develop the code to run on the Raspberry Pi. (If you want to see the full project code, skip ahead to "The Complete Code" on page 290.) Here's the main() function:

```
def main():
    print 'starting piweather...'
    # create parser
❶  parser = argparse.ArgumentParser(description="PiWeather...")
    # add expected arguments
    parser.add_argument('--ip', dest='ipAddr', required=True)
    parser.add_argument('--port', dest='portNum', required=True)

    # parse args
    args = parser.parse_args()

    # GPIO setup
❷  GPIO.setmode(GPIO.BOARD)
❸  GPIO.setup(18, GPIO.OUT)
❹  GPIO.output(18, False)
    # start server
❺  run(host=args.ipAddr, port=args.portNum, debug=True)
```

At ❶, you set up a command line argument parser with two required arguments: --ip for the IP address where the server should be started and

--port for the server port number. At ❷, you start the GPIO pin setup. You use BOARD mode to indicate you'll be using the pin-numbering convention based on the board's physical layout. At ❸, you set up pin #18 as an output because you plan to write data out to it to control the LED, and at ❹, you set the pin value to False so the LED is turned off when you start. Then you start Bottle by supplying the IP address and port number, and set debug to True to monitor any warning messages ❺.

Handling Sensor Data Requests

Now let's take a quick look at the function that handles sensor data requests:

```
❶ @route('/getdata', method='GET')
❷ def getdata():
❸     RH, T = Adafruit_DHT.read_retry(Adafruit_DHT.DHT11, 23)
       # return dictionary
❹     return {"RH": RH, "T": T}
```

This method defines a route called /getdata ❶. When the client accesses the URL */getdata* defined by this route, the getdata() method is called ❷, which uses the Adafruit_DHT module to retrieve humidity and temperature data ❸. At ❹, the retrieved data is returned as a dictionary, which will be available on the client as a JavaScript Object Notation (JSON) object. JSON objects consist of lists of name-value pairs that can be read in as objects. In this case, getdata() returns a JSON object with two pairs: one for the humidity reading (RH) and one for temperature (T).

Plotting the Data

The plot() function handles the client's plot requests. The first part of this function defines the HTML <head> section, which sets the Cascading Style Sheets (CSS) style and loads the necessary JavaScript code, as shown here:

```
@route('/plot')
def plot():
❶     return '''
<html>
<head>
    <meta http-equiv="Content-Type" content="text/html; charset=utf-8">
    <title>PiWeather</title>
    <style>
    .demo-placeholder {
    width: 90%;
    height: 50%;
    }
    </style>
        <script language="javascript" type="text/javascript"
      src="jquery.js"></script>
        <script language="javascript" type="text/javascript"
      src="jquery.flot.js"></script>
        <script language="javascript" type="text/javascript"
      src="jquery.flot.time.js"></script>
```

The plot() function is a Bottle route for the */plot* URL, which means that the plot() method will be called when you connect to this URL. At ❶, plot() returns the entire HTML data as a single string, which will be displayed by the client's web browser. The initial lines in the listing are the HTML headers, CSS size declaration for the plot, and code to include the flot library—all similar to the setup that produces the flot chart example in Figure 14-4.

The <body> element of the code shows the overall structure of the HTML.

```
<body>
        <div id="header">
❶              <h2>Temperature/Humidity</h2>
        </div>

        <div id="content">
            <div class="demo-container">
❷                  <div id="placeholder" class="demo-placeholder"></div>
            </div>
❸          <div id="ajax-panel"> </div>
            </div>
    <div>
❹          <input type="checkbox" id="ckLED" value="on">Enable Lighting.
❺          <span id="data-values"> </span>
        </div>

</body>
</html>
```

At ❶, you simply add a title for the plot. Add a <placeholder> element at ❷, which will be filled later by the flot JavaScript code. At ❸, you define an HTML element with the ID ajax-panel, which will display any AJAX errors, and at ❹, you create a checkbox element with the ID ckLED, which controls the LED connected to the Raspberry Pi. Finally, you create another HTML element with the ID data-values ❺, where you display sensor data when the user clicks a data point in the plot. The JavaScript code will use all of these IDs to access and modify the corresponding elements.

Now let's dive in to the embedded JavaScript code that initiates sensor data requests as well as toggles the LED on and off. This code goes into the <script language="javascript"...> tag under the <head> of the HTML data.

```
❶ $(document).ready(function() {

    // plot options
❷    var options = {
        series: {
            lines: {show: true},
            points: {show: true}
                },
```

```
❸          grid: {clickable: true},
❹          yaxes: [{min: 0, max: 100}],
           xaxes: [{min: 0, max: 100}],
       };

       // create empty plot
❺      var plot = $.plot("#placeholder", [[]], options);
```

The ready() function at ❶ is called by the browser when the HTML data has been fully loaded. At ❷, you declare an options object to customize your plot. In this object, you tell the plot to display both lines and points, and at ❸, you allow the plot grid to be clicked (for querying values). You also set the axes limits at ❹. At ❺, create the actual plot by calling plot() with three arguments: the ID of the element in which you want the plot to appear, an array of values (which is empty to start), and the options object you just set up.

Next let's look at the JavaScript code that gets the sensor data:

```
       // initialize data arrays
❶      var RH = [];
       var T = [];
       var timeStamp = [];
       // get data from server
❷      function getData() {
           // AJAX callback
❸          function onDataReceived(jsonData) {
❹              timeStamp.push(Date());
               // add RH data
❺              RH.push(jsonData.RH);
               // removed oldest
❻              if (RH.length > 100) {
                   RH.splice(0, 1);
               }
               // add T data
               T.push(jsonData.T);
               // removed oldest
               if (T.length > 100) {
                   T.splice(0, 1);
               }
❼              s1 = [];
               s2 = [];
               for (var i = 0; i < RH.length; i++) {
                   s1.push([i, RH[i]]);
                   s2.push([i, T[i]]);
               }
               // set to plot
❽              plot.setData([s1, s2]);
               plot.draw();
               }
```

```
                         // AJAX error handler
     ⑨          function onError(){
                             $('#ajax-panel').html('<p><strong>Ajax error!</strong> </p>');
                         }

                         // make the AJAX call
     ⑩          $.ajax({
                             url: "getdata",
                             type: "GET",
                             dataType: "json",
                             success: onDataReceived,
                             error: onError
                         });
                     }
```

At ❶, you initialize empty arrays for the temperature and humidity values, and a timeStamp array that stores the time when each value is collected. You define a getData() method at ❷ that you'll call periodically using a timer. At ❸, you define a onDataReceived() method that you'll set as a callback method for the AJAX call. Because in JavaScript you can define functions within functions that can be used like regular variables, you can define onDataReceived() within the getData() function and then pass it to the AJAX call as a callback function.

The onDataReceived() function stores a timestamp for the data point at ❹ by creating a JavaScript Date object. Data from the server is passed into OnDataReceived() using the jsonData object, and at ❺, you push the temperature data from this object into an array. At ❻, you remove the oldest element in the array if the number of elements exceeds 100, which produces a scrolling graph similar to the one you created for the Arduino light sensor project in Chapter 12. You process the humidity data the same way.

At ❼, the collected data is formatted to make it suitable to be passed to the plot() method. Since you're plotting two variables simultaneously, you need an array with three layers of the form:

$$[[[i_0, RH_0], [i_1, RH_1],...], [[i_0, T_0], [i_1, T_1]]]$$

The data is set and plotted at ❽.

At ❾, you define an error callback, which AJAX will use in case of a failure to display errors, using the HTML element with the ID ajax-panel that you set up previously. At ❿, you make the actual AJAX call, which specifies the URL *getdata*, the Bottle route. The call uses the HTTP GET() method to request data from the server in the json format. The AJAX setup call sets the OnDataReceived() method as the success callback and onError() as the error callback. This AJAX call returns immediately, and the callback methods are activated asynchronously when data becomes available.

The update() Method

Now let's look at the update() method that calls getData() every second.

```
        // define an update function
        function update() {
            // get data
❶          getData();
            // set timeout
❷          setTimeout(update, 1000);
        }

    // call update
        update();
```

The update() method first calls getData() at ❶ and then uses the Java-Script setTimeout() method at ❷ to call itself after 1,000 milliseconds. As a result, getData() is called every second to request sensor data from the server.

The JavaScript Handler for the LED

Now let's look at the JavaScript handler for the LED checkbox, which sends an AJAX request to the web server.

```
        // define the click handler for the LED control button
❶       $('#ckLED').click(function() {
❷           var isChecked = $("#ckLED").is(":checked") ? 1:0;
❸           $.ajax({
                url: '/ledctrl',
                type: 'POST',
                data: { strID:'ckLED', strState:isChecked }
            });
        });
```

At ❶, you define a click handler for the checkbox with the ID ckLED that you created earlier in the HTML. This click handler function is called each time the user clicks the checkbox. The function stores the state of the checkbox ❷; then the code at ❸ calls AJAX with the URL */ledctrl* and the HTTP request type POST, which sends the checked state as data.

The server-side handler for this AJAX request sets the GPIO pin of the Pi to on or off as per the request.

```
❶ @route('/ledctrl', method='POST')
  def ledctrl():
❷     val = request.forms.get('strState')
❸     on = bool(int(val))
❹     GPIO.output(18, on)
```

At ❶, you define the Bottle route for the URL */ledctrl*, which is a decorator for the ledctrl() method that handles this request. At ❷, you use the Bottle request object to access the string value of the strState parameter sent by the client code, which is converted to a Boolean at ❸. Use the GPIO.output() method on pin #18 to toggle the LED connected to this pin on or off ❹.

Adding Interactivity

You also want to provide some interactivity for the plot. The flot library provides a way for users to click data points to get values, which you enabled earlier by passing clickable:true in options when you called the plot() function. Here, you define the function to be called when a data point is clicked:

```
    $("#placeholder").bind("plotclick", function (event, pos, item) {
        if (item) {
❶          plot.highlight(item.series, item.datapoint);
❷          var strData = ' [Clicked Data: ' +
                        timeStamp[item.dataIndex] + ': T = ' +
                        T[item.dataIndex] + ', RH = ' + RH[item.dataIndex]
                        + ']';
❸          $('#data-values').html(strData);
        }
    });
});

</script>
</head>
```

This function calls the flot highlight() method at ❶ to draw a ring around the point clicked. At ❷, it prepares a string to be displayed in the HTML element with the ID data-values. When a data point is clicked, flot passes in an item object to the function, which has a member called dataIndex. You use this index to retrieve the relevant data from the timestamp, temperature, and humidity arrays defined in the ready() function. Finally, the string is added to the HTML element ❸.

This concludes the embedded JavaScript in your Python code, but you need one more Bottle route to find the JavaScript files that the web page needs, as shown here:

```
@route('/<filename:re:.*\.js>')
def javascripts(filename):
    return static_file(filename, root='flot')
```

This code tells the Bottle server to find these files in the subdirectory *flot/* at the same level as your program.

The Complete Code

You can find the complete code listing for this project at *https://github.com/electronut/pp/tree/master/piweather/piweather.py*.

```
from bottle import route, run, request, response
from bottle import static_file
import random, argparse
import RPi.GPIO as GPIO
from time import sleep
import Adafruit_DHT
```

```python
@route('/hello')
def hello():
    return "Hello Bottle World!"

@route('/<filename:re:.*\.js>')
def javascripts(filename):
    return static_file(filename, root='flot')

@route('/plot')
def plot():
    return '''
```
```html
<html>
<head>
    <meta http-equiv="Content-Type" content="text/html; charset=utf-8">
    <title>PiWeather</title>
    <style>
     .demo-placeholder {
    width: 90%;
    height: 50%;
    }
    </style>
    <script language="javascript" type="text/javascript"
        src="jquery.js"></script>
    <script language="javascript" type="text/javascript"
        src="jquery.flot.js"></script>
    <script language="javascript" type="text/javascript"
        src="jquery.flot.time.js"></script>
    <script language="javascript" type="text/javascript">
```
```javascript
$(document).ready(function() {

    // plot options
    var options = {
        series: {
            lines: {show: true},
            points: {show: true}
                },
        grid: {clickable: true},
        yaxes: [{min: 0, max: 100}],
        xaxes: [{min: 0, max: 100}],
    };

    // create empty plot
    var plot = $.plot("#placeholder", [[]], options);

    // initialize data arrays
    var RH = [];
    var T = [];
    var timeStamp = [];
    // get data from server
    function getData() {
        // AJAX callback
        function onDataReceived(jsonData) {
            timeStamp.push(Date());
```

```
            // add RH data
            RH.push(jsonData.RH);
            // removed oldest
            if (RH.length > 100) {
                RH.splice(0, 1);
            }
            // add T data
            T.push(jsonData.T);
            // removed oldest
            if (T.length > 100) {
                T.splice(0, 1);
            }
            s1 = [];
            s2 = [];
            for (var i = 0; i < RH.length; i++) {
                s1.push([i, RH[i]]);
                s2.push([i, T[i]]);
            }
            // set to plot
            plot.setData([s1, s2]);
            plot.draw();
        }

        // AJAX error handler
        function onError(){
            $('#ajax-panel').html('<p><strong>Ajax error!</strong> </p>');
        }

        // make the AJAX call
        $.ajax({
            url: "getdata",
            type: "GET",
            dataType: "json",
            success: onDataReceived,
            error: onError
        });
    }

    // define an update function
    function update() {
        // get data
        getData();
        // set timeout
        setTimeout(update, 1000);
    }

    // call update
    update();

    // define click handler for LED control button
    $('#ckLED').click(function() {
        var isChecked = $("#ckLED").is(":checked") ? 1:0;
        $.ajax({
            url: '/ledctrl',
            type: 'POST',
```

```
                    data: { strID:'ckLED', strState:isChecked }
                });
            });

        $("#placeholder").bind("plotclick", function (event, pos, item) {
            if (item) {
                plot.highlight(item.series, item.datapoint);
                var strData = ' [Clicked Data: ' +
                                timeStamp[item.dataIndex] + ': T = ' +
                                T[item.dataIndex] + ', RH = ' + RH[item.dataIndex]
                                + ']';
                $('#data-values').html(strData);
            }
        });
});

</script>
</head>

<body>
    <div id="header">
        <h2>Temperature/Humidity</h2>
    </div>

    <div id="content">
        <div class="demo-container">
            <div id="placeholder" class="demo-placeholder"></div>
        </div>
        <div id="ajax-panel"> </div>
    </div>
    <div>
        <input type="checkbox" id="ckLED" value="on">Enable Lighting.
        <span id="data-values"> </span>
    </div>

</body>
</html>
'''

@route('/getdata', method='GET')
def getdata():
    RH, T = Adafruit_DHT.read_retry(Adafruit_DHT.DHT11, 23)
    # return dictionary
    return {"RH": RH, "T": T}

@route('/ledctrl', method='POST')
def ledctrl():
    val = request.forms.get('strState')
    on = bool(int(val))
    GPIO.output(18, on)

# main() function
def main():
    print 'starting piweather...'
```

```
# create parser
parser = argparse.ArgumentParser(description="PiWeather...")
# add expected arguments
parser.add_argument('--ip', dest='ipAddr', required=True)
parser.add_argument('--port', dest='portNum', required=True)

# parse args
args = parser.parse_args()

# GPIO setup
GPIO.setmode(GPIO.BOARD)
GPIO.setup(18, GPIO.OUT)
GPIO.output(18, False)
# start server
run(host=args.ipAddr, port=args.portNum, debug=True)

# call main
if __name__ == '__main__':
    main()
```

Running the Program

Once you've connected the Raspberry Pi to the DHT11 and LED circuit, SSH into the Pi from your computer and enter the following (substituting the IP address and port you have set up for your Pi):

```
$ sudo python piweather.py --ip 192.168.x.x --port xxx
```

Now open a browser and enter the IP address and port for your Pi into the browser's address bar in this form:

```
http://192.168.x.x:port/plot
```

You should see a plot similar to the one in Figure 14-7.

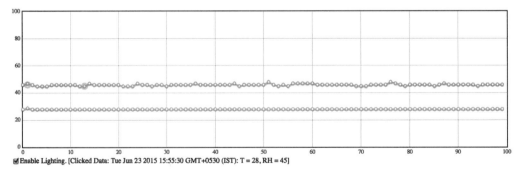

Figure 14-7: The resulting web page and chart from a sample run of piweather.py

If you click any data point in the graph, the Clicked Data section should update to show more information about that point. After 100 points are collected, the graph will start scrolling horizontally as new data comes in. (Click the Enable Lighting checkbox to toggle the LED on and off.)

Summary

In this project, you built a Raspberry Pi–based weather monitor that plots temperature and humidity data over a web interface. These were some of the concepts covered in this project:

- Setting up a Raspberry Pi
- Using Raspberry Pi GPIO pins to talk to hardware
- Interfacing with the DHT11 temperature and humidity sensor
- Creating a web server using the Bottle Python web framework
- Making charts using the flot JavaScript library
- Building a client-server application
- Controlling hardware over a web interface

Experiments!

Try refining this project with these modifications:

1. Provide a way to export the sensor data. One simple way would be to maintain a list of (T, RH) tuples on the server, then write a Bottle route for */export*, and, in this method, return the values in CSV format. Modify the */plot* route so that it includes HTML code to place an Export button on the web page. When the button is clicked, have the corresponding AJAX code call the export() method on the server, which will send the CSV values to be displayed in the browser. These values can then be copied or saved by the user from the browser window.

2. The program plots the DHT11 data, but after 100 values, it starts scrolling. What if you want to see historic data over a longer period? One way would be to maintain a longer list of (T, RH) tuples on the server and then modify the server code to send HTML data with a button and the necessary JavaScript code to toggle between plotting the full range of data or just the most recent 100 values. How will you retrieve old data from before the Pi was switched off? (Hint: write the data to a text file when the server exits and load old data when it starts.) To really make this project scalable, use a database, such as SQLite.

A

SOFTWARE INSTALLATION

In this appendix, I will cover how to install Python, as well as the external modules and code used in the book. Since I've already covered the installation of several Raspberry Pi–specific projects in Chapter 14, I'll skip those instructions here. The projects in this book have been tested with both Python 2.7.8 and Python 3.3.3.

Installing Source Code for the Book's Projects

You can download source code for the book's projects from *https://github .com/electronut/pp/*. Use the Download ZIP option at this site to retrieve the code.

Once you download and extract the code, you need to add the path to the *common* folder in the downloaded code (generally *pp-master/common*) to your PYTHONPATH environment variable so that modules can find and use these Python files.

On Windows, you can do this by creating a PYTHONPATH environment variable or adding to one if it already exists. On OS X, you can add this line to your *.profile* file in your home directory (or create a file there if needed):

```
export PYTHONPATH=$PYTHONPATH:path_to_common_folder
```

Linux users can do something similar to OS X, in their *.bashrc*, *.bash_profile*, or *.cshrc/.login* as appropriate. You can use the echo $SHELL command to see the default shell.

Now, let's look at how to install Python and the modules used in this book on Windows, OS X, and Linux.

Installing on Windows

First, download and install Python from *https://www.python.org/download/*.

Installing GLFW

For the OpenGL-based 3D graphics projects in this book, you need the GLFW library, which you can download at *http://www.glfw.org/download.html*.

On Windows, after you install GLFW, set a GLFW_LIBRARY environment variable (type **Edit Environment Variables** in the search bar) to the full path of the installed *glfw3.dll* so that your Python binding for GLFW can find this library. The path will look something like *C:\glfw-3.0.4.bin.WIN32\lib-msvc120\glfw3.dll*.

To use GLFW with Python, you use a module called pyglfw, which consists of a single Python file called *glfw.py*. You don't need to install pyglfw because it comes with the source code for the book; you can find it in the *common* directory. But just in case you need to install a more recent version, here is the source: *https://github.com/rougier/pyglfw/*.

You also need to ensure that your graphics card drivers are installed on your computer. This is a good thing in general since many software programs (especially games) make use of the graphics processing unit (GPU).

Installing Prebuilt Binaries for Each Module

The simplest way to install the necessary Python modules on Windows is to get prebuilt binaries. The links for each module are listed here. Download the appropriate installers (32 or 64 bit) for each. Depending on your Windows setup, you may need to run these installers with administrator privileges.

pyaudio
   http://www.lfd.uci.edu/~gohlke/pythonlibs/#pyaudio

pyserial
   http://www.lfd.uci.edu/~gohlke/pythonlibs/#pyserial

scipy

http://www.lfd.uci.edu/~gohlke/pythonlibs/#scipy
http://sourceforge.net/projects/scipy/files/scipy/

numpy

http://www.lfd.uci.edu/~gohlke/pythonlibs/#numpy
http://sourceforge.net/projects/numpy/files/NumPy/

pygame

http://www.lfd.uci.edu/~gohlke/pythonlibs/#pygame

Pillow

http://www.lfd.uci.edu/~gohlke/pythonlibs/#pillow
https://pypi.python.org/pypi/Pillow/2.5.0#downloads

pyopengl

http://www.lfd.uci.edu/~gohlke/pythonlibs/#pyopengl

matplotlib

http://www.lfd.uci.edu/~gohlke/pythonlibs/#matplotlib

The `matplotlib` library depends on `dateutil`, `pytz`, `pyparsing`, and `six`, and you can get those from the following links:

dateutil

http://www.lfd.uci.edu/~gohlke/pythonlibs/#python-dateutil

pytz

http://www.lfd.uci.edu/~gohlke/pythonlibs/#pytz

pyparsing

http://www.lfd.uci.edu/~gohlke/pythonlibs/#pyparsing

six

http://www.lfd.uci.edu/~gohlke/pythonlibs/#six

Other Options

You can also build all the required packages yourself on Windows by installing the appropriate compilers. See *https://docs.python.org/2/install/index.html #gnu-c-cygwin-mingw* for a list of compatible compilers. Another option is to install the special Python distributions at *http://www.scipy.org/install.html*, which have most of these packages preinstalled.

Installing on OS X

Here are the recommended steps for installing Python and the necessary modules on OS X.

Installing Xcode and MacPorts

The first step is to install Xcode. You can get it through the App Store, or if you are running an older version of the operating system, you can get a compatible version of Xcode from the Apple developer website at *https://developer.apple.com/*. Once you install Xcode, make sure you also have the command line tools installed. The next step is to install MacPorts. You can refer to the MacPorts guide (*http://guide.macports.org/#installing.xcode*), which has detailed installation instructions to help you with this process.

MacPorts installs its own version of Python, and it's simplest to just use that version for your projects. (OS X also comes with Python built in, but installations on top of it are fraught with problems, so it's best left alone.)

Installing Modules

Once you have MacPorts installed, you can install the required modules for the book using the port' command in the Terminal application.

Use this command in a terminal window to check the versions of Python:

```
$ port select --list python
```

If you have multiple Python installations, you can make a particular version of Python active for MacPorts using this command (Python version 2.7 is selected here):

```
$ port select --set python python27
```

Then you can install the required modules. Run these commands one by one in a terminal window.

```
sudo port install py27-numpy
sudo port install py27-Pillow
sudo port install py27-matplotlib
sudo port install py27-opengl
sudo port install glfw
sudo port install py27-scipy
sudo port install py27-pyaudio
sudo port install py27-serial
sudo port install py27-game
```

MacPorts usually installs its Python in */opt/local/*. You can ensure you get the right version of Python in a terminal window by setting the PATH environment variable in your *.profile*. Here is how I have it set up:

```
PATH=/opt/local/Library/Frameworks/Python.framework/Versions/2.7/bin:$PATH
export PATH
```

This code ensures that the right version of Python is available to run from any terminal.

Installing on Linux

Linux usually comes with Python built in, as well as all the development tools needed to build the required packages. On most Linux distributions, you should be able to use pip to get the packages required for the book. See the following link for instructions on installing pip: *http://pip.readthedocs.org/en/latest/installing.html*.

You can install a package using pip like this:

```
sudo pip install matplotlib
```

The other way to install a package is to download the module source distribution for it, which is usually in a *.gz* or *.zip* file. Once you unzip these files into a folder, you can then install them as follows:

```
sudo python setup.py install
```

You need to use one of these methods for each package needed for the book.

B

BASIC PRACTICAL ELECTRONICS

 In this appendix, I briefly cover some basic terminology, components, and tools related to building electronic circuits. *Electronics* is a branch of engineering that deals with the design and construction of electrical circuits that use active and passive electrical components.

This topic is vast, so I am barely going to scratch the surface.[1] But from a hobbyist or DIY (do-it-yourself) perspective, you don't need to know a whole lot to get started with electronics. You can learn as you build, and from my own experience, I can tell you that this is a fun and addictive hobby. I hope a quick tour through the following topics will inspire you to start reading up on the subject and put you on the path to designing and building your own circuits.

---

1. For a comprehensive reference on electronics, I recommend Paul Scherz and Simon Monk, *Practical Electronics for Inventors, 3rd ed.* (San Francisco: McGraw-Hill, 2013).

Common Components

Most electronic components use materials that fall into the *semiconductor* category. Semiconductors have special electrical properties that make them an ideal choice for the construction of electronic devices.

In this section, we look at some of the most common components used in circuits. Figure B-1 shows these components alongside the symbols used to represent them in circuit diagrams.

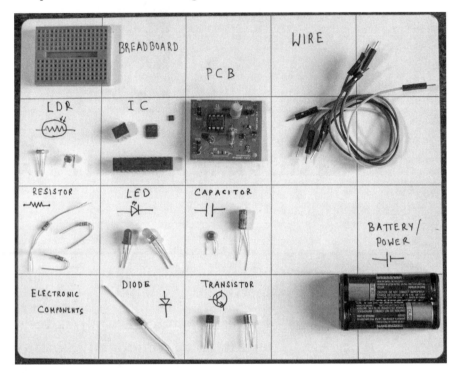

Figure B-1: Common electronic components and their corresponding symbols

Breadboard

A breadboard is a perforated block used for prototyping electronic circuits. The holes in a breadboard have spring-loaded clips in them and are interconnected in a simple way, allowing for easy experimentation. Instead of having to solder each connection, you plug in the components to the breadboard and use wires to connect them.

Light-Dependent Resistor (LDR)

An LDR is a type of resistor whose resistance decreases with the intensity of light falling on it. It is used as a light sensor in electronic circuits.

Integrated Circuit (IC)

An IC is a device that contains a complete electronic circuit. ICs are quite small and can contain billions of transistors in a square centimeter.

Each IC usually has a specific application in mind, and the data sheet from the manufacturer provides the necessary schematics, electrical and physical characteristics, and sample applications to aid the user. A common IC that you may encounter is the 555, which is used mostly as a timer.

Printed Circuit Board (PCB)

To make an electronic circuit, you need a place to assemble the components. You typically do this on a PCB, a board consisting of an insulator with one or more layers of a conductive material (typically copper) on top of it. The conductive layer is shaped in such a way that it forms the wiring of the circuit.

The components are mounted onto the PCB either as *through-hole* components or *surface-mounted* components and soldered to form an electrical connection with the conducting layer.

Wires

Not very high-tech, but you can't make circuits without wires. You'll use copper wires insulated by plastic.

Resistor

A resistor is one of the most common components found in a circuit. A resistor is used to decrease current or voltage in a circuit and is specified in terms of its resistance, which is measured in *ohms*. For example, a 2.7k resistor has a resistance of 2.7 kilohms, or 2,700 ohms. A resistor has color-coded bands that indicate its resistance value, and two leads that are interchangeable because it has no polarity.

Light-Emitting Diode (LED)

LEDs are the little blinking lights you see in many circuits. An LED is a special type of diode, however, so it also has polarity and needs to be connected accordingly. It is often used in conjunction with a resistor, which limits the current flowing through it so it doesn't get damaged. LEDs of different colors have different minimum "turn-on" voltages.

Capacitor

A capacitor is a device with two leads that is used to store an electrical charge. It is measured in terms of *capacitance*, which has units of *farads*. A typical capacitor has a capacitance measured in microfarads (μF). Capacitors come in polarized and unpolarized versions.

Diode

A diode is an electronic device that lets a current pass only in one direction. Diodes are commonly used as *rectifiers*—devices that convert AC current to DC. A diode has two leads: an anode and a cathode. That means it has polarity, so the two leads need to be matched up correctly with the rest of the circuit.

Transistor

A transistor can be thought of as an electronic switch. A transistor can also act as an amplifier of current or voltage. As a basic building block of integrated circuits, it is one of the most important electronic components. Transistors come in several types, but the most common ones are the bipolar junction transistor (BJT) and the metal-oxide-semiconductor field-effect transistor (MOSFET). A transistor usually has three leads. For the BJT, they are named *base, collector,* and *emitter,* whereas for a MOSFET, they are named *gate, source,* and *drain.* When the transistor is used as a switch, the current to the base for the BJT—or voltage to the gate in the case of MOSFET—is what enables the flow of current through the collector and emitter, thus acting as an on/off switch for an external load like an LED or a relay.

Battery/Power Supply

Most electronics work on small voltages ranging from 3 to 9 Volts, and this voltage can be supplied using batteries or power adapters that plug in to a wall AC outlet.

Essential Tools

In addition to the components just described, you also need some basic tools to get started with electronic circuits. Figure B-2 shows what you would typically find on the workbench of a hobbyist. Some of these essential tools are described next.

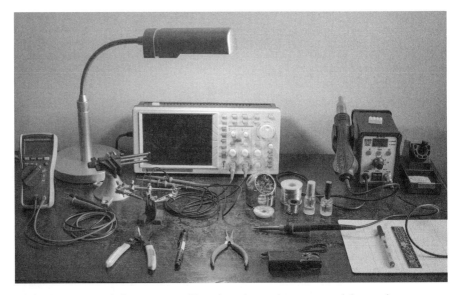

Figure B-2: A typical electronics workbench, with a multimeter, a task lamp, clamps, a wire stripper, a screwdriver, needle-nose pliers, a loupe, solder, flux, an oscilloscope, and a soldering station.

Multimeter

A multimeter is an instrument used to measure the electrical characteristics of a circuit, such as voltage, current, capacitance, and resistance. It is also often used to measure *continuity* in a circuit, which indicates a continuous flow of current. A multimeter is quite useful when you're trying to debug your circuit.

Soldering Iron and Accessories

Once you are satisfied that your circuit works on a breadboard, the next step is to transfer it to a PCB, and this requires *soldering*. Soldering is the processing of joining two metals using a heated filler metal. The filler, or *solder*, used to contain lead, but these days lead-free solder alloy is typically used, which is more environmentally sound. To solder a component, place it on the PCB, apply *flux* (a chemical that makes the soldering process easier), and apply the hot solder with the iron. When the solder cools, it forms a physical bond and an electrical connection between the component and the copper layer.

Oscilloscope

An oscilloscope is an instrument used to measure and display voltages from electronic circuits. It is a useful tool for analyzing electrical waveforms. For example, you could use it to debug digital data coming out of a sensor or measure analog voltage coming out of an audio amplifier. It also has other specialized measurement functions like fast Fourier transform (FFT) and root mean square (RMS).

Figure B-2 shows some other useful items for building circuits: a multi-bit screwdriver, needle-nose pliers, wire stripper, clamps to hold your PCBs while soldering, a good table lamp for a well-lit work area, a magnifier that will help you inspect small components and solder joints, and a cleaner for your soldering iron tip.

Building Circuits

When building a circuit, start with a circuit diagram or *schematic*, which tells you how the components are connected to each other. Typically, you then construct this circuit on a breadboard, plugging in components and connecting them using wires. Once you have tested the circuit to your satisfaction, you might consider moving it to a PCB. Although the breadboard is convenient, it looks a bit like a rat's nest, and all those loose wires can make it unreliable for deployment.

You can either use a general-purpose PCB, which has fixed patterns of copper laid out in the bottom, or design your own PCB. The former works fine for small circuits. Typically, you solder in your components, use the copper connections that are already present, and then hack the rest by soldering additional wires as needed. Figure B-3 shows a schematic, the breadboard prototype, and the PCB construction for a simple circuit.

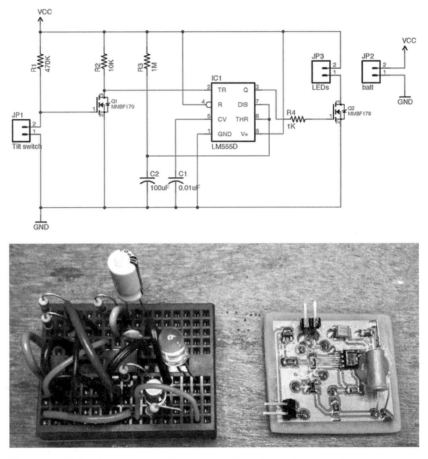

Figure B-3: Going from a schematic to a breadboard prototype to a PCB circuit

If you want a really nice-looking PCB, you can design one yourself and have it manufactured inexpensively. Several software packages are available for designing your PCB, but the most common (free) ones include EAGLE[2] and KiCad.[3] EAGLE software has a Light edition that is free as long you use it only for nonprofit applications. It has certain restrictions (for instance, only two copper layers, a maximum PCB size of 4×3.2 inches, and one schematic per project), but these shouldn't be too problematic for a hobbyist. EAGLE has a steep learning curve, however, and a somewhat confusing interface in my opinion. Before you get started, I recommend that you first watch some video tutorials.[4]

A typical work flow in EAGLE is as follows. First, you create a circuit diagram in the schematic editor. For this, you need to add components

2. CadSoft EAGLE PCB design software, *http://www.cadsoftusa.com/eagle-pcb-design-software/*.

3. KiCad EDA software suite, *http://www.kicad-pcb.org/display/KICAD/KiCad+EDA+Software+Suite/*.

4. Jeremy Blum, "Tutorial 1 for Eagle: Schematic Design," YouTube (June 14, 2012), *https://www.youtube.com/watch?v=1AXwjZoyNno*.

used in your circuit and then wire them. A huge number of component libraries are available for EAGLE, and chances are that your components are already listed in one of those libraries. (EAGLE also lets you create your own custom components.) Once you are done with your schematic, EAGLE can generate a PCB from it, which brings up a physical representation of your components. You then need to *place* and *route* your circuit to design the connection paths of the copper layer on the PCB. A typical EAGLE design is shown in Figure B-4. To the left is the schematic, and to the right is the corresponding board. Using EAGLE takes a bit of practice, but the YouTube tutorial will get you started.

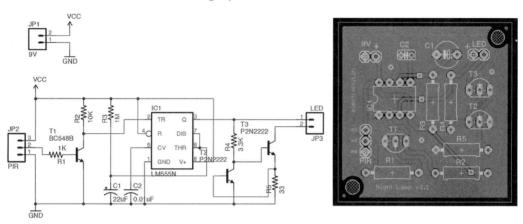

Figure B-4: A circuit schematic and the matching PCB design created with EAGLE

Once you have designed the PCB, you need to manufacture it. Some techniques for making PCBs can be done at home,[5] which can be fun, but a more professional technique is to send your design to a PCB manufacturer. These companies typically accept a design format called *Gerber*, and you can generate these files right from EAGLE with a little setup.[6] Many companies make PCBs. One that I have used with good results is OSH Park.[7]

Once you have your PCB built and components soldered, consider an enclosure for your project. Current manufacturing technologies allow you to design and build professional-looking enclosures using techniques like laser printing and 3D printing. You can use a combination of 2D[8] and 3D[9] software to design your creations. A nice project by Rich Decibels illustrates the whole build process discussed here.[10]

---

5. Some techniques for making PCBs at home can be found at *https://embeddedinn.wordpress.com/tutorials/home-made-sigle-sided-pcbs/*.

6. Akash Patel, "Generating Gerber files from EAGLE," YouTube (April 7, 2010), *https://www.youtube.com/watch?v=B_SbQeF83XU*.

7. *https://oshpark.com/*.

8. For 2D software, see Inkscape, *http://www.inkscape.org/en/*.

9. For 3D software, see SketchUp, *http://www.sketchup.com/*.

10. Rich Decibels, "Laser-Cut Project Box Tutorial," Ponoko (August 9, 2011), *http://support.ponoko.com/entries/20344437-Laser-cut-project-box-tutorial/*.

Going Further

You can approach practical electronics from two angles. The first is from the ground up, where you learn to put together simple circuits, learn about analog and digital circuits, and eventually go on to learn about micro-controllers and interfacing circuits with computers. The other approach is from the programming angle, where you start with hardware-friendly boards like the Arduino and the Raspberry Pi and then learn about circuits by building sensors and actuators for these boards. Both approaches are fine, and most of the time you will likely find yourself somewhere in between.

I wish you grand success with your electronics projects, and once you build something, I hope you will take the time to document it and share it with the world. On websites like Instructables (*http://www.instructables.com/*), you can share your projects or find inspiration from projects by other DIYers around the globe.

RASPBERRY PI
TIPS AND TRICKS

As you learned in Chapter 14, the Raspberry Pi is a full computer with an operating system, which means it requires some setup procedures before you can start using it. I covered basic setup in that project, but here are some additional tips and tricks to prepare the Pi for your projects.

Setting Up Wi-Fi

In Chapter 14, I recommended using the built-in WiFi Config utility to set up Wi-Fi on your Raspberry Pi. However, there's a quicker way to do the same thing using the command line. First, enter the following in the terminal to bring up the configuration file in the nano editor:

```
$ sudo nano /etc/wpa_supplicant/wpa_supplicant.conf
```

This is what my file looks like:

```
ctrl_interface=DIR=/var/run/wpa_supplicant GROUP=netdev
update_config=1

network={
    ssid=your-WiFi-network-name
    psk=your-password
    proto=RSN
    key_mgmt=WPA-PSK
    pairwise=TKIP
    auth_alg=OPEN
}
```

Edit the contents of your file and set ssid and psk to match your Wi-Fi settings. If the whole network section is missing, enter the settings (filling in the details that match your own Wi-Fi setup).

Checking Whether Your Pi Is Connected

You can use the ping command from another computer to check whether your Pi is connected to the local network. Here is what a ping session looks like:

```
$ ping 192.168.4.32
PING 192.168.4.32 (192.168.4.32): 56 data bytes
64 bytes from 192.168.4.32: icmp_seq=0 ttl=64 time=13.677 ms
64 bytes from 192.168.4.32: icmp_seq=1 ttl=64 time=8.277 ms
64 bytes from 192.168.4.32: icmp_seq=2 ttl=64 time=9.313 ms
--snip--
```

This ping output shows the number of bytes sent and the time it took to get a reply. If you see the message "Request timeout..." instead, then you know your Pi is not connected to the network.

Preventing the Wi-Fi Adapter from Going to Sleep

If you are unable to ping your Pi or SHH into it after a while, your USB Wi-Fi adapter may have gone to sleep. You can prevent this from happening by disabling power management. First, use this command to open the file that controls power management:

```
$ sudo nano /etc/modprobe.d/8192cu.conf
```

Then add the following to this file:

```
# disable power management
options 8192cu rtw_power_mgnt=0
```

Reboot your Pi and the Wi-Fi adapter should stay awake now.

Backing Up Your Code and Data from the Pi

As you put more and more code on your Raspberry Pi, you need a way to back up your files. rsync is a great utility that synchronizes files between two folders, even if they exist on different machines on a network. The rsync utility is extremely powerful, so do not meddle with it unless you are paying attention—or else you might end up deleting your original files. If you are playing around with it for the first time, back up your test files first and use the -n, or "dry run," flag. That way, rsync only tells you what it would do without actually doing it, and you have a chance to get comfortable with the program without accidentally deleting anything. Here is my script to back up my code directory (recursively) from the Raspberry Pi onto my computer running OS X:

```
#!/bin/bash
echo Backing up RPi \#1...

# set this to Raspberry Pi IP address
PI_ADDR="192.168.4.31"

# set this to the Raspberry Pi code directory
# note that the trailing slash (/) is important with rsync
PI_DIR="code/"

# set this to the local code (backup) directory
BKUP_DIR="/Users/mahesh/code/rpi1/"

# run rsync
# use this first to test:
# rsync -uvrn pi@$PI_ADDR:$PI_DIR $BKUP_DIR
rsync -uvr pi@$PI_ADDR:$PI_DIR $BKUP_DIR

echo ...
echo done.

# play sound (for OS X only)
afplay /System/Library/Sounds/Basso.aiff
```

Modify this code to match your directories. For Linux and OS X users, rsync is already built in. Windows users can try grsync.[1]

---

1. You can download grsync—an rsync port for Windows—from *http://grsync-win.sourceforge.net/*.

Backing Up Your Entire Pi OS

Backing up the OS on your Pi is a good idea. That way, if the filesystem on your SD card gets corrupted as a result of improper shutdown, you can quickly rewrite the OS to the SD card without having to go through the whole setup. You can also use your backup for cloning your existing install on to another Pi. One solution, posted on StackExchange,[2] involves using the dd utility on Linux and OS X or the Win32 Disk Imager software on Windows.

Logging In to Your Pi with SSH

In Chapter 14, I discussed how you can conveniently use SSH to log in to your Pi and work. If you do this not only frequently but also from the same computer, you'll probably find it annoying to enter the password every single time. With the ssh-keygen utility that comes with SSH, you can set up a public/private key scheme so you can securely log in to your Pi without entering the password. For OS X and Linux users, follow the next procedure. (For Windows users, PuTTY lets you do something similar.[3]) From a terminal on your computer, enter the following, modifying your Pi's IP address as needed:

```
$ ssh-keygen
Generating public/private rsa key pair.
Enter file in which to save the key (/Users/xxx/.ssh/id_rsa):
Enter passphrase (empty for no passphrase):
Enter same passphrase again:
Your identification has been saved in /Users/xxx/.ssh/id_rsa.
Your public key has been saved in /Users/xxx/.ssh/id_rsa.pub.
The key fingerprint is:
--snip--
```

Now, copy this key file to the Pi:

```
$ scp ~/.ssh/id_rsa.pub pi@192.168.4.32:.ssh/
The authenticity of host '192.168.4.32 (192.168.4.32)' can't be established.
RSA key fingerprint is f1:ab:07:e7:dc:2e:f1:37:1b:6f:9b:66:85:2a:33:a7.
Are you sure you want to continue connecting (yes/no)? yes
Warning: Permanently added '192.168.4.32' (RSA) to the list of known hosts.
pi@192.168.4.32's password:
id_rsa.pub                                    100%  398     0.4KB/s   00:00
```

---

2. You'll find instructions for backing up your Raspberry Pi's SD card on Stack Exchange. "How do I backup my Raspberry Pi?" StackExchange, *http://raspberrypi.stackexchange.com/ questions/311/how-do-i-backup-my-raspberry-pi/*.

3. "How to Create SSH Keys with PuTTY to Connect to a VPS," DigitalOcean (July 19, 2013), *https://www.digitalocean.com/community/tutorials/how-to-create-ssh-keys-with-putty-to-connect-to-a-vps/*.

Then, log in to the Pi:

```
$ ssh pi@192.168.4.32
pi@192.168.4.32's password:

$ cd .ssh
$ ls
id_rsa.pub  known_hosts

$ cat id_rsa.pub >> authorized_keys
$ ls
authorized_keys  id_rsa.pub  known_hosts
$ logout
```

The next time you log in to the Pi, you won't be asked for a password. Also, note that I am using an empty passphrase in ssh-keygen, which is not secure. This setup may be fine for Raspberry Pi hardware projects in which you aren't very concerned about security, but for further discussion on working with SSH passphrases, see "Working with SSH Key Passphrases," a helpful GitHub article.[4]

Using the Raspberry Pi Camera

If you want to take pictures with your Pi, a dedicated camera module is available.[5] The module has a camera with a fixed focal length and focus, and the camera supports both image capture (5 megapixels) and video capture (1080 pixels at 30 frames/second). It connects to your Pi via a ribbon cable. Once you install the camera module, you can use the raspistill command to take photos or videos. Make sure camera support is enabled when you first boot up your Pi. Before you install the camera, take a look at the installation video.[6] This video also covers using the raspistill command.

Enabling Sound on Your Pi

The Raspberry Pi comes with an audio output jack. If you are unable to get any sound on your Pi, you may need to install ALSA utilities. The installation is covered by an informative page by CAGE Web Design.[7]

---

4. "Working with SSH Key Passphrases," GitHub Help, *https://help.github.com/articles/working -with-ssh-key-passphrases/*.

5. Refer to the product page for the Raspberry Pi camera module, *http://www.raspberrypi.org/ product/camera-module/*.

6. TheRaspberryPiGuy, "Raspberry Pi—Camera Tutorial," YouTube (May 26, 2013), *https:// www.youtube.com/watch?v=T8T6S5eFpqE*.

7. "Raspberry Pi—Getting Audio Working," CAGE Web Design (February 9, 2013), *http:// cagewebdev.com/index.php/raspberry-pi-getting-audio-working/*.

Making Your Pi Talk

Once the sound is working on your Pi, getting your Pi to talk isn't that hard. First, you need to install `pyttsx`, which is a Python text-to-speech library.[8] Install it as follows:

```
$ wget https://pypi.python.org/packages/source/p/pyttsx/pyttsx-1.1.tar.gz
$ gunzip pyttsx-1.1.tar.gz
$ tar -xf pyttsx-1.1.tar
$ cd pyttsx-1.1/
$ sudo python setup.py install
```

Then you need to install espeak, as shown here:

```
$ sudo apt-get install espeak
```

Now connect speakers to your Pi's audio jack and run this code:

```
import sy:
import pyttsx

# main() function
def main():
    # use sys.argv if needed
    print 'running speech-test.py...'
    engine = pyttsx.init()
    str = "I speak. Therefore. I am.  "
    if len(sys.argv) > 1:
        str = sys.argv[1]
    engine.say(str)
    engine.runAndWait()

# call main
if __name__ == '__main__':
    main()
```

Making HDMI Work

You can plug your Raspberry Pi in to your monitor or TV using an HDMI cable. To ensure it works the first time you boot the Pi, open the Pi's SD card in your computer and edit *config.txt* in the top-level directory, as shown here:

```
hdmi_force_hotplug=1
```

Now, when your Pi boots, you should be able to see the output via HDMI.

---

8. You'll find the GitHub repository for pyttsx, a Python text-to-speech library, at *https://github.com/parente/pyttsx/*.

Making Your Pi Mobile

You can always use a power adapter for your Raspberry Pi. At some point, however, you might want to make your Pi mobile without the hassle of wires. For this, you need a battery pack. One option that works nicely is a rechargeable battery pack with a compatible micro USB output. I've had great results with the Anker Astro Mini 3000mAh External Battery, which can be found online for about $20.

Checking Your Raspberry Pi Hardware Version

Raspberry Pi comes in several flavors. You can check the hardware version of your Pi by logging in to your Pi and entering this in a terminal:

```
$ cat /proc/cpuinfo
```

Here is what the output looks like on my terminal:

```
processor : 0
model name : ARMv6-compatible processor rev 7 (v6l)
BogoMIPS : 2.00
Features : swp half thumb fastmult vfp edsp java tls
CPU implementer : 0x41
CPU architecture: 7
CPU variant : 0x0
CPU part : 0xb76
CPU revision : 7

Hardware : BCM2708
Revision : 000f
Serial : 00000000364a6f1c
```

To understand the revision number, refer to the hardware revision history table at *http://elinux.org/RPi_HardwareHistory*. In my case, I have the Model B, with PCB Rev 2.0, made in Q4 2012.

INDEX

B

backing up Raspberry Pi
    code, 313
    OS, 314
base, 306
battery, 306
battery pack, 256
Berra, Yogi, 87
billboarding, 160, 165–166
blending, 164
    of 3D volumetric data, 192
    Open GL, 164
Boids simulations, 71
    adding a boid, 79–80
    animation, 81
    boundary conditions, 74–75
    drawing, 75–76
    initial conditions, 73
    limiting vector magnitude, 81
    obstacle avoidance, 86
    rules, 72, 77–79
    scattering, 80
    tiled boundary conditions, 74
    time step, 81
bootloader, 237
Bottle web framework, 274, 278, 280
breadboard, 236, 239, 284, 304, 307

C

camera, Raspberry Pi, 315
capacitance, 305
capacitor, 305
cellular automaton, 41
central processing unit (CPU), 133
centroid, 79
circuit diagram, 307
collections module, 61
collector, 306
color cube, 194
color representation, 195
command line arguments.
        See argparse module
computer-generated swarms.
        See Boids simulations
computer simulations. *See* Boids
        simulations; Conway's
        Game of Life; Karplus-
        Strong algorithm

config.txt, 316
constant time operation, 61
continuity, circuit, 307
Conway, John, 41
Conway's Game of Life, 41
    boundary conditions, 43–44
    cells, 42
    glider, defining, 46
    Gosper Glider Gun, 52
    initial conditions, 45–46
    patterns
        blinker, 51, 52
        block, 51, 52
        glider, 51, 52
        loaf, 51, 52
    rules, 42, 44
    toroidal boundary conditions,
        43, 46–47
CPU (central processing unit), 133
cpuinfo, 317
CT scan, 191

D

DC motor, 250
dd utility, 314
decorators, 280
depth encoding, 120
depth map, 120
depth perception, 119
deque class, 61, 241
    appendleft, 242
    pop, 242
deque container, 242
    example, 61
    ring buffer, 62
DHT11, 273, 274. *See also* weather
        monitor
dictionaries, 5
    items method, 6
diodes, 305
Document Type Declaration (DTD), 5
double buffering, 146

E

EAGLE software, 308
electrical waveform, 307
Embedded PostScript (EPS), 29
emitter, 306

enclosure, 309
epitrochoids, 20
EPS (Embedded PostScript), 29
equation of motion, particle
systems, 162
espeak, 316
Extensible Markup Language (XML), 4
extracting duplicate tracks, 7

F

face culling, 195
farad, 305
far plane, 138
fast Fourier transform. *See* FFT
FBO (frame buffer objects), 195
FFT (fast Fourier transform), 252, 307
    amplitude, 252
    example, 253
    frequency, 253
    sampling rate, 254
field of view, 138
file handles, 105
fixed-function graphics pipeline, 135
flocking behavior. *See* Boids simuations
flot library, 274
    adding interactivity with, 290
    installing, 279
    plotting with, 281–282
flux, 307
fountain particle systems, 160
    animation, 166
    Camera class, 173–174
    clipping, 170
    equation of motion, 162
    fragment shader, 171
    gravity, 162
    initial velocity, 163
    keyboard handler, 185
    mathematical model, 161
    parabola, 161
    particle velocity, 162
    random velocities, 168
    spherical coordinates, 163
    time lag, 163, 168
    vertex shader, 169–171
fractions module, 24
fragment shader, 136
frame buffer objects (FBO), 195
frequency, 55
    fundamental, 56, 57

G

Game of Life. *See* Conway's Game
of Life
GCD (greatest common divisor), 21
gcd method, 24
geometric primitive, 138
Gerber, 309
GL_CCW, 196
GLFW, 134, 196, 227
    glfwCreateWindow, 143, 183
    glfwGetTime, 145, 185
    glfwInit, 143, 183
    glfwMakeContextCurrent, 143, 183
    glfwPollEvents, 145, 186
    glfwSetKeyCallback, 144, 184
    glfwSetMouseButtonCallback, 144, 184
    glfwSetTime, 145
    glfwSetWindowSizeCallback, 144, 184
    glfwSwapBuffers, 145, 186
    glfwTerminate, 145, 186
    glfwWindowHint, 143, 183
    glfwWindowShouldClose, 145, 185
    keyboard events, 144
    window resizing events, 144
GL_QUAD, 136
GLSL (OpenGL Shading
Language), 191–192
    clamp method, 170
    compiling, 140
    computing position, 149
    discard method, 150
    example, 139
    float, 169
    fragment shader, 136, 140, 171
    gl_FragColor, 201
    gl_FragCoord, 215
    gl_Position, 139, 170, 201, 214
    in, 139, 169
    length, 215
    linking, 140
    mat4, 139, 200, 214
    mod method, 170
    normalize, 215
    out, 140, 169
    rasterization, 140
    sampler2D, 214
    sampler3D, 214
    setting fragment color, 150
    shader, 133

GLSL (OpenGL Shading Language),
 continued
 texture, 215
 texture2D, 171
 uniform, 139, 169, 200, 214
 vec2, 169, 214
 vec3, 139, 169
 vec4, 139, 200, 214
 vertex shader, 136, 149, 169–171
glTexImage3D, 198
GL_TRIANGLES, 195
GL_TRIANGLE_STRIP, 141
GND (ground) connection, 239
graphics processing unit (GPU),
 133, 191
grayscale
 images, perceiving, 90
 values, 90
greatest common divisor (GCD), 21
ground (GND) connection, 239
guitar, 56

H

harmonics, 58
hdmi_force_hotplug, 316
high-definition multimedia interface
 (HDMI), 273, 316
histograms, 5, 10
homogeneous coordinates, 138
hot glue, 254
humidity sensor. *See* DHT11; weather
 monitor
hypotrochoid, 20

I

IC (integrated circuit), 304–305, 306
ICSP (in-circuit serial
 programming), 237
illusions. *See* autostereograms
image based rendering, 192
in-circuit serial programming
 (ICSP), 237
integrated circuit (IC), 304–305, 306
iTunes playlists, parsing
 collecting track statistics, 8–9
 command line options, 10–11
 plotting track statistics, 9–10

J

JavaScript Object Notation (JSON)
 object, 285
jQuery library, 280
 and flot, 281
JSON (JavaScript Object Notation)
 object, 285

K

Karplus-Strong algorithm, 57–59
 low-pass filter, 58
KiCad software, 308

L

laser, 249
 patterns, generating, 250–253
 pointer, 250
laser printing, 309
LDR (light-dependent resistor), 239,
 304, 305
LED (light-emitting diode), 289, 305
light intensity, 240
light sensor, 304
linear spacing, 118, 119
list comprehension, 31
loops, avoiding, 77
low-pass filter, 58
luminance, 93

M

magnitude, of vectors, 73
 limiting, 81
major scale, 60
mapping, grayscale values to ASCII
 characters, 90
matplotlib library, 5, 44, 65
 animation, 44, 48
  FuncAnimation, 76
 axes, 243
 figure, 243
 imshow, 44, 45
 interpolation, 44
 mouse button press, 79
 mpl_connect, 79
 pyplot, 9
 set_data, 243
matrix multiplication, 138

medical data, 193
metal-oxide-semiconductor field-effect
    transistor (MOSFET),
    256, 306
microcontroller, 310
microfarad, 305
min method, 122
minor pentatonic scale, 60
mirrors, 250, 254–255
modelview matrix, 201
modelview transformations, 138
modulus (%) operator, 46
MOSFET (metal-oxide-semiconductor
    field-effect transistor),
    256, 306
motor control, 251–252
MRI, 191
multimeter, 307
musical scales, 60

N

N-body simulation, 72
nearest neighbor search problem, 116
near plane, 138
normal vectors, 165–166
numpy library, 104, 142
    abs, 263
    arrange, 59, 168
    arrays, 44, 48, 147
        applying operations to
            elements, 9
        concatenate method, 79, 198
        repeat, 168
        reshape, 46, 76, 93, 105
        shape, 93, 105
        slice, 46
        sum, 77
        zeros, 46, 48
    average, 93, 105
    broadcasting, 73
    cross, 172
    fft, 263
    frombuffer, 263
    image.crop, 94
    linalg.norm, 172
    optimization, 77
    random module
        choice, 45, 64
        rand, 73
    sin, 59
    sum, 263

O

ohms, 305
OpenGL, 134
    3D graphics pipeline, 136
    3D transformations, 137–139
        modelview, 138
        projection, 138
    alpha blending, 164
    alpha channel, 164
    billboarding, 165
    binding, 134
    blending, 164
    clamp texture, 156
    color representation, 195
    context, 142
    depth buffer, 173
    displaying, 142
    face culling, 195
    geometric primitive, 137
    glActiveTexture, 148, 172, 203
    glBindBuffer, 147, 167, 203, 220
    glBindFramebuffer, 203
    glBindRenderbuffer, 204
    glBindTexture, 148, 156, 173,
        198, 203
    glBindVertexArray, 147, 148, 167, 173,
        203, 206, 220
    glBlendFunc, 173
    glBufferData, 147, 167, 203, 220
    GL_CCW, 196, 206
    glCheckFramebufferStatus, 204
    glClear, 145, 185
    glClearColor, 143, 183
    GL_CULL_FACE, 205
    glDepthMask, 173
    glDrawArrays, 148, 173
    glDrawElements, 206
    GL_ELEMENT_ARRAY_BUFFER, 203
    glEnable, 143, 173
    glEnableVertexAttribArray, 147, 220
    glFramebufferRenderbuffer, 204
    glFramebufferTexture2D, 204
    glfwSwapBuffers, 145
    glGenBuffers, 147, 167, 203, 220
    glGenFramebuffers, 203
    glGenRenderbuffers, 203
    glGenTextures, 156, 198, 203
    glGenVertexArrays, 147, 167, 203, 220
    glGetUniformLocation, 146
    glPixelStorei, 156, 198
    GL_POINTS, 163

OpenGL, *continued*
> GL_QUAD, 136
> glRenderbufferStorage, 204
> GLSL. *See* GLSL
> glTexImage2D, 156, 204
> glTexImage3D, 198
> glTexParameterf, 156, 198
> glTexParameteri, 203
> GL_TEXTURE0, 173
> GL_TRIANGLES, 195
> GL_TRIANGLE_STRIP, 137, 141
> glUniform1f, 148
> glUniform1i, 148, 173
> glUniformMatrix4fv, 148, 172, 205
> glUseProgram, 146, 148
> glVertexAttribPointer, 147, 220
> glViewport, 143, 183
> linear filtering, 156
> rasterization, 136
> sparks, drawing, 163–164
> state machine, 134
> texture mapping, 141
> texture unit, 148
> vertex array object (VAO), 141
> vertex buffer object (VBO),
> 141, 168
> vertex shader, 169

OpenGL Shading Language. *See* GLSL
orthographic projection, 138
oscilloscope, 307
os module
> listdir, 104, 197
> path, 65
>> abspath, 104, 197
>> join, 104, 197
overtones, 56

P

parabola, 161
parallel processing, 133
parametric equations, 18
> for a circle, 19
> for a Spirograph, 19–22
particle systems, 159. *See also* fountain
> particle systems
pass keyword, 7
pattern, laser, 251
PCB (printed circuit board), 305
> manufacturers, 309

pentatonic scale, 60
performance analysis, 78
peripherals, recommended for
> Raspberry Pi, 276
perspective projection, 138, 139
photomosaics, 101
> averaging color values, 103,
> 105–106
> command line options, 110
> creating, 108–109
> grid, 102, 106
> matching images, 104, 106–107
> measuring distance, 104
> reading input images, 104
> RGB values, 104, 107
> splitting target image, 103, 106
photoresistor, 239, 304, 305
--piano option, 69
Pillow module, 23, 92, 104, 121
PIL. *See* Python Imaging Library (PIL)
ping command, 312
playlists. *See* iTunes playlists, parsing
p-list (property list) files, 5
plistlib module, 5
> readPlist, 6
position vectors, 77
power adapter, 317
power management, Raspberry Pi, 312
power supply, 306
printed circuit board (PCB), 305
> manufacturers, 309
Processing, 238
projection matrix, 201
projection transformations, 138
property list (p-list) files, 5
prototyping, 304
public/private key, 314
PuTTY, 314
PWM pins, 252
pyaudio module, 261
> get_device_count, 261
> get_device_info_by_index, 261
> open, 262
> paInt16, 262
> stream, 263
pygame module, 61, 63
> event, 69
> mixer, 63
> type, 69
PyOpenGL module, 142, 196

set.intersection method, 8
set object, 8
shaders, 133, 139
    fragment, 140
    vertex, 139–140
signature, email, 89
sine wave, 55, 59
sketches, 238, 240. *See also* Arduino
soldering, 307
sound
    amplitude, 58
    frequency, 55
    fundamental frequency, 56
    overtones, 56
Sparkfun TB6612FNG, 251
    connecting, 257
spectral plot, 56
speech API, 316
spherical coordinates, 163
split, 243
Spirographs. *See also* turtle module
    equations, 19–22
    periodicity, 21
SSH, 314
ssh-keygen utility, 314
state machine, 134
struct.pack, 265, 266
surface-mounted component, 305
Suzuki, Shunryu, 1
system resources, 105

T

TB6612FNG, SparkFun, 251
    connecting, 257
temperature sensor. *See* DHT11
text-based graphics. *See* ASCII art
texture mapping, 141–142
texture unit, 148
through-hole component, 305
timeit module, 78
time module, sleep, 64
timing, 78
tkinter module, 23
    canvas.postscript, 29
tones, 60
transistor, 306
translation matrix, 138
turn-on voltage, for LEDs, 305
turtle module, 22
    down, 22
    drawing a circle, 22

drawing a Spirograph, 25
hiding the cursor, 29
listen, 30
mainloop, 22
onkey, 30
ontimer, 27
setpos, 22
setting the cursor, 23–24
setup, 30
showturtle, 29
title, 30
up, 22
window_height, 26
window_width, 26

V

VAO (vertex array object), 141
VBO (vertex buffer object), 141
vectors
    magnitude of, 73
        limiting, 81
    normal, 165
    position, 77
    velocity, 73
velocity vectors, 73
vertex array object (VAO), 141
vertex buffer object (VBO), 141
vertex shader, 136
volume rendering, 191
    2D slices, 196, 220
        computing texture
            coodinates, 222
        fragment shader, 223
        keyboard handler, 223–224
        rendering, 221
        vertex shader, 222
    3D texture coordinates, 193
    color cube, 194
        computing rays, 195
        defining, 202
        drawing, 205–206
        drawing front-faces, 205
        geometry definition, 201–202
        rendering back-faces, 204–205
        setting up FBO, 203–204
    keyboard handler, 228
    maximum intensity projection
        (MIP), 232
    ray casting, 195–196
        algorithm, 212
        blending, 216

Python Playground is set in New Baskerville, Futura, Dogma, and TheSansMono Condensed. The book was printed and bound by Lake Book Manufacturing in Melrose Park, Illinois. The paper is 60# Husky Opaque Offset, which is certified by the Sustainable Forestry Initiative (SFI).

The book uses a layflat binding, in which the pages are bound together with a cold-set, flexible glue, and the first and last pages of the resulting book block are attached to the cover. The cover is not actually glued to the book's spine, and when open, the book lies flat and the spine doesn't crack.